Roman Encounters

Gerhard Cardinal Müller

Roman Encounters

The Unity of the Faith and the Holy See's Responsibility for the Universal Church

Translated by Susan Johnson

EWTN PUBLISHING, INC.
Irondale, Alabama

EWTN Publishing, Inc.
5817 Old Leeds Road, Irondale, AL 35210

Distributed by Sophia Institute Press, Box 5284, Manchester, NH 03108.

ISBN 978-1-68278-123-4

Library of Congress Control Number:2019946726

First printing

"But those who exist must not be governed badly:
The rule of many is not good; let one be the ruler."

—Aristotle, *Met.* 1076a

"Peter does not abandon the helm
of the Church which he undertook."

—Leo the Great, Sermo 3, 3

"Strengthen your brothers"—in faith.

—Lk 22:32

Contents

Roman Encounters

1

All Roads Lead to Rome

It is one of those beautiful spring days in Rome that everyone living in the Eternal City longs for. The large number of pilgrims and tourists will rave about it for a long time to come when they get back home. You sit al fresco drinking your cappuccino. With a bit of luck, you'll find a seat in a café on the Via della Conciliatione that offers you a view of St. Peter's Basilica—an image of eternity in the ocean of time. You're still bursting with the large papal audience and can brag a little about how close you got to the Holy Father—perhaps even in the front row. What a joy to be able to post a fantastic photo for friends online. Or there's the not exactly timid young woman who has pushed her way forward and snatched a selfie with a smiling Pope.

There is always a multi-lingual, even pentecostal feeling about Trastevere. The jumble of languages there has nothing dissonant and threatening about it. The pilgrims from all corners of the globe get an almost physical sense of the unifying power of the Catholic faith. That is *Roma aeterna*—unmistakable and unique in its dignity and serenity.

The Rome of Saints Peter and Paul—that is the visible center of the Catholic Church. For 3,000 years, this city has been a melting pot of the nations. The universality of the *Ecclesia Catholica* with Her mission to all mankind is represented in the Bishop of the Church of Rome. For Her founder "placed blessed Peter over the other Apostles, and instituted in him a permanent and visible source and foundation of unity of faith and communion" (*Lumen Gentium* [LG] 18). Upon this Rock the Lord continues to build the Church that He founded permanently in Peter. Since the apostle's martyrdom under Emperor Nero, the successors of Peter have been the Popes. It is because of them that many people still regard the city of Rome as the *caput mundi*.

It is, of course, not the sophistication of the citizens of the world—in the *civitas terrena*—that lends Christian Rome its luster but rather the citizenship of the Kingdom of Heaven enjoyed by the faithful—in the *civitas Dei*. And believers and seekers alike hasten to the portals of the churches in which these two Princes of the Apostles, Peter and Paul, are buried—*ad limina Apostolorum*—simply in order to venerate them. On account of the Pope's office as universal teacher and shepherd, the Roman Church is acclaimed throughout the world as the mother and teacher of all churches—*mater et magistra omnium ecclesiarum*.

The same Lord Jesus who placed Simon at the head of his disciples to profess for all ages in his successors: "You are the Messiah [Christ], the Son of the living God" (Mt 16:16) also handed him the keys of the Kingdom of Heaven. Now it is the Pope who holds the keys of Peter in his hands. Even in the face of headwinds and tempests, he must steer the Barque of Peter through raging seas, keeping it on course to Christ.

For only Jesus, the divine Word that took on our flesh (cf. Jn 1:14), is "the way, and the truth, and the life" (Jn 14:6). No one comes to God except through him. He unites the disciples in the Triune God and establishes the community of the disciples among each other. "He is the head of the body, the church.... For in him all the fullness of God was pleased to dwell, and through him God was pleased to reconcile to himself all things, whether on earth or in heaven, by making peace through the blood of his cross" (Col 1:18-20).

The Risen Lord said to the eleven apostles, and "first, Simon, also known as Peter" (Mt 10:2): "All authority in heaven and on earth has been given to me. Go therefore and make disciples of all nations, baptizing them in the name of the Father and of the Son and of the Holy Spirit, and teaching them to obey everything that I have commanded you. And remember, I am with you always, to the end of the age" (Mt 28:18-20).

St. Ignatius, the Bishop of Antioch who was martyred in about A.D. 110, was the first to call the universal, orthodox Church of Christ *the Catholic Church*. "Wherever the bishop shall appear, there let the multitude [of the people] also be; even as, wherever Jesus Christ is, there is the Catholic Church" (IgnSmy 8, 2). He writes to "the Church which is beloved and enlightened by the will of Him that wills all things which are according to the love of Jesus Christ our God, which also presides in the place of the region of the Romans, worthy of God, ... and which presides over love" (IgnRom, Prol.). In its self-designation as "catholic" the universal Church dissociates itself from apostates, schismatics and heretics. These are those who are baptized members of the Catholic Church but have abandoned the faith, i.e., Catholics who have renounced full communion with the Church or who have diminished or falsified the truth of Her apostolic teaching. But the word "catholic" also establishes the identity of Christians in the unity of the Church and the truth of the faith. "Catholic," with its orientation towards the primacy of the Church of Rome, can be seen as a synonym for "orthodox," a badge of orthodoxy. But the Church is also "evangelical" (scriptural) since her creed is identical with the gospel of the Kingdom of God. She is Christian since she is the Church of Christ. In the 4th century, St. Pacian, Bishop of Barcelona, put this in a nutshell: "Christian is my name, but Catholic my surname.... Wherefore our people when named Catholic are separated by this appellation from the heretical name—*Christianus mihi nomen est, catholicus vero cognomen*" (Ep. 1 c.7-8).

In his famous catechetical lectures given to the newly baptized in the Church of the Holy Sepulchre in 348 A.D. Archbishop Cyril of Jerusalem says of the Church: "It is called Catholic then because it extends over all the world, from one end of the earth to the other; and because it teaches universally and completely one and all the doctrines which ought to come to men's knowledge, concerning things both visible and invisible, heavenly and earthly; and because it brings into subjection to godliness the whole race of mankind, governors and governed, learned and unlearned; and because it universally treats and heals the whole class of sins, which are committed by soul or body, and possesses in itself every form of virtue which is named, both in deeds and words, and in every kind of spiritual gifts" (Cat. XVIII, 23).

The one and only Church of Christ is catholic and apostolic because She serves the universal—after all, that is what "catholic" means—salvific will of God, "who desires everyone to be saved and to come to the knowledge of the truth" (1 Tim 2:4) through the one mediator between God and humankind (cf. 1 Tim 2:5). Nowhere does the Church show Herself a more tender mother to the faithful than in Rome, taking all Her children into Her arms and giving them the feeling of being at home in God's family. Catholics feel in their hearts, wherever they participate in the Eucharist and whatever language it is celebrated in: *I am at home everywhere.* Although we are merely guests on earth, we journey among the ranks of the pilgrims seeking the city that is to come (cf. Heb 13:14). And there judgement awaits us on our lives; but at the same time we confidently place our hope in the undeserved grace of our Judge. "But our citizenship is in heaven, and it is from there that we are expecting a Savior, the Lord Jesus Christ. He will transform the body of our humiliation so that it may be conformed to the body of his glory, by the power that also enables him to make all things subject to himself (Phil 3:20f.). For we have full citizenship in the present and coming Kingdom of God. We are not torn this way and that in a dialectic of this world and the next. The melancholy of transience does not cloud our understanding. And our hearts do not die of pain and anger that in the end everything has been in vain. How often have you heard people obsessed with eternal youth heave a bitter sigh when their age can no longer be denied: "So that was it, was it?"

There is only one cure for ontological and existential nihilism: Christian positivism. It is better to be than not to be. "God saw everything that he had made, and indeed, it was very good" (Gen 1:31). Only someone who has been born has the prospect of eternal life. "For God created us for incorruption, and made us in the image of his own eternity" (Wis 2:23).

And the being (*Sein*) from which everything that lives and thinks proceeds as from an inexhaustible wellspring is a being for life and not for death. The meaning of being is love. It is stronger than death. "Many waters cannot quench love, neither can floods drown it" (Song 8:7).

Therefore all that is, is one, good and true—*omne ens est unum, verum, bonum*. God is the first principle and last end of mankind and the world—*Deus est principium et finis omnium rerum*. It was not some invented supreme being, a postulate of moral reasoning or an ideal of speculative reasoning, but rather the living God with his universal salvific will who revealed his name to Moses on Mount Horeb, the Mountain of God: "I am who I am" (Ex 3:14). The divine majesty stoops down towards a shepherd and does not shun the desert dust. For he is our keeper and shepherd. We are made from the dust of the earth and yet crowned with God's glory and honor (cf. Ps 8:5). For those who persevere through the wilderness, the Garden of Eden awaits them with the tree of knowledge and the waters of life (cf. Gen 2:9).

God did not have to wait for the powdered, bewigged philosophers of an 18th-century Paris salon to indignantly open the door to Him and mockingly grill Him on the problem of theodicy. He cannot be embraced by the concepts of finite reason or manipulated with the magic of the culture industry. The divine intellect, which is reason in person, has no need of being made to see reason by the criticism of mortals.

God Himself opens our hearts and draws near to us as the Savior: God said to Moses, "I am who I am." He said further, "Thus you shall say to the Israelites, 'I am has sent me to you'" (Ex 3:14). He is the God of Abraham, Isaac and Jacob and the God and Father of Jesus, his Son, the Word that took on our flesh. "This is my name for ever, and this my title for all generations" (Ex 3:15). God eludes our objectifying question of whether, like an object of sensual perception or an abstract concept, He exists or not.

The "Memorial" of the philosopher and mathematician Blaise Pascal, written in "the year of grace 1654" on his soul's being touched with the joy of the nearness of God, contains the solution of the opposition between the thinking of the heart and cold reason:

Feu
« *DIEU d'Abraham, DIEU d'Isaac, DIEU de Jacob* »
non des philosophes et des savants. Certitude. Certitude. Sentiment.
Joie. Paix. DIEU de Jésus-Christ.
Deum meum et Deum vestrum.
« *Ton DIEU sera mon Dieu.* »[1]

---

[1] *Oeuvres complètes*, Gallimard, Paris 1954 m 554.

Fire
"GOD *of Abraham,* GOD *of Isaac,* GOD *of Jacob,"*
not of the philosophers and of the learned.
Certitude. Certitude. Feeling. Joy. Peace.
GOD *of Jesus Christ.*
Deum meum et Deum vestrum.
"Your GOD *will be my God."*

God, in His inscrutable mystery, reveals Himself in His words and deeds and most profoundly in His *name.* And so we enter into an I-to-I relationship with Him. God is a person in relation to Himself within the Trinity and to us in salvation history, in the Incarnation, Cross, and Resurrection of Christ. His name is " 'Emmanuel', which means, 'God is with us' " (Mt 1:23). Referring to Jesus Christ, Peter states: "there is no other name under heaven given among mortals by which we must be saved" (Acts 4:12). We are baptized "in the *name* of the Father and of the Son and of the Holy Spirit" (Mt 28:19). And according to Jesus' instructions, we pray daily: "Our Father in heaven, hallowed be your name" (Mt 6:9).

What the dense crowds packing St. Peter's Square and the millions watching on television experience at Christmas and Easter when they see the Pope appear on the loggia of St. Peter's is a salvation history and a universal Church that seem accessible to them. Like "Peter, standing with the eleven" (Acts 2:14) at Pentecost, the Pope, too, appears in public and, lifting up his voice, begins to tell them of the crucified Jesus, "that God has made him both Lord and Messiah" (Acts 2:36). The universality of God's salvific will, which desires to bring all people together in Christ's Church, is realized with the Holy Spirit's being poured out upon all flesh (cf. Acts 2:17): "For the promise is for you, for your children, and for *all who are far away* [Is 57:19], everyone whom the Lord our God calls to him" (Acts 2:39).

Roman Encounters

Then the young theologian quotes an ancient Church Father: "One who does not have the Church as mother cannot have God as Father" (Cyprian, De unit. eccl. 6) so devoutly that the two girl servers sitting at the same table as him in the café are astonished at such erudition. In the highly symbolic act of Urbi et Orbi, the Pope blesses everyone "in Christ with every spiritual blessing in the heavenly places" (Eph 1:3). Even those who have distanced themselves from the Church and been disappointed by life, those of other faiths and even a few skeptics sense a hint of the Christian faith that unites peoples and kindles hope.

Whether they are attracted by its classical antiquities or by Christian Rome, everyone is seized by the same elation that led Johann Wolfgang von Goethe to sigh on All Saints Day 1786, at the end of his Italian journey: "Well, at last I am arrived in this great capital of the world."[2] And in the entry for 3 December he adds: "As I fared with natural history, so I do here also; for the history of the whole world attaches itself to this spot, and I reckon a new birthday,—a true new birth from the day I entered Rome" (ibid. 147). Rome is in every respect a symbol of the unity of the faith, the Church and the whole of humanity.

But neither in Rome nor anywhere else can enthusiasm for a popular Pope drown out the Supreme Pastor's concern for the Church all over the world—*sollicitudo omnium ecclesiarum*. The creeping and openly pursued de-Christianization of the western world, the unity of Christendom under the one Shepherd Jesus Christ, the antagonism of the political powers—all these issues require him, together with the bishops and all the faithful, to show an active commitment to re-evangelization, to the ecumenical

---

[2] *Italienische Reise: Hamburger Ausgabe* 11, 123. Engl. transl. *The Works of J. W. von Goethe*, Volume 12, *Letters from Italy*, Part VI, translated by Alexander James William Morrison, 222

route towards the reunification of all believers into the one flock of Christ and to exercise his moral authority in upholding the global validity of human rights, social justice and peace among the family of nations.

So the Catholic understands in a more profound spiritual way why "all roads lead to Rome"—"*tous les chemins vont à Rome.*" Even Voltaire was right about that. However, the Catholic does not think first and foremost of Rome as the capital of an empire that Caesar Augustus marked as the center of his power with the Golden Milestone (*Milliarium Aureum*) he had erected in the Roman Forum. Nor does the Catholic think of Rome as the cultural center of Europe in the Renaissance and Baroque periods. Rather, before his mind's eye he has the Kingdom of God and the unity of mankind in their belief in Jesus Christ in the communion of his Church—*una fides, una ecclesia* (cf. Eph 4:4-6).

The golden milestone of the whole history of the world and of mankind is no longer bound to a specific place and time; rather, it is directly present to every human being in each and every time and place in one person. "But when the fullness of time had come, God sent his Son, born of a woman, born under the law, in order to redeem those who were under the law, so that we might receive adoption as children" (Gal 4:4f.).

That is why, as even the Gallicans and Febronians conceded, the Rome of the Princes of the Apostles Saints Peter and Paul is also not the *centrum unitatis* of a socio-religious empire with its provinces and peripheries but the *principium unitatis* of the community of local churches. The Roman Church is not the continuation of the Imperium Romanum but rather surpasses it. The Pope is present in the local churches and the local churches are united in Peter as the visible Catholic Church with Her Creed, Her liturgy, and hierarchical-sacramental constitution. For, in the strict sense, it is Christ who is the head and center of both the universal Church and the local churches — their *fundamentum principale* — and their soul is the Holy Spirit. He gives life to the members of this body and unites Christ's disciples in faith, hope and love. The apostles and their successors in the episcopal office of preserving and proclaiming the teaching of the apostles and the Church are only in a secondary sense the principle and foundation of the unity of the visible Church in that the Risen Lord speaks His word audibly through them and acts through them in the sacraments for our salvation.[3] The Church does not desire world dominion, nor does She seek to be close to the powerful, to privilege, and the social media — and if She does so, it is only in order to implant the ethical imperative in the secular power. "The Church is only the Church when it exists for others" (Dietrich Bonhoeffer, *Letters and Papers from Prison*), i.e., when She prays, suffers, and works for the coming of God's kingdom.

Peter was crucified in Rome like his Lord, only head downwards; Paul as a Roman citizen was beheaded with a sword. That is the martyrological justification of the authority of the Holy Roman Church. "We proclaim Christ crucified, a stumbling-block to Jews and foolishness to Gentiles" (1 Cor 1:23). The authority of the true apostle is attested by a critical distance to the world and not by crafty chumminess and diplomatic agreements with those who are "wise by human standards [and] powerful" (1 Cor 1:26), "so that your faith might rest not on human wisdom but on the power of God" (1 Cor 2:5).

And how must the Christian message that "you are no longer a slave but a child, and if a child then also an heir, through God" (Gal 4:7) have sounded in the ears of the vast multitudes of slaves in pagan Rome who were robbed of their human dignity and bereft of all hope? And that goes for us, too, today and tomorrow. Anyone

---

[3] Thomas Aquinas, *In Symb.Apost* 9.

who has, despite secularization and the blunting of feeling, retained the least trace of a sense of the fragility of human existence will be wrenched out of the lethargy of forgetfulness of God by the gospel of Christ. For none other than the Son of God and Savior of the world guarantees us the hope that brings comfort to all the suffering of the world: "that the creation itself will be set free from its bondage to decay and will obtain the freedom of the glory of the children of God" (Rom 8:21).

Ultimately, it is of no consequence at all whether someone tops the Forbes list of the richest men and women in the world. What does matter is who has the last word. Whoever is stronger than death is right. Those on God's list do not merely survive until the next danger comes along but rather have life forever.

The tourist just takes a look at Rome and returns home with his or her impressions, not really knowing what to do with them. The Catholic comes as a pilgrim to the sites of the apostles Peter and Paul so as to reinforce his or her faith in the witness they bear to Jesus the Christ. The Catholic then returns home as an 'expressionist' who lives being a Christian in the Church and the world expressively and filled with hope. At the tomb of St. Peter, the Catholic professes in the words of the first among the apostles: "You are the Messiah [Christ], the Son of the living God" (Mt 16:16). Without any clever sophistry, he takes seriously every dimension of the words of the Lord that follow this statement: "And I tell you, you are Peter, and on this rock I will build my church" (Mt 16:18). There is only one "household of God, which is the church of the living God, the pillar and bulwark of the truth" (1 Tim 3:15).

Not only symbolically but also in reality the one, holy, catholic and apostolic Church is "in Christ like a sacrament or as a sign and instrument both of a very closely knit union with God and of the unity of the whole human race—*cum Deo unionis totiusque generis humanae*" (LG 1). In the communion of the local churches of and in which the Catholic Church consists, the Church of Rome holds the primacy of teaching and governing. It preserves the faithful in the unity of faith against heresies and schisms. The Holy Roman Church was commissioned by Christ to lead all Christians into full unity with the Catholic Church.

The Catholic Church is one in Her foundation, unique in Her mission, and united in Her life (*una, unica et unita*) because it is in Christ that She has Her foundation and true head, which is visible in the apostle Peter. No Catholic comes to Rome without knowing "that he is making a pilgrimage to the chair of Peter (*cathedra Petri*) and the principal Church, the source of episcopal unity, and without remembering that it is Romans whose fidelity to the faith the apostle praises and extols and to whom erroneous faith can have no access" (Cyprian of Carthage, Ep. 59,14). That is the Roman Church's mission in world history. The justification for its primacy lies solely in its role of safeguarding and promoting the unity in faith of the universal Church. Combined with this is its commission to promote the unity of the family of mankind, to fight for the dignity of every human being and to remind each one of them of his or her divine calling. The Pope is the highest moral authority of mankind because he articulates natural moral law unambiguously: to do good and to avoid evil.

These are the first thoughts that spontaneously go through the head of a faithful Catholic when moved by the aura of the city of the Princes of the Apostles.

Once, as a cardinal was making his way home through the colonnades after the Papal Mass on a high feast day, a gesticulating journalist shouted out to him from among the crowds: "Are we going to be seeing each other later today at the German Embassy to the Holy See?" The Cardinal gestured yes.

2

A Spring Evening at the German Embassy

Not only German citizens are invited to the reception at the German Embassy to the Holy See. Everyone who is anyone in Roman Church circles enjoys getting together there. So there is nowhere in the world that the German church is less provincial and more noticeably a worldwide Church than at the German Embassy to the Holy See. Every language spoken by Catholics and non-Catholics in Rome is to be heard there. But all of them are able to make themselves understood to each other in Italian and English, too. A wide circle of people has turned up. The mild weather attracts them all out into the beautiful garden. Different groups form at the various tables. Topics are touched on briefly rather than discussed in depth. What this produces is a barometer of the general mood and a rumour market about events in the Church and politics. Anyone who has ears to hear will learn many a thing.

When the Cardinal enters, all eyes turn to him. In Rome a cardinal is rated—hard though it is to believe—according to his political market value at the papal court. Theological competence counts for little and is neutralized by the caricature of the scholar in his ivory tower. The presumed goodwill of His Holiness and friendship with his closest confidants promises more reliable information as well as the eagerly awaited chance to get really, really close to the Pontiff and be honored with an office. That explains why most of those present speak in somewhat hushed voices and the outsider has difficulty deciphering all the metaphors and allusions. You need the password to get to the right page.

A pinch of German directness brings a little relief when the Curial paths are all too sinuous. You may not make yourself popular with it, but you do render both the Church and ecumenism a good service if you remind people, with a touch of Germanic defiance, that what is meant by the invisibility of the Church cannot be the power games, personnel policies, alliances and nepotism that take place behind the scenes. One only has to think of the Second Vatican Council, which recalls the classic definition of the relationship between the visible and the invisible dimension of the one Church. The invisible Church is the higher goal of the sacramental Church, i.e., communion with God in grace by virtue of faith, hope and love. "So ... does the visible social structure of the Church serve the Spirit of Christ, who vivifies it, in the building up of the body" (LG 8). Thus, treating the sacred in an all-too-human way stands in stark contrast to the incarnationally grounded human shape in which salvation is mediated.

In the first circle of chairs

German bishop

Looking at the cheering crowds in St. Peter's Square gives you the feeling that the Church is young and dynamic. We are a Church of new departures, setting off in new directions. Let's see where the Spirit leads us. What's all this talk of empty churches, monasteries, convents, and seminaries back home? Where there's something being offered, people are there. The Pope comes across positively. With the Francis effect, we're no longer pilloried by the left-wing liberal media. The Church has broken out of Her own blockade and is now walking hand in hand with the world. We are no longer a foreign body in the modern age. In mysticism and asceticism people used to speak of *conformitas cum Christo*. Nowadays what is called for is to be "mainstream" and "politically correct." You'll only be close to the people if you get on well with the media. A good bishop doesn't rub people the wrong way but rather lets himself be guided by what they say and tells them what they want to hear. They're ravenous for a shared Eucharist, and there's no stopping their willingness to get involved. Wasn't that cabaret artist greeted with frenetic applause at the *Katholikentag* (German Catholic Congress) when he quite rightly pointed out our common responsibility for creation? It's a bit of a sloppy way of putting it, I admit, but he did put the battle over "the wafers at the Eucharist" in perspective, didn't he. I'll just leave it at that and wait and see where it takes me.

What each individual believes is something they have to sort out with their own conscience. Beware of those who carry the Creed and dogmas in front of them like a monstrance. All they do is absolutize their own fusty opinions, opinions you can't get over to anyone any more. Just a few flexible parish priests are infinitely preferable to a crowd of conservatives slamming on the brakes.

A fellow German-speaking bishop declares his solidarity with him
Before Francis, we were ridiculed as a relic from the Middle Ages. Now we're not just having the last laugh, we're on the same side as those who are laughing. That is, so to speak, the popular front of religious and atheistic liberals against the orthodox and reactionaries on all sides. And now my eyes are seeing us connect with the modern age after all. So I'd like to update Simeon's *Nunc dimittis* in the Temple. And didn't Cardinal Martini complain quite correctly that the Church was lagging two hundred years behind the Enlightenment? The hard work of the St. Gallen Group is now bearing rich fruit. Now it's not that the people come to the Church—that was the old-fashioned method. Now the Church

has merged into the world—or been submerged in it, depending on how you look at it.

An aide from the Secretariat of the German Episcopal Conference
Without giving up anything of the nonnegotiable values, what is called for today is a new flexibility, which must not, incidentally, be confused with arbitrariness. The necessary pluralization of Christianity and the differentiation of society cannot be crudely suspected of relativism. The Pope knows exactly why he does not trot out eternal truths and strict moral precepts to the people. They are not going to change anything any more. But he scores points with environmentalism, immigrants, criticism of neo-liberalism—and he's excommunicated the Mafia! Dogmatism isn't going to help anybody. It's individual pastoral care and not abstract doctrines that people need today in all their fragility. Compassion towards those who have failed, not the self-righteousness of teachers of the law, is, after all, what Jesus would also preach today, isn't it?

And his commitment to the poor opens the hearts of dyed-in-the-wool socialists, too, who even recognize him as the secret leader of their Internationals. Who could have imagined it: the Pope hated by the Right and a hero to the Left? The best thing about Benedict's pontificate was his abdication. So now Francis can reduce the backlog of reforms. The goal of the St. Gallen Group, namely, to heave a liberal Pope on to the Chair of Peter, has finally been achieved. Cardinal Danneels of Brussels, who was a fearless defender of the spirit of the Council against pre-Conciliar thinking, has himself confirmed this. We can now finally carry on from where the reforms of Vatican II were halted. The restorative phase under John Paul II and its continuation under Benedict XVI embroiled us in a battle with modernity that we cannot win.

There is never going to be any re-evangelization unless we at long last—and as far as I'm concerned, the Pan-Amazon Synod can make a start here—get married priests, unless there are female deacons, so that women finally feel valued, and unless there are no more barriers to marriage for all. I know a lot of homosexual couples who live up to values and take on responsibility. And, lastly, Communion for remarried divorcees and Protestants, too, really must finally be allowed—naturally, just in individual cases. One theologian has recently discovered that, on account of God's universal salvific will, the sacraments are simply signs of what has already happened anyway. This renders obsolete the Catholic doctrine that the sacraments are necessary for salvation. After all, God doesn't use the sacraments like instruments in order to mediate grace with tools. That's a completely material, not a personal, way of thinking. It brings us pretty close to the 'clockmaker god' of the Deists. We simply must not cling so stubbornly to antiquated dogmas any more or confuse liturgy with magic and superstition.

The German bishop once again
With this agenda we're killing two birds with one stone. It decreases the distance from Protestantism and clears away all the obstacles to being a Church that is in touch with the people. Why should we stand among the 40,000 Christian denominations like an erratic bloc claiming, completely unrealistically, to be the sole representative of Christianity—as was attempted again in 2000 with the unhappy declaration "Dominus Iesus." You know we just bore people today with those old slogans of "winning people for Christ" or "living from the faith." We have to take on social topics if we want to be sought after as dialogue partners in politics and the media. It's better to be in a well-attended talk show than alone before the tabernacle. The Belgian church has got it right. Since no one is interested in the faith any longer, they've set out a modern agenda with which they're attracting attention: the abolition of celibacy, the priesthood of women, the blessing

of homosexual couples, compassion for young people who suffer sickness and stress caused by a strict code of sexual morality, and Communion for remarried divorcees. We can leave aside the lax treatment of pedophile clerics—conservative Catholic countries are no better here either.

I dream that we shall simply become part of a secular religion. Dialogue instead of head-on evangelization. Then there would not be any public hostility towards Catholics any more. Then even the conservative fundies could no longer misuse the words of the apostle just to prevent the necessary modernization of the Church: "Do not be conformed to this world, but be transformed by the renewing of your minds, so that you may discern what is the will of God" (Rom 12:2). When Paul says "For no one can lay any foundation other than the one that has been laid; that foundation is Jesus Christ" (1 Cor 3:11), what he means is, after all, dialogue as the basis for living together, not that we should force our belief in Christ on others. The fundamentalism of John Paul II is over, and so is Ratzinger's.

Polish priest

We are proud of our fellow countryman. He's the greatest Pole in the whole of history. But what Catholicism in our country cannot be is traditionalist if it survived two dictatorships with their bloody persecutions for over fifty years. It was you Germans who got us into the whole dilemma with your Hitler. You have 120 seminarians; we have 3,500 young men testing their vocation to this sacred ministry. John Paul II played a considerable part in bringing about the downfall of the inhuman regimes in the Soviet Bloc. Incidentally, the first democratic constitution in Europe came from Poland in 1791, before your enlightened rulers in Austria, Russia and Prussia brought my homeland under the rule of their empires. The greatest series of uprisings in Europe against domination by foreign and domestic dictators took place in our country in the 19th and 20th centuries. We are a nation of freedom fighters. If our country was cut off from its Christian roots, Poland would be just a territory that is home to a mindless consumer society. And that's the end of freedom and human dignity.

German bishop

But now materialism is digging in massively in Poland, too. So, as sociological analyses confirm, the conditions of a modern secular culture are going to bring about a normalization of the Church there, too. The West is the dominant culture in the world. You must follow the example of the German church. We know better how the Church survives in a secular culture, that is, in a democratic pluralist society. We don't have a lack of priests in Germany at all. We just put the parishes together. We had 700 parishes in my diocese. With 300 priests, we were short of 400 in the parishes. Our planning team also used AI. The decision taken at our three-year diocesan synod was unanimous. Now we're putting the pastoral plan into practice come what may. We've already trimmed down to 120 pastoral units, each with a parish priest at its head. And we've already got a surplus of clerics. We don't know what to do with all the surplus of priests. And it's better if you don't meet a priest around every corner anyway. The laity want to develop their own charisms for a change. The Catholic Church has had to wait since the Tridentine restoration for this opportunity. The time has come to head for new shores. The trend to almost nil of new entrants to the seminary is by no means a sign of decline. It actually offers us a great opportunity to increase the amount of responsibility the parishes take for themselves. So now the clericalist constriction of the Church can be actively overcome.

And if you will keep on holding our empty churches up to us, I have to point with pride to all our social activities and institutions and to our theological faculties. The German church is a world champion in that. Anyway, liturgy is just one dimension of the Church among others. Caritas and diakonia are just as important, if not more so, in today's world. There the Church is closer to the people. And I really can't stand the self-righteousness of the conservatives when they accuse the progressives in Belgium, Holland and France of contributing to the collapse. Without the courageous reformers there, things would be even worse. Apart from that, the criteria the conservatives employ are only those of counter-reformation Catholicism. After all, the relevance of faith isn't displayed in frequent confession, regular Mass attendance, church weddings, or in whether you can recognize priests and religious in the street by their dress.

The Church must become poor and serving, simple but conspicuously compassionate. You just put people off with the fusty old vocabulary of sin and repentance. What people need is understanding for their weaknesses. For no one can guarantee to live up to every ideal. The Pope is quite right to say we have to admit the injured to our field hospital instead of subjecting them to an inhuman re-education process. We'll earn more brownie points with first aid than with long and expensive rehabilitations.

The Roman Cardinal

It's actually not that convincing, my dear confrere, when the basic functions of the Church are played off against one another. I get the impression you're making yourself believe the crisis is rather less serious than it is. Deluding oneself is also a breach of the Eighth Commandment. When you've lost the gold of faith, it's not much consolation to think that you'll no longer have to drag it around. And anyway, Vatican II emphasized the sacramental reality of the Church precisely in the modern world. Pope Francis is continually warning against a secularized Church. The Church is not, he says, an NGO, a secular organization that draws attention to itself with what it has to offer spiritually and socially. The Council did indeed sum up the whole mission of the Church in the three functions of proclamation, liturgy and pastoral care as the sacrament of the salvation of the world in Christ. Nevertheless, the Eucharistic sacrifice remains "the source and summit of the whole Christian life" as *Lumen Gentium* puts it so strikingly in Article 11. And, you know, Sunday Mass is not a burdensome duty if Jesus commands us at the Last Supper to celebrate the giving of his Body and Blood on the Cross in the Eucharist "in remembrance of me" (Lk 22:19; 1 Cor 11:25).

So we don't need priests just as team leaders for a vast pastoral area; we need them locally as good shepherds. When a father lives far from home, this seems pretty unnatural to his wife and children. They all long to be together again. The idea of priests being close to their people is a really good one. Let's not forget that Jesus must have had something in the back of His mind when He called the apostles, thus also making the sacramental priesthood foundational in the construction of His Church. The Church's self-secularization according to the model of liberal Protestantism does not represent the first step towards Her modernization but rather the last before Her self-abolition. "Yesterday we were still standing on the edge of the abyss, but today we've taken a step forwards"—I hope that's not the title of your pastoral handout.

An African religious sister

I really don't understand what you're talking about here and why you're arguing. What's so difficult about believing in Jesus and living the gospel? Jesus gave His Church the seven sacraments. Why don't we just simply celebrate the grace as the Church lays it down in Her liturgy? Christianity is growing back home in Africa—and not because we still have the Enlightenment ahead of us. You're being taken in by the Enlightenment if you let yourselves be persuaded that religion is something for the uneducated, preferably the illiterate. There is no truer enlightenment about the mystery of mankind than the Good News of Christ. Where the gospel is, that's always the front. Yet you think that the superstition and fanaticism of religion in Africa could be overcome with your parochially European reason.

Your 20th-century substitute religions didn't show themselves to be all that rational, just and tolerant, did they? So what is your exporting of ideologies that are inimical to life other than neo-colonialism? What annoys us most about you is that you continue to treat us like children the schoolmaster wags his finger at. I studied theology in Europe. I am familiar with religious criticism, but Jesus persuades me more because He doesn't destroy our hope and joy—because, on the contrary, He gives our lives meaning. Your nihilism is just spiritual night—inhuman and unnatural—even if you do try to instill it into us with Nietzschean profundity. In our country the sun shines. It's not easy for your northern gloom to spread there. The self-doubts of Christians in the West are something we cannot understand—and we certainly don't want to live like that. A word from the mouth of God weighs more than the hundreds of millions of dollars we are supposed to sell our hearts for.

German bishop

I am frequently in touch with professors from our theological faculty. And they assure me that under the conditions of the modern age—and currently we need to add the post-modern age—a paradigm shift is urgently needed. We cannot turn back time. We are very well placed in developing countries with our international charitable organizations of Misereor, Adveniat, Missio and Renovabis. We are so important for the worldwide Church, and financially for the Vatican, too, that we can lay claim to having a sort of pioneering role in the universal Church with our brilliant theology. False modesty would be out of place here. We're glad to help, but the others must let us give them a leg-up. You know what they say: he who pays the piper calls the tune. But as far as the truth is concerned, we're flexible. They should each take their own paths. We call that inculturation. That's why we make bold use of the teaching competence of the episcopal conferences. Incidentally, we translate our texts into many languages. What the Romans can do, so can we. The others should get to know what's going on here and what would be good for them, too.

A German professor offers his support
Kant already established in his *Critique of Pure Reason* (1781) that we do not perceive reality as it is but rather only as it appears to us. Our subjective forms of perception and the categories of reason only permit us to perceive the thus constituted compound phenomena. The very idea of objectively knowing God and supernatural revelation is inconceivable. God, soul and world are merely ideals of pure reason. That is something all our students learn in their first semesters: "A Supreme Being is, therefore, for the speculative reason, a mere ideal, though a faultless one—a conception which perfects and crowns the system of human cognition, but the objective reality of which can neither be proved nor disproved by pure reason" (KrV B 670). A speculative theology as understood by the Fathers and Scholasticism is therefore no longer possible. We are no longer dealing with the abstract truths of revelation; rather, it is a matter of their practical application as a means of shedding light on and coping with life. Historicism and constructivism later showed us conclusively that all seemingly absolute truths are historically, societally, culturally and neurophysiologically determined. Our revealed truths, too, are merely the code for a time-conditioned, subjective experience of something higher, which, however, we are incapable of perceiving. Thus, atheists are in some way anonymous

believers in God, just as Christians are anonymous atheists or, if you like, also unitarian or trinitarian theists or polytheists and pantheists. It is only a false image of God that they refuse to accept.

That offers an enormous opportunity for dialogue between religions. Their claim to truth is no longer an impediment, nor is there any longer a potential for violence. One sun — many rays. That is the motto of religious pluralism — a bit like the Global Ethic, but with a marzipan flavor. Monotheism in particular, not just in Islam but also already in the Old Testament, has always been a source of danger unless refined by the Enlightenment. If the orthodox interpretation of so-called revelation is not tamed by reason, all monotheisms tend towards intolerance and dogmatism.

Even if a Christian does not have a psychological predisposition to violence, his faith's absolute claim to truth can nevertheless lead to a temptation to intolerance. The Crusades, the Inquisition and the persecution of witches all offer us unambiguous historical evidence of this. Incidentally, the patriarchal image of God in the three Abrahamic religions contains a huge problem as regards women. Since Christianity has been through the Enlightenment, it has become more tolerant because we have learnt to relativize our truths. All truths of the faith are merely symbols pointing to the unknown mystery beyond being. Violence seems to be naturally inherent in intolerance towards the truth of other gods beside the sole Creator. I don't know whether you are familiar with the work of the Egyptologist Jan Assmann on this: *Die Mosaische Unterscheidung oder der Preis des Monotheismus*. Munich 2003. [English: *The Mosaic Distinction or The Price of Monotheism* (2009)]. And Freud already enlightened us as to the psycho-social mechanisms of its origins in his *Der Mann Moses und die monotheistische Religion* (1939). [English: *Moses and Monotheism* (1939)]. So we must be careful about our feelings of superiority towards other religions, especially Asian ones, which conceive of the divine as being greater than a person.

A Spring Evening at the German Embassy

Paradoxically, we in fact owe the New Atheism of Dawkins, Dennet, Hitchens, Oddifreddi and Michel Onfray, etc. to the kind of religious fundamentalism that wishes to go back before the Enlightenment. In view of the abuse and the reactionary course pursued by the Church leadership in Rome, you can to a certain extent sympathize with their concern. Looking at the conservative theologians, you can scarcely deny that religion and science are at odds with one another. It is only with a pragmatic concept of religion, one that dispenses with absolute truths, that we can enter into a dialogue with these revenants of the old humanism without God and their admittedly somewhat peculiar naturalistic monism. Society has become so pluralistic and confusing that any homogeneity in faith, prayer and action turns out to be impossible. A reconciled heterogeneity in which each individual finds his or her own salvation and everyone likes each other in some way or other — that is sufficient for the unity of the Church in our times.

A progressive theologian seconds the previous speaker

Fiction

Dogmatic unity was, anyway, only held together artificially by means of suppressing several other traditions. The idea of a continuity of the Church's tradition is simply a fiction that owes its existence solely to the repressive measures of the Magisterium. What we need to rediscover is the unintegrable plurality of approaches. Then we would automatically have the unity in diversity that we need. The days of national churches to which the majority of the population belongs are finally over, even if people in Poland and Africa still refuse to admit this. We can only survive as a creative minority. So we have to throw overboard the whole baggage of dogmas and no longer 'liveable' morals. By the way, I am proud of our neologism of *Lebbarkeit* (liveability) because it does not sound as banal as "*Leben*" (life, to live) and is good to use at educational events. A slimmed down but 'smart' Church is the model for tomorrow. I am not afraid that we shall be digging our own grave. We are well cushioned for a fall.

And anyway, I regard the accusation of Protestantizing the Catholic Church as a compliment. After all, quite unlike us, the Protestants have already fully arrived in the modern age. That is the aim of the gospel, isn't it? For it to be blended with the self-understanding of a mature person who is responsible only to his or her own conscience? That is what I call—loosely based on Gadamer—the hermeneutics of the fusion of horizons. Modernity does not understand itself any longer as an alternative to Christianity, but rather as its product—even though many people today no longer realize that their values of self-determined freedom, subjectivity and absolute autonomy all come from modern Christianity. By that I mean the Reformation as opposed to the medieval Catholicism that was kept alive for another few centuries by the Council of Trent—so to speak as a living corpse. So we have killed two birds with one stone in achieving unity in ecumenism and the fusion of the Church with the world. If the Ultramontanists, with their fixation on Tradition, the authority of the Magisterium and the dogmas of Trent and Vatican I, had not failed to keep pace with the modern world, we would have spared ourselves the *Kulturkampf* [the struggle between Church and state, esp.1872-1887 in Germany; culture wars]. The United Christian Church of Germany (VCKD) would have already become a reality back then. A hundred and fifty wasted years for ecumenism. The Protestants would not buy the idea of an infallible Pope remote from the world; but one like today's smiling Pope, who waves to everyone around him, reaches out to people and is popular with the media—that is one they would have accepted even then.

With this last stage of the de-confessionalization of the Catholic Church the opposition between the denominations is overcome, as is the distance between the Church and the world. For without noticing it the world has become Christian, albeit without the now superfluous packaging of Christianity's core message in dogmas, sacraments, moral precepts and ecclesial laws. The true Church has always been hidden, just as in kenotic theology Jesus' divinity is completely hidden in his humanity. What we have is an internalized Christianity of attitude, not one of institutions with their splendid liturgy, clergy and cloisters, seminaries, Catholic kindergartens, schools and hospitals, with catechisms learnt by heart and theological textbooks that are only written by professors for professors. Maybe the Pentecostals are the external manifestation of Christianity pointing the way forward in the new world. And please let's not have any ecumenism that talks of returning to the fold. Everyone should stay where they are. Whether there are two or seven sacraments simply depends on how the respective theological schools define their sacramental understanding, so that doesn't really have much to do with salvation, does it? Augustine knew nothing of there being seven sacraments, and he's not someone the conservatives of all people can claim is not a Catholic. Yet they are still fond of appealing to him and his semi-Manichaean sexual morals and to his pessimistic idea of Original Sin, none of which are at all suited to our times any more. The sacraments are not instrumental causes in mediating our salvation any more, that would be magical thinking from the Middle Ages with its substance metaphysics. We are all already redeemed through the universal salvific will, and we are simply made aware of this in religious signs. The main thing is to be a Christian, whatever that means.

The concept of civil religion that was already developed by Jean-Jacques Rousseau in 1762 in his *Social Contract* is actually not too bad at all—at least better than Kant's new version of Christianity as a secular rational religion, which is far too complicated for ordinary people. But Catholic theologians really should be recommended to use Kant's *Religion within the Limits of Reason*

Alone (1793) as the level on which to engage in dialogue with critical intellectuals. Friedrich Daniel Ernst Schleiermacher already showed us brilliantly how to do this in 1799 with his *On Religion: Speeches to its Cultured Despisers.* Surely a statement like the following unites everyone—whatever their religion or none—in the experience of being secure in the universe: "Do try to surrender your lives out of love for the universe. Strive here already to destroy your individuality in order to live in the One and the All; strive to be more than yourselves so that you lose little when you lose yourselves; and when you have flowed together with the universe, as much as you find of it here, and a greater and holier longing has arisen in you, then let us further converse about the hopes that death gives us and about the infinity to which we infallibly soar aloft as a result of it.... God is not All in religion, but One, and the universe is more; nor can you believe Him arbitrarily or because you wish to use Him for consolation and help, but rather because you must. Immortality must not be a desire if it has not first been a task that you have solved. To become One with the Eternal in the midst of eternity and to be little in a moment, that is the immortality of religion."[4]

I have quoted this at such length in order to show that these ideas can be declaimed just as easily at the cremation of a member of the Giordano Bruno Foundation as at the interment of a theology professor who has caught up with the modern age. They can even be devoutly recited as the ashes of a Hindu flow down the Ganges. How uniting and all-embracing! It is only with such a breadth of religion, which must not be sneered at being one-size-fits-all, that we shall rid ourselves of the reputation for being stuck in medieval thinking with this substantializing of truths. In faith there is nothing unreasonable, and therefore nothing that goes beyond

---

[4] From the end of the Second Speech (= PhB 225, 73f.).

reason either. I'll say it again — there is no going back behind the Enlightenment. We must have the courage to rethink everything.

I am saying this with deep and utter conviction, a conviction I share with all my open-minded and receptive contemporaries. Pope Francis is getting it right: instead of repeating antiquated dogmas, he makes pleasing gestures. Pure genius — and twenty million followers confirm that the Vatican's new media policy is in good shape. You don't get through to young people with books and boring sermons but with commercials and tweets, if need be with You Tube, too.

The Cardinal

That sounds to me like when someone records his own requiem in advance so as to give himself the creeps over and over again by listening to it. Once the clearance sale is over, the shop closes down. There is a great deal of ideology in all this but very little understanding of the particular nature of the Catholic faith. You cannot make a virtue out of necessity by sugar-coating apostasy as a way of making the true nature of faith visible. Faith is both an inward and an outward profession of Jesus Christ, the Son of God. As Paul puts it: "If you confess with your lips that Jesus is Lord and believe in your heart that God raised him from the dead, you will be saved" (Rom 10:9). The Incarnation, Cross and Resurrection are realities that determine our relationship to God. And the sacramental and ecclesial mediation of communion with God is neither an invention of Trent and Vatican I nor a passing variant of Catholicism but rather its distinctive property. Look it up in Irenaeus! As early as the 2nd century, the Bishop of Lyon was confronted with the same problems when, against the highly enlightened Gnostics, he prevented a reinterpretation of the Catholic faith that turned it into an ideology. If we relinquish truth, we also forfeit freedom. The agnostic does not become tolerant but rather a slave to the majority opinion, which is borne along on the drifting sands of the interests of the powerful. By the way, it would be nice if you as a man of the Church would get beyond using the word "dogma" in an everyday sense. That assumes the affected attitude of an Enlightenment philosopher in dismissing dogma as an apodictic assertion that is neither rationally nor empirically provable but employed for purposes of retaining power. Their argument is that the Church has to keep its clients immature and sheep-like since enlightenment would cause it to lose its influence among minds that had become critical. As a technical term in Catholic theology, however, "dogma" has since the 18th century meant—where did you study your theology anyway?—simply the highest degree of certainty of a truth believed by the Church and revealed by God. Without dogmas the Church does not become more human but instead cheats humanity out of the truth of the Word of God that became flesh and dwells among us. No one is capable of teaching who has not first learnt. The word "dogma" in the specific usage of scientific theology fulfills Jesus' commission to the Apostles and their successors: "Go therefore and make disciples of all nations, … teaching them to obey everything that I have commanded you" (Mt 28:19f.). Faith in the form of Church dogma tells us that our salvation is grounded in God's truth and not in the utopias and visions of fallible human beings. If the Word of Christ is the proclamation of divine reason, how can the hermeneutics of a finite mind—even that of a Kant—be the yardstick by which it is measured?

In the second circle of chairs

The Rome correspondent of Spiegelwelt

I would never have believed that the Church would once again connect with the modern world. Pope Francis is not a reformer of the old school, where they always pussyfooted around, talking in myths and Church-speak about a renewal of our faith in Christ and following the crucified and risen Lord. Francis is a real revolutionary, who pushes ahead uncompromisingly with his agenda and—as one of his friends has actually said—makes it irreversible. There won't be a dry eye left in the house, and nothing will be the same as it once was. The Church hasn't overcome the Enlightenment nor the Enlightenment the Church. But what really gives you a thrill is that the Church has overcome itself through self-enlightenment.

The traditionalist

It's all the fault of the French Revolution. Joseph de Maistre was quite right with his 1819 book *Du pape*. Only a new alliance between the Church and the conservative intellectuals and politicians can halt the decline now. With Vatican II, Modernism broke into the world. *Gaudium et Spes* gives in to the anthropocentric thinking of the modern age. You mustn't start with man but with God. Didn't even the Reformed theologian Karl Barth reject liberal theology and defend the theocentric approach against the Lutheran Adolf von Harnack, the pope of cultural Protestantism? *Deus dixit* does after all mean that God has spoken—and we have to obey. Enough said! And then that disastrous Declaration on Religious Freedom. Pope Pius VI immediately rejected the 1789 Declaration of the Rights of Man as it was not theonomically based. His successors, too, have stated clearly that truth does not permit everyone to choose his or her own religion. And yes, I do know the difference between natural and supernatural religious freedom. In his spiritual nature man feels the duty to obey the call of truth and the principle of good, but as he understands them and free from outside coercion. But supernatural religious freedom is about elevating and perfecting freedom in faith and love, strengthened by the Holy Spirit. However, I regard this as nitpicking. Truth is truth, and it alone has a right to be right. Error, even innocent error, has no right whatsoever to be regarded as right in state and society. The task of the State is not just to ensure the earthly wellbeing of its citizens but rather—working closely together with the Church—their eternal salvation.

And the worst modernism of all happened with the reform or rather the destruction of the liturgy. The only remedy in this crisis of faith that would stop the Church falling apart would be to return to the Mass of All Time in the 1962 *Missale Romanum*. It is only in this form that the content of the Mass is available to us in every detail. Everything is equally important and unchanging. The fact that the priest no longer celebrates towards Christ but faces the people is convincing proof of a capitulation before the anthropocentric shift of modern times. And now we even have a Pope who favors the Modernists and either mercilessly lambastes us conservatives or pushes us out of the Church.

A student from Latin America

Our Holy Father is Catholic. After all, he touches the statue of Our Lady every morning and is up praying his breviary in front of the tabernacle at 4 a.m.—and he always goes quite demonstratively to confession, too. You can see everywhere how humbly he kneels down in front of his confessor. A monumental documentary made by an internationally famous director shows what a great personality lies hidden behind his humility. That's how you tell the difference in my country between us and the Protestants, or sects as we call them. Well, they come from the gringos, don't they, who we can't stand anyway. We're proud that one of us has become Pope. It's time that the Europeans learnt something from us for a change. Our professor always said that European Christianity is too Platonic and dualistic. But Liberation Theology has rediscovered a holistic perspective. It's a matter of integral development. Pope Francis has even created a special dicastery for this. That's what we need to be talking about, not your Egel—you know, that philosopher whose name starts with an unpronounceable 'h', the 'hache'. If there's anything we can learn from Karl Marx, then it's the statement: "The philosophers have only interpreted the world in various ways; the point, however, is to change it." Our professor for philosophical propaedeutics kept on quoting this from Marx's *Theses on Feuerbach* and even knew that it was Thesis 11. It corresponds exactly to early Christianity's precedence of orthopraxis over orthodoxy. It was only Scholasticism that turned lived faith into a scientific system. The Pope wants a poor Church for the people, not a Church of professors for the intellectuals. There's been a lot of talk about reforming the Curia. Now everyone's just afraid that he'll be next on the list. Hence the opposition in the Curia against the Pope, who after all only wants what is good and hates evil.

A professor with a Cluster of Excellence

For me, as a cultural historian with a background in natural science, it is clear that a religion with a dogmatic, i.e., exclusive, claim to truth does not stand a chance in our global world and has no right to exist. Catholicism especially is now faced with the task of disarming itself dogmatically. The untested acceptance of axioms and dogmas is incompatible with freedom of research. Much less can some long-established tradition and the authority of the so-called Magisterium tell us what we have to believe. Our enlightened contemporaries are not going to let freedom of thought be taken away from them again. Our approach is one of methodological atheism. Only a theology that does not immediately come up with God, the Trinity or the Incarnation can connect with the modern world. Without supernatural revelation, we become able to connect and enter into dialogue with people today. That is something our fundamentalists still have to learn. We only become relevant to today's world once belief in God and all the transcendental talk have become irrelevant for us. The Church must locate itself in this world. If, for example, we leave out the stuff about the Real Presence of Christ at Mass and interpret the distribution of the wafers as a gesture of welcome on the part of everyone in our community, then we already have ecumenical unity among Christians through Intercommunion. Transubstantiation is a thing of the past. It's simply embarrassing when the priest recites the biblical words: "Whoever eats my flesh and drinks my blood." Mindless magic if you take it literally. Let's leave dogmas and sacraments aside. We must break free from the tyranny of truth and set out for the paradise of relativism. The next world doesn't interest anyone any more. Don't they say: "Let the dead bury their own dead"? If everything ends with death, we must let the music play in the here and now.

Catholic dogmas anyway presuppose the metaphysics of the Ancient Greeks. That's all old hat! And we know that since Kant no metaphysics of reality is possible any more. Religious beliefs are our notions of God, the soul and the world, but they are not based on objective knowledge. Truth lies in the eye of the beholder. Each of us has their own truth. Colleagues of mine have already stated that. But I want to stress it again. I don't want to go as far as Feuerbach's Projection Theory. In contrast to Karl Marx, I believe that religion can also play a positive, let us say therapeutic role for human beings. Religion or the religions should be pragmatically based. Let's do without theoretical speculations in a post-metaphysical age of "weak thought"—what was the name of the Italian philosopher who came up with that term? I remember, Vattimo. That's why I welcome it that in its current strategy the Vatican doesn't keep on repeating the teaching we all know quite well enough but instead prioritizes the pastoral aspect, which focusses on the individual. Truth for everyone is not what counts; individual pastoral care is the order of the day. What is called for today is not dogmas and an insistence on what is intrinsically evil about a moral act, but rather dialogue and tolerance. Indifferentism is still socially more tolerable than fundamentalism. The individual's conscience decides — not what is in itself good and evil, but what is good and bad for me. So feeling good is the criterion here. Identity is nowadays defined through sexual preferences, not through religious convictions. To confess to being a Christian is embarrassingly forthright; to out yourself as gay — now that's what I call courage.

We should ask forgiveness for all the suffering we have brought upon humanity with rigorous laws. Jesus would never have wanted anyone to suffer being lonely and having to do without sex just because they are not allowed a second, better partner after the first one has disappeared. That's typical of people who care about the letter and not the spirit of God's commandments. Those are the closed minds. When you maintain absolute truth, the step to violence is not far off.

Just look at the Thirty Years War in our country with all its brutality in the name of the true faith! I am a member of my Church — if for no other reason than consideration for our family tradition — even though as a natural scientist I cannot take things like creation and resurrection from the dead literally. Religious myths should not be abolished if we do not want the aesthetics of the soul to freeze to death in cold rationality. But I can easily warm to Bultmann's existential interpretation. "The Profession of Faith of the Savoyard Vicar" can unite the reasonable people who exist in every religion into a community of *Gutmenschen* (idealistic do-gooders). How often do you think I've read Chapter 5 of that genius Rousseau's *Emile ou de l'Education* (1762)? The revealed religions' claim to truth divides people and causes enmity, coercion and violence towards unbelievers or those of other faiths. Natural religion makes universal friendship possible. (*And he hums bits of Schiller's "Ode to Joy" to himself with an expression of rapture*): "*Seid umschlungen, Millionen! / Diesen Kuss der ganzen Welt! / Brüder, überm Sternenzelt / Muss ein lieber Vater wohnen!*" (Be embraced, you millions. Share this kiss throughout the world! Brothers, far above the starry canopy a loving father must reside).

Its positive dogmas do not result from the illogical and contradictory assertions of Christian revelation but are the expression of a social conscience that holds together a free and caring society.

It suffices if we assume the existence of an omniscient, good omni-deity, life after death—however one may imagine it—the rewarding of the good and punishment of the bad, and adherence to the social contract and the law. And as far as Robespierre is concerned, he thoroughly misunderstood his teacher Rousseau when he practised terror in the name of virtue. But in his defense, it can be said that, after all, he simply wanted to make the revolution irreversible.

A Christian socialist politician

We want nothing to do with terror in the name of the revolution. Violence has no place in our democracy, which we established on the basis of the human rights in European states after the State terror perpetrated by the Nazis and Communists. And we have also defended it against the terror of the Red Brigades and all the civil wars in the Third World and all the misery resulting from left- and right-wing dictatorships. Such things keep being brought up every now and then by the thought leaders on our Programme Committee. All the same, we do need religion in our free democratic constitutional order to supply the values that hold together our pluralistic society. Everyone must surely recognize the Ten Commandments, and as a Christian I also take my bearings from the Sermon on the Mount. I think that is actually the most important thing about Christianity. The rest is all about such difficult topics that the theologians should discuss amongst themselves. Pope Francis, who speaks so humanly and generally comprehensibly, has himself quoted Patriarch Athenagoras to argue that the denominations and religions would already be closer to each other if the theologians were put on an island. They simply disturb the peace of the ordinary people, who are much more advanced. Young people in particular cannot cope without being taught values. And that is where the churches have a great task to fulfill. So in fact Church Taxes benefit everyone; and how good it is that we have excellent schools run independently by the churches. That saves us a lot of money.

A post-communist politician

If you disregard Church Tax and other ways of funding the churches with my taxes, I, too, value the Church's social work for peace and disarmament, in protecting the environment and combatting climate change. We proved our new closeness to the Church by, unlike other parties, putting a picture of Pope Francis on our election posters. But privately I stick to my agnostic standpoint and thus to our tradition; but when religion teaches values, I find it good. So don't let anyone say I'm incapable of learning. I profess my support for the freedom of every individual whether it be for or against religion.

In the third circle of chairs

The first professor of feminist anthropology

I thank you that I as a woman am also being given a chance to speak. The real problem is, of course, that the Church continues to be a men's church. In the 19th century we lost the working classes; now we are losing the women. As always, the Church is reacting too late. That comes as no surprise given the celibate clergy's phobia of women. The Protestants cope all right, don't they? The real antagonisms in history are not, as Marx held, the class struggles. After all, the subjugation of women already starts in the biblical creation story. And that was written by men, which is why it can only conceive of God as a patriarch. This chain of thought leads directly to having only male priests in positions of power. Jesus broke through the patriarchal system, but then men turned back the wheel of time. I'm not blaming anyone. They themselves were still altogether captive to the spirit of the times.

But two thousand years later there is no excuse any more. Science has established that men and women are equal, even that in many respects women are superior to men. It is time to abolish the restrictive regulations of Canon Law. John Paul II's *Ordinatio Sacerdotalis* is out of date. Exegesis has shown that there were already women in every office in the Early Church, which means that there are no longer any obstacles to the priesthood and diaconate. Pope Francis recently named Mary Magdalene the '*Apostola apostolorum*'. That means that now women, too, can become successors to the apostles in the office of bishop and priest. That at least is a revolution from above and unlike those fighting for a female diaconate trying to capture the office from the bottom rung. The proof that Jesus wanted women priests can be adduced from precisely those sources that were spirited away. And conversely, the suppression of the proof-texts for the early Christian female priesthood is evidence that it did exist. Let me just cite Junia, who was "prominent among the apostles" (Rom 16:7): a little 's' was added to her name to turn her into a man—although they otherwise rant and rave on moral grounds against gender reassignment. Can't everyone choose the body they feel at home in? If there is a conflict between the soul and the body, it's better to correct the body than the soul—but okay, I'm not a medical doctor.

In any event, we are claiming the right for men and women to be treated equally. If I have the wish to realize myself in the vocation of a priest, I shall not let anyone talk me into believing that it is a question of objective calling and the sacramental nature of the office. Nor are we going to allow ourselves to be distracted by the strategy of appointing a higher proportion of women to leadership roles in the Church. Only when we stand at the altar like our male colleagues will the emancipation of women in the Catholic Church be achieved. And then we can talk about re-evangelization, communicating the faith or belief in God. That is the *conditio sine qua non*. Without women in priestly vestments there is no way forward because that alone is proof that in this my Church, which has always failed to see the signs of the times, the emancipation and equal status of women has finally and irreversibly arrived. The Pope is quite rightly against the clericalization of the laity. The situation in which more and more lay people have to take on the work of the clergy in the absence of priests can only be avoided with a female priesthood of equal status. Our open-minded Pope has made a start here with the Study Commission on the Women's Diaconate and showed the direction we should be going in.

A female philosopher of religion

I share many of your goals, but I am not entirely in agreement with the reasoning. I have succeeded—albeit with quite a struggle—in bringing up my five children very lovingly and at the same time having an academic career. My husband and I have not been in some kind of competition with one another but have done everything together. I cannot accept that some kind of class warfare exists between man and woman; after all, it was in the distinction between the two sexes that God laid the foundation for marriage and family. For us Christians, marriage is a symbol of the love between Christ and the Church, and it is in this that the vocation of husband and wife can be fulfilled in the love of God. It was not a deficiency in creation that brought conflict into even the most intimate fellowship of man and woman but rather the sin of Adam and Eve. However, Jesus has overcome sin, and we must follow Him, including in daily reconciliation and in the growth of love.

It is true that the social framework of marriage and the family has also changed — to a large extent for the better, too. Let us just think of medical advances with respect to infant mortality and the dangers to mothers when giving birth. We are also struggling to ensure that working conditions are organized in such a way as to make career and family compatible with one another. I am firmly convinced that the concerns of women are better served by a Christian anthropology than by some ism or other. And in the same way, women, too, regard social justice as being served better in the hands of Catholic Social Teaching than those of Socialism. We no longer have any need of feminism with militant rhetoric; what we need now is an in-depth theology of men, women and the relationship between the two sexes in their complementarity and mutual benefit. And when all is said and done, the Son of God came into the world for us and for our salvation and not as a referee in battles over power and prestige.

Through Baptism we have fellowship with Him, and in Holy Communion we receive the food for eternal life. A person is ordained priest in order to serve the Church and not in order to compensate for individual or collective affronts and satisfy ambitions. I am confident that the Magisterium made its decisions in accordance with revealed truth. It was certainly not driven by self-seeking gender interests in order to defend old bastions of male domination — that is completely absurd. My wish would be for us not to start with an ideological a priori such as that history is a series of class struggles and will end in the victory of the working class and victory parades trooping past the nomenklatura on Red Square in Moscow. The philosophical and theological a priori is: open your eyes and ears and your heart very wide. For faith comes from hearing. "For one believes with the heart and so is justified, and one confesses with the mouth and so is saved. The scripture says, 'No one who believes in him will be put to shame'" (Rom

10:10f.). It is better to live for ever in the house of the Lord than to spend a short time in an earthly paradise admiring the heroes of Socialism who lie dead as doornails by the walls of the Kremlin.

A Christian philosopher

I think that belief in God is the crucial question for modern man. We are made in His image and likeness. From that we derive our knowledge of our own dignity and our respect for our fellow human beings. That is why I refuse to accept a functional use of religion. I feel that to be an instrumentalization of my conscience, in which I am convinced of the truth. You see, for us truth is not the knowledge of facts but rather a relationship to the person of Jesus Christ. The cognitive community of persons is a higher truth than the mere knowledge of facts. What good does it do a young man when presenting his beloved with a rose if he tries to demonstrate his knowledge of cell biology with it instead of using it to reveal the passion of his love?

Furthermore, the agnostics think they can assume a loftier stance in their observation of the world and their use of reason as compared to believers. They imagine they can penetrate my inmost convictions by alleging that we are, whether consciously or unconsciously, controlled by interests. They maintain that whenever it proclaims the truth, the Church — and here they are thinking in a pre-conciliar manner only of the clergy and not of the salvific community — is really only concerned with power or other highly material interests. The relativists are inconsistent because they fail to apply the principle of the non-cognizability of the objective truth to their own theory and, despite their skepticism, still think they can read the minds of others. Even if the conviction that God exists and the fact of God's historical self-revelation in Jesus Christ cannot be deduced from man's finite reason, why should they be considered unreasonable? But anyway, the spontaneity, singularity and eventfulness of a person's commitment in love cannot be deduced with mathematical logic; nevertheless, reason certainly can react to it in freedom and allow itself to be moved by it. The spirit, with all its expressions, surely has ontologically no lesser being than the material world. In this respect, faith, as it understands the meaning of human existence as love, is more reasonable than the denial that leaves me perplexed and bereft of salvation.

The Roman Cardinal

I am delighted with your courage to bear witness and even more with your rational argumentation. After all, we must always be ready to make our defense to anyone who demands from us an account of the hope that is in us (cf. 1 Pet 3:15). A purely functional justification of religion both contradicts the Catholic faith's self-understanding and fails to do justice to the human striving after the truth. Maybe a doctor can be satisfied if his placebo helps a hypochondriac. But human beings do not imagine their mortality, death, mental and physical ailments or the loss of loved ones. It would be nothing more than a subtle deception to fabricate some fake truth about such things. And no one can be expected to deceive either himself or other people. What we Christians proclaim, we ourselves also believe. What was it Paul wrote to the doubting Corinthians: "My speech and my proclamation were not with plausible words of wisdom, but with a demonstration of the Spirit and of power, so that your faith might rest not on human wisdom but on the power of God" (1 Cor 2:4f.).

A sea captain

When I listen to the jumble of opinions here, I wouldn't like to hire a crew like this on my ship. I've steered many a huge tanker through heavy seas. But seeing that in recent years I've brought thousands of people safely back to harbour on cruise ships, I really can't resist drawing an analogy with the Barque of Peter. It is not the first task of a captain to show himself from his most charming side at lavish parties on board his ship with a little kiss here and a wave there. No, no. It's his damned duty to get the passengers into the harbour safe and sound. As a boy I used to dream dreams of the nautical life, imagining that a captain can do whatever he likes on his ship. There was a colleague who steered his ship close to the shore, concerned only for the sensation it offered those watching but forgetting the rocks beneath the keel. Yes indeed, a captain has supreme responsibility for his ship. But he also needs to trust his team and know that he can rely on them. And he must also have learnt his trade and acknowledge that he has to respect the requirements of wind and sea as well as the limits of technology if he doesn't want his ship to run aground on a sandbank or be smashed on the cliffs. You cannot put a good team together from individualists who just want to do their own thing and don't stick to the rules of navigation. In the Church, the rules will presumably be what is contained in revelation. And the collegiality of the bishops is called team spirit, too. The spirit of Christian seafaring is not blind obedience to rules so as to ingratiate oneself with the captain but rather acting on the basis of expert knowledge, thinking for yourself and taking on responsibility — everyone and everything in pursuit of a common goal. And that is not achieved by just sailing along the coast. You have to venture out into the open seas.

The Roman Cardinal

Those are the closing words. And I could not have put it better. For me they also call to mind what Paul has to say when he appeals to his listeners' sense of honor as bearers of the name Christian: "Now I appeal to you, brothers and sisters, by the name of our Lord Jesus Christ, that all of you should be in agreement and that there should be no divisions among you, but that you should be *united in the same mind and the same purpose — in eodem sensu eademque sententia*" (1 Cor 1:10). This principle of the identity of the faith of the Church, even as the theological and secular sciences progress, had already been formulated by Vincent of Lérins in his *Commonitorium* and was adopted by Vatican I (DH 3020)[5] and developed by Vatican II (*DV* 8). Preservation and progress, identity and relevance — these are the legs upon which the body of the faith community both stands and advances. Conservatism and progressivism are the broken wings that may still flap mightily but will no longer lift the bird into the air. Let's just hear what that early Church Father had to say to his fellow Christians 1600 years ago: "But someone will say, perhaps, shall there, then, be no progress in Christ's Church? Certainly; all possible progress. For what being is there, so envious of men, so full of hatred to God, who would seek to forbid it? Yet on the condition that it be real progress, not alteration of the faith. For progress requires that the subject be enlarged in itself, alteration, that it be transformed into something else. The intelligence, then, the knowledge, the wisdom, of individuals as well as of all, of one man as well as of the whole Church, ought, in the course of ages and centuries, to increase and make much and vigorous progress; but yet only in its own kind; that is to say, in the same doctrine, in the same sense, and in the same meaning" (Comm. 23).[6]

Parting exchange

After two and a half hours, the reception is over. On the way out, the Rome correspondent meets the Cardinal and comments that he found the discussion quite contentious. There was not much left of the much-vaunted unity of Catholics under the Magisterium, he

---

[5] DH: Denzinger, Latin-English 43rd ed. (2012), ed. Peter Hünermann.

[6] Vincent of Lérins, *Commonitorium*, ed. Michael Fiedrowicz, Mühlheim/Mosel 2011, 267. (English transl. cited from New Advent, Fathers of the Church.)

said. There were as many different voices as among the Protestants. And how the Catholic Church could be, to use an expression from Vatican II, an "instrument" of "the unity of the whole human race" (*LG* 1) remained a complete mystery to him. The Cardinal promises him that he will try to come up with a common thread running through all the afternoon's bits and pieces of ideas. As always, he has a quotation handy and cites Aristotle: "*Sapientis est ordinare et iudicare.*"[7] The highest and best thing for reason is to recognize grounds and connections. That hits the nail on the head as St. Thomas never ended a discussion with claims to power or one-sided partisanship; rather, it was through taking all the arguments seriously that he led the discussion onto the path of knowledge and insight. In order to pre-empt any kind of ideological appropriation, St. Thomas states the goals of his theological studies to be the wish to know not only what others have thought but also ultimately how the matter stands — *sicut res se habet.*

The following morning, in the Cardinal's sunlit study.

   The daily celebration of Holy Mass is the center of a priest's life. Theological thinking does not begin with books but springs from encountering Christ, the divine Word, in the "Most Blessed Eucharist [which] contains the entire spiritual boon of the Church" (PO 5). After that, the Cardinal soon goes to his study. He wants to prepare a short study on the topics that were discussed somewhat contentiously the day before at the German Embassy.

   The Cardinal walks up and down the room deep in thought.

The antagonism between a traditionalist and a modernist wing has a paralyzing effect and leads to defeatism. It turns the dove of the Holy Spirit, the Church as *una colomba*, as the Church Fathers

---

[7] *Met.* 982a; Thomas Aq., *S.th.* I q.1 a.6

called Her, into a lame duck. Apocalyptic nightmares of the great apostasy preceding the return of Christ haunt the blogosphere. There are secret murmurings about Francis being the last Pope, and he milks the idea.

But the *genius loci* of Rome inspires the Cardinal's thoughts on the unity and reform of the Catholic Church. He takes courage once more, and his thoughts and feelings begin to take shape more clearly. The magnificent view of the dome of St. Peter's fortifies him. It keeps the divine mission and the sacred commission of St. Peter constantly in sight. Popes come and go. How much failure in its ranks and how many enemies has the papacy already survived? And the Pope is still the successor of Peter. How often have we been beaten about the head with the anti-Roman prejudices and stereotypes with which historical painters blight people's imaginations and which earn public-opinion leaders a good deal of money? As a pastor, he knows enough about the human weaknesses of men of God and servants of the Church, too. But people also have to be warned against the cheap polemic that is always pushed along in front like dirt before a road-sweeper. The agitation against the Church is the bow wave of unbelief. The believer "keeps alert" (1 Pet 5:8) and he knows that: "While Christ, holy, innocent and undefiled [Heb 7:26] knew nothing of sin [2 Cor 5:21], … the Church, embracing in its bosom sinners, at the same time holy and always in need of being purified, always follows the way of penance and renewal" (*LG* 8). Penetrating the fog of sadness at what is all too human in the Church, the apathy of the indifferent and the hatred of Her enemies comes Jesus' clear promise that the gates of hell will not overcome Her — "*et portae inferi non praevalebunt adversus eam*" (Mt 16:18). God is the Lord of history. God's government of the world is not thwarted by human confusion. *Hominum confusione — Dei providentia.* The true consolation of the faithful lies in God's providence (cf. Rom 8:26-30). He preserves the Church in the unity of faith and the truth of the Word that became flesh. It is in order that the Church should be preserved in the unity of faith that the primacy of the Roman Church exists. So what is "this teaching about the institution, the perpetuity, the meaning and reason for the sacred primacy of the Roman Pontiff"? Vatican II put it clearly and concisely: "And in order that the episcopate itself might be one and undivided, he placed blessed Peter over the other apostles, and instituted in him a permanent and visible source and foundation of unity of faith and communion — *perpetuum ac visibile unitatis et communionis principium et fundamentum*" (LG 18).

The Cardinal surveys his library, and immediately all the minds gathered there beckon him to dialogue and disputation.

Here the scholar is surrounded by his books as by his teachers and friends; but also beleaguered by his spirits of contradiction. His library is where he feels spiritually at home. Amidst the philosophers from Plato and Aristotle, Hume and Kant to Hegel and Heidegger, and the Church Fathers, Scholasticism, the Reformers, the more recent theologians and philosophers, he is inspired by the relationship between revelation and reason. As Origen carefully weighed the arguments of the philosopher Celsus against the logic of faith and refuted them, so one today should also "be ready to make your defense to anyone who demands from you an account (*logon*) of the hope that is in you" (1 Pet 3:15).

It is not the epigones of the philosophers of materialism, of critical philosophy, of the metaphysics-smashers and the God-is-dead prophets along with all their parrots who are the dialogue partners of controversial theology. No, it is instead these in the original. In an ecumenical spirit, the great authors of Orthodoxy and of Protestant theology are consulted, too.

Scholarly books do not lead their thinking readers into a world of anemic abstractions that are meaningless for the cares and constraints of the daily life of the masses. For every human being has the right to understand the nature of the meaning and goal of his or her life, and every teacher has the duty to know what he or she is talking about, just as every politician must reflect on and weigh up the principles and consequences of his or her decisions.

Theology is a form of worshipping God, a necessary function of the Church. In the words of Dietrich Bonhoeffer: "Theology is the self-understanding (*Selbstverständigung*) of the Church about Her own nature on the basis of Her understanding (*Verständnis*) of God's revelation in Christ; and this self-communication necessarily always begins where there is a new turn in the Church's self-understanding (*Selbstverständigung*)."[8]

A scientifically competent theology and one that is firmly located within the Church is a "protest against any form of the church which does not honor the question of truth above all things."[9] That is what the young theologian said to those who wanted to play off theology against praxis in the ecumenical movement. "For those who despise wisdom and instruction are miserable" (Wis 3:11). No one can proclaim the gospel without first having been a pupil of the divine teacher. For a false or abridged presentation of doctrine will provoke the mockery of the opponents and jeopardize even more the salvation of those who are called to faith and eternal life through the light of Christ (cf. Jn 1:7).

The truth of the faith is the foundation and wellspring of Christian life. Without the teaching of the faith, the *sana et vera doctrina fidei*, good pastoral care is not possible because it is in faith that we "believe and know the truth" (1 Tim 4:3). Christ the Teacher and Christ the Good Shepherd, the *bonus pastor*, are one and the same person.

---

[8] *DBW* 11, 327f. English translation from: Volume 11: *Ecumenical, Academic, and Pastoral Work: 1931–1932.*

[9] Ibid. 328.

Priests are "servants of the word" (Lk 1:2), who are urged to "proclaim the message; be persistent whether the time is favorable or unfavorable; ... For the time is coming when people will not put up with sound doctrine, but having itching ears, they will accumulate for themselves teachers to suit their own desires" (2 Tim 4:2f.). The priest receives with humility the Apostle's exhortation: "As for you, always be sober, endure suffering, do the work of an evangelist, carry out your ministry fully" (2 Tim 4:4). Theology is not a matter of keeping oneself intellectually occupied but rather an encounter with the word of God in the service of the Church. Theological books are written and read to the glory of God in order that faith might be fixed and deepened in the hearts of the faithful. Theology is dialogue with God in His Word and in the power of the life-giving Holy Spirit. For "one does not live by bread alone, but by every word that comes from the mouth of God" (Mt 4:4). Faith is not a vague sense of the supersensory; it is the knowledge of God in Jesus Christ unto eternal life (cf. Jn 17:3). The Church needs scholarly theology. Jesus said to His disciples: "Therefore every scribe who has been trained for the kingdom of heaven is like the master of a household who brings out of his treasure what is new and what is old" (Mt 13:52).

That is why the teacher of the sacred sciences does not have the same feelings in his library as Goethe's Faust once had in his study. He lets himself be inspired by the Spirit of God, who always affirms, not by the spirit who denies. At one point, Mephistopheles joins Faust, who wishes to recognize the force "that binds creation's inmost energies" (Faust I, Night. In a high- vaulted, narrow Gothic chamber). He offers Faust the following as his visiting-card:

> *Ich bin der Geist, der stets verneint!*
> *Und das mit Recht; denn alles, was entsteht,*
> *Ist wert, dass es zugrunde geht;*

Roman Encounters

Drum besser wär's, dass nichts entstünde.
So ist denn alles, was ihr Sünde,
Zerstörung, kurz, das Böse nennt,
Mein eigentliches Element.
(*Faust* I, Studierzimmer).

The spirit I, which evermore denies!
And justly; for whate'er to light is brought
Deserves again to be reduced to naught;
Then better 'twere that naught should be.
Thus all the elements which ye
Destruction, Sin, or briefly, Evil, name,
As my peculiar element I claim.
(*Faust* I, Study)[10]

For the scholar of the sacred sciences it is quite different. In his study he feels more like St. Jerome, the only cardinal among the Fathers of the Church, in his study. In Dürer's famous engraving of him the saint is sitting at his writing and reading desk. He is studying the Bible in order thus to become more deeply acquainted with the mystery of man and his divine calling. For "Ignorance of Scripture is ignorance of Christ" (Comm. in Isaias. prol.). The skull on the windowsill reminds the observer that in Adam we were all doomed to die. But the cross on the corner of the table assures us of our redemption from our sins and from eternal death. In the Cross is life and hope — that is the message of salvation that our Church Father draws from Sacred Scripture. "We know that Christ, being raised from the dead, will never die again; death no longer has dominion over him. The death he died, he died to sin, once for all; but the life he lives, he lives to God. So you also must consider yourselves dead to sin and alive to God in Christ Jesus" (Rom 6:9-11).

---

[10] Project Gutenberg e-text: May 2004.

And unlike Faust with his shaggy poodle, Jerome with his grateful lion, out of whose foot he had removed a thorn, knows that in the beginning was not the deed but rather the Word through whom all things came into being. And "in him was life, and the life was the light of all people" (Jn 1:4).

Man's destiny does not lie in seizing power, but in giving thanks. Deed without word is *brutum factum*, brute force. But the deeds of salvation that spring from the Word are spirit and life (cf. Jn 6:63). Our role-model is not the Titan storming the heavens but rather the humble Son of the Father, who for us human beings and for our salvation came down from heaven. He came "that the creation itself will be set free from its bondage to decay and will obtain the freedom of the glory of the children of God" (Rom 8:21). "The accuser of our comrades . . ., who accuses them day and night before our God" (Rev 12:10) rejoiced too soon over the death of the sinner. Mephistopheles's shout of triumph at the perdition of an unhappy soul: "She is condemned!" is met with a "Voice from above" at the very moment when all seems lost uttering the judgement of grace: "She is redeemed!" (Faust I, Final scene in the Dungeon).

To cynicism about life, nihilism about being, and despair of hope the believer shows his ID-card with its unique PIN, which does not react to the password "curse" but only to "blessing." The Holy Spirit does not teach us "A scurvy song. Faugh! a political song, A filthy song" (*Faust* I, Auerbach's Cellar in Leipzig) but rather the "cheerful song" of the redeemed:

> *Der Christ, das ist der Mensch, der stets bejaht!*
> *Und das mit Recht; denn alles, was entsteht,*
> *Ist wert, dass es nie zugrunde geht;*
> *So ist denn alles, was ihr Gnade,*
> *Versöhnung, kurz, die Liebe nennt,*
> *Des Höchsten eigentliches Element.*

Roman Encounters

Drum besser war's, dass entstand,
was der Schöpfer selbst sehr gut genannt.

The Christian I, who evermore affirms!
And justly; for whate'er to light is brought
Deserves ne'er to be reduced to naught;
Thus all that you well describe as grace,
Atonement, too, in love's embrace,
Is God's peculiar element.
Then better 'twas it was brought to light
What was *very good* in the Creator's sight.

The Cardinal is somewhat consoled, in the face of this confusion of spirits and the ice-cold power politics of many a clique, about how he should promote the unity of the Church and Her reform in Christ.

But spiritually he feels called to render this service to the Church since before his Passion the Son of God Himself prayed for the unity of the Church. We must not withdraw into the peace of contemplation when rough hands are ripping apart the Lord's seamless garment (cf. Jn 19:23). As long as we are pilgrims on this earth, we belong to the Church Militant, Christ's militia (cf. Eph:10-20). "Indeed, we live as human beings, but we do not wage war according to human standards; for the weapons of our warfare are not merely human, but they have divine power to destroy strongholds. We destroy arguments and every proud obstacle raised up against the knowledge of God, and we take every thought captive to obey Christ" (2 Cor 10:3-6).

At the Last Supper, Jesus said to His Father: "I ask not only on behalf of these, but also on behalf of those who will believe in me through their word, that they may all be one. As you, Father, are in me and I am in you, may they also be in us, so that the world may believe that you have sent me. The glory that you have given me I have given them, so that they may be one, as we are one, I in them and you in me, that they may become completely one, so that the world may know that you have sent me and have loved them even as you have loved me" (Jn 17:20-23).

The Pentecost event springs to mind here, too, when through the preaching of the apostles the Holy Spirit gathered together the first Church from among all the languages of the world. And everyone could see "that the whole group of those who believed were of one heart and soul" (Acts 4:32). The inner unity of the Church in faith and love came about as "they devoted themselves to the apostles' teaching and fellowship, to the breaking of bread and the prayers" (Acts 2:42).

But it is shattering if you just take a look at Paul's communities. There are reports of divisions, bickering and strife. And the apostle sharply admonishes his Corinthians: "What I mean is that each of you says, 'I belong to Paul', or 'I belong to Apollos', or 'I belong to Cephas,' or 'I belong to Christ.' Has Christ been divided? Was Paul crucified for you? Or were you baptized in the name of Paul?" (1 Cor 1:12f.).

The unity of the Church has nothing to do with romantic feelings of the commingling of God and the world or the idyll of a cozy gathering over coffee and cakes. The Lord's Supper can only be celebrated in God's Church as an efficacious sign of unity if "when you come together as a church" there are no "divisions (*schismata*) among you" (1 Cor 11:17f.). "Indeed there have to be factions (*nam oportet et haereses esse*) among you, for only so will it become clear who among you are genuine" (1 Cor 11:19).

The bishops have a particular responsibility for the unity of the Church in the truth of Christ. That is why the famous Father of the Church Cyprian of Carthage, when writing against those who had become apostates, heretics and schismatics during the persecution, brought out the unity of the Church as the foundation for Her mediation of salvation: "Does he who does not hold this unity of the Church think that he holds the faith? Does he who strives against and resists the Church trust that he is in the Church, when moreover the blessed apostle Paul teaches the same thing, and sets forth the sacrament of unity, saying, 'There is one body and one spirit, one hope of your calling, one Lord, one faith, one baptism, one God?' (Eph 4:4-6).

"And this unity we ought firmly to hold and assert, especially those of us that are bishops who preside in the Church, that we may also prove the episcopate itself to be one and undivided. Let no one deceive the brotherhood by a falsehood: let no one corrupt the truth of the faith by perfidious prevarication. The episcopate is one, each part of which is held by each one for the whole. The Church also is one, which is spread abroad far and wide into a multitude by an increase of fruitfulness. As there are many rays of the sun, but one light; and many branches of a tree, but one strength based in its tenacious root" (Cyprian, *De unit.* eccl. 4-5).

The fact that the unity of the Church is instituted by God and makes the sacramental nature of the Church recognizable in faith means that it is logical for the same to be applied to the unity of the Catholic faithful in the Church, the unity of all the baptized with the Catholic Church and the Catholic Church's service of the unity of the human race.

If "Christ is the light of nations," it follows that "the Church is in Christ like a sacrament or as a sign and instrument both of a very closely-knit union (*unio*) with God and of the unity (*unitas*) of the whole human race" (*LG* 1).

Just as the first outlines of the subject of the reform and the unity of the Church are taking shape before his mind's eye, there is a ring at the door of the Cardinal's apartment. The journalist from yesterday arrives with a French cultural theoretician. They apologize for disturbing him and settle down for a long meeting.

The Cardinal

Welcome, gentlemen, but I'm just working on the first outlines of my new book on the reform and unity of the Church in faith. Naturally I'm proceeding systematically, as I learnt to from my academic teachers and always urged my own students to when I was supervising their work, right down to doctoral and post-doctoral dissertations. Well, what strikes us first is that in both creeds, the longer Nicene-Constantinopolitan and the shorter Apostolic, unity is the first of the four marks of the Church to be named, followed by Her other attributes.

It seems to me that unity not only comes first but is, in fact, the foundational mark of the Church. It is, as it were, the root of the trunk from which the others grow like three branches. For the unity of the Church is grounded in the unity of God and reflects it. The Church results from God's self-revelation, from which it emerges as the house and people of God, the Body of Christ and the temple of the Holy Spirit. "Thus, the Church has been seen as 'a people made one with the unity of the Father, the Son and the Holy Spirit'" (*LG* 4). The Second Vatican Council adopted this sentence from Cyprian of Carthage and used it as the basis for the systematics of its ecclesiology.

Hence at Holy Mass on Sundays and Feast Days we profess our faith in God the Father, the Son and the Holy Spirit along with their works in creation and salvation history; later we say: "I believe in one, holy, catholic and apostolic Church." This by no means indicates a political and organizational entity or refers to something along the lines of absolutist princes and the leaders of totalitarian states who unite all power in one hand. *Un roi, une lois, une foi* was a political slogan of the absolutism of Louis XIV and his countless imitators. He considered himself the greatest luminary in his solar system, the Sun King. Here religion was subordinated to raison d'état. Later, the Church was completely eliminated in atheistic states and the social function of religion was replaced by a totalitarian ideology. With rallying cries such as *"Ein Volk, ein Reich, ein Führer"* and "The Party is always right," they demanded complete control over hearts and minds. All religions and morals founded on divine authority counted as enemies of freedom and progress and were fought against tooth and nail. And how easily deadly political enemies forged the grand coalition of anticlericalism. The Liberals and Socialists who pushed through the separation of Church and State in France in 1905 raged against the Cross of Christ just as much as the Nazis did in Germany and the League of the Militant Godless in the Soviet Union. What must be going on in their hearts for them to be so terrified by the image of the Crucified Christ? Why is such fear aroused by him of whom it is said that he came "that he might create in himself one new humanity in place of the two, thus making peace, and might reconcile both groups [Jews and Gentiles] to God in one body through the cross, thus putting to death that hostility through it" (Eph 2:15f.).

When Jesus, on the other hand, promises that "there will be one flock, one shepherd" (Jn 10:16), He is not thinking of a secular claim to power of people over people but rather recalling His giving His life for us, through which the Church comes into being as a community in faith, hope, and love. The unity among the many believers with all their different charisms and talents is a gift of God to His Church. They belong together organically like the many members of a body, and their Head is Christ.

It was only by brute force that the Caesars of various types came to exercise autocratic rule. They sacrificed the life of others for themselves whereas Jesus sacrificed His own life for others. That is what makes the crucial difference when we speak of the Kingdom of

God as opposed to worldly kingdoms: here the King on the Cross; there the imperial pomp of impermanence. Christ did not amass His kingdom like the rulers of this world with the military might of the legions and the manipulations of cunning propaganda.

Before Pilate, Jesus identifies Himself as a king of quite a different kind: "You say that I am a king. For this I was born, and for this I came into the world, to testify to the truth. Everyone who belongs to the truth listens to my voice" (Jn 18:37). The unity of Christians is grounded in the unity of Jesus with His Father in the Most Holy Trinity. And since He took on our humanity in the Incarnation, it is the God-Man, the Head of the Church, who unites the many members, i.e., the baptized individuals, in one body. In accordance with this Pauline image of the Church as the Body of Christ united with its Head, St. Augustine came up with the famous formulation: "The one and whole Christ, Head and Body, with the many members—*unus et totus Christus, caput et corpus et membra*" (Sermo 341, 9, 11).

So it is not a collective unity but rather an organic and personal one in community with Christ and each other. Paul underlines the personal reality of the Church: "… for all of you are one in Christ Jesus" (Gal 3:28). He does not say just that we are one as if this were just the unity of a shared ethos; rather, we are one as head and body are one. The Church is a person in Christ, and the members of Christ's Body are in reality joined together in a sacramental unity. That is why with relation to Christ, the Bridegroom, the Church can also be called His *bride* and with respect to the faithful their *mother*.

In this historic hour of the Church, the Catholic faithful can certainly expect a spiritual and moral reorientation from Rome, the city of the Princes of the Apostles, Peter and Paul. That is my firm conviction and one based on the leadership role given by Christ to the Roman church. Didn't Irenaeus of Lyon as early as the 2nd century counter the gnostic doubts regarding its legitimacy by highlighting the vital principle of the unity of Catholics in the truth of Christ. Referring to the "Church founded and organized at Rome by the two most glorious apostles, Peter and Paul," he states: "For it is a matter of necessity that every Church should agree with this Church, on account of its preeminent authority, that is, the faithful everywhere, inasmuch as the tradition has been preserved continuously by those [faithful men] who exist everywhere" (*Haer.* III, 3, 2).

The greatest obstacle would seem to be the substitution of an ideology for faith or the fact that the Church—instead of reassuring Herself of Her universal mission in Christ—manuvers politically back and forth between the ideological parties. How often do you hear people say that the Church must be virtually refounded in order to be able to hold Her own in a secularized world? The Church is faced with the tragic alternative of either retaining Her identity and thereby losing Her relevance or adapting to the modern world whatever the cost, even that of losing Her identity.

The French cultural theorist

The project of 18th-century Enlightenment philosophy, whose ultimate aim was a "humanism without God,"[11] currently seems to have come very close to achieving its aim in the program of the complete dechristianization of European culture and civilization. Let me call to mind the beginnings of this tsunami with the Jacobins of the French Revolution. In his radical newspaper *Père Duchesne*, Jacques René Hébert, who himself ended up on the guillotine on 24 March 1794, demanded the radical obliteration of every trace of France's

---

[11] Cf. Henri de Lubac, *Le Drame de l'humanisme athée*, Paris 71983 (1944) ; Engl. *The Drama of Atheist Humanism*, San Francisco 1995 (London 1949).

Christian history. The first issue of the extremely anti-clerical paper appeared under the title "Down with the Bells." Christian symbols, feasts and names were to disappear: out of sight, out of mind. Belief in God was replaced by the "Cult of Reason." The Jacobins were the willing executors of Enlightenment criticism of religion. But every revolution produces such monsters. You Germans have your own Hébert in the anti-Christian and antisemitic Nazi demagogue Julius Streicher with his inflammatory paper *Der Stürmer*. He, too, ended ignominiously on the gallows in Nuremberg on 16 October 1946. Militant atheism in the Soviet Union was similarly brutal with its aim of totally destroying Christianity. In a report published in the government broadsheet *Izvestia* (13 October 1922, No. 231), Leon Trotsky, whom Stalin will have murdered in Mexico on 21 August 1940, writes: "Religion is a poison precisely during a revolutionary epoch.... If man is promised a hereafter, a kingdom without end, then is it worth shedding his own and his brothers' and his children's blood for the establishment of a kingdom just like this here in *this* world?... We must go to them [the people] with the propaganda of atheism, for only this propaganda defines the place of man in the universe and draws out for him a circle of conscious activity here on earth."[12] This is, of course, a typical figure of thought of modern atheism with its primitive juxtaposition of the hereafter and this world as if orientation towards God and responsibility for the world were not mutually dependent. Whereas in the political atheisms the aim is to speed up the expected certain death of religion by exterminating its adherents, in liberal circles the natural death of religion is expected imminently. They maintain that with the rise of science and technology a process of "disenchantment of the

[12] Leon Trotsky, *The Position of the Republic and the Tasks of Young Workers* (Report to the 5th All-Russian Congress of the Russian Communist League of Youth 1922). Quoted from Leon Trotsky Internet Archive (www.marxists.org) 2002.

world"—as the great sociologist Max Weber put it—has begun which condemns religion to extinction. All the same, in view of facts displaying the opposite, the plausibility of the secularization theory has recently been called into question. I can see you have books by Charles Taylor here, which makes me think in particular of his *A Secular Age* (2007).[13] Hans Joas' critique of Max Weber in his book *Die Macht des Heiligen. Eine Alternative zur Geschichte von der Entzauberung* (The Power of the Sacred: An Alternative to the Narrative of Disenchantment) has met with great success.[14] Nor do I want to forget Volker Gerhardt's attempt at a new justification of rational theology in his book *Der Sinn des Sinns: Versuch über das Göttliche.*[15]

But let's go back. In his absolute Idealism, Hegel had still made a stand against materialism, the Enlightenment's stance of this-worldliness (*Diesseitigkeit*) without transcendence. He wanted to understand world history, including the death of God on the Cross, the hour of triumphant atheism, as the dialectical self-fulfillment of the Absolute Spirit (*Geist*). Which includes in itself the revelation of the truth of religion and philosophy.

Reaching into the shelves, the Professor takes down Hegel's Lectures on the Philosophy of World History (I/B) *and goes straight to the following quotation:*

"For that history [= world history] is the exhibition of the divine, absolute development of Spirit in its highest forms—that gradation by which it attains its truth and consciousness of itself."[16] As the revelation and implementation of God's plan, the goal of world

---

[13] Charles Taylor, A Secular Age, Cambridge Mass. 2007.

[14] Berlin 2017.

[15] Munich 2014.

[16] PhB 171a, 75. Engl. *The Philosophy of History.* Kitchener, Ontario 2001, 69.

history is not just the subjective salvation of mankind, which would be purposively directed only towards the next world.

The Professor skips a large number of pages and, landing in Part C, sums up:

"Now according to the religious view, the purpose of spiritual activity, like that of natural existence, is the glorification of God. This is indeed the worthiest purpose of the spirit and of history." (PhB 171a, 181).

But the 19th century materialists and atheists once again draw on their predecessors in English empiricism and the Encyclopédistes of the French Enlightenment.

The French professor refers to the "Preliminary Discourse" that D'Alembert wrote in 1751 for the Encyclopédie that he and Diderot edited and which most purely embodies the spirit of this-worldliness of the modern age. The neo-atheists revere the Encyclopédie like an icon and its authors like heroes.

An interpretation of the whole of humanity's intellectual and religious history was offered by Auguste Comte in his *Discours sur l'Esprit positif* (1844) (A General View of Positivism, London 1856, 1865). Convinced of the superiority of positivist thinking, he develops the Law of the Three Stages, arguing that the progress of world history necessarily reveals "the law of the growth of the human mind." It begins, he contends, with the theological or fictitious stage, is succeeded by the metaphysical or abstract stage, and finally culminates in the positive and real stage. Only what is positively given and empirically verifiable is real, meaning that all theology is based on fiction. In its theory and practical application in technology, modern positivist science is in principle incompatible with both theology and belief in one God or in transcendent powers. The true God is Humanity, which celebrates itself in an artificial religion.

Let me recall the other narrative of modern times, one that does not, however, end in man's apotheosis but rather reduces him to the level of an animal. According to Sigmund Freud, as a result of scientific progress the naïve narcissism of the human consciousness has suffered first cosmological, then biological and finally psychological injury: through Copernicus he was banished from the center of the cosmos; through Darwin he was forced to learn that he was descended from the animal kingdom, meaning that there was merely a gradual difference between man and animal, and this "destroyed man's supposedly privileged place in creation."[17] Through Freud's discovery of the unconscious it has become clear to man that he is not master in his own house.

This can be compared with class-war materialism and Feuerbach's projection theory with its image of history, which leads to the pure immanence of humanity without leaving the place of the Absolute empty. The personal God of the Word and the Holy Spirit is replaced by the idea of progress, science and humanity, whose interests are represented by a party or a leader. Instead of being liberated, man is now at the mercy of man because there is no longer any authority to which he could appeal or to whom his conscience ought to be answerable.

But by its very nature history is not a succession of class struggles inevitably leading to the earthly paradise of the working population. Nor is it the opposite. In my opinion, history is the progression of time in which individuals and states and religious communities serve the *bonum commune* without its being possible to require them all to be convinced of the idea of inner-worldly perfection. For to do so would mean placing secularism, which is but one ideology among others, in the position of the absolute. Secularism is not, as it were, the norm against which religions orientated towards

---

[17] *Vorlesungen zur Einführung in die Psychoanalyse* (1917): S. Freud, Studienausgabe I, ed. A. Mitscherlich, Frankfurt a. M. 2000, 283f. (Engl. *Introductory Lectures on Psycho-Analysis*, Lecture XVIII).

transcendence would have to justify their right to exist and their usefulness. This self-contradiction is something our laicists have up to now not yet worked out; otherwise they would be more tolerant and conciliatory.

Responsibility for the world is perfectly compatible with being convinced of a supernatural divine calling to beatitude in God. The hope of a supernatural perfection releases more commitment to love of neighbor than the illusion of a material paradise on earth from which I shall be shut out again through death.

What these ideologies have in common is their absolute certainty that progress in education, the blessings of technology and the struggle against oppression, exploitation, hunger and war will inevitably lead to the extinction of belief in God and the religion and morals associated with it, i.e., Christianity. And the creation of the New Man must be accelerated by destroying religion, which is the "opium of the people." "The criticism of religion is, therefore, in embryo, the criticism of that vale of tears of which religion is the halo."[18]

The journalist on a Christian weekly magazine

Perhaps I can finally get a word in. Apparently, people weren't quite so convinced of these axioms after all if they thought they had to help the objective course of the historical process of emancipation along by subjecting Christians to the cruellest of persecutions. Honest believers are vilified for their religion as incurably sick opium addicts. There are states today that pursue their battle against narcotics by murdering addicts. That's what comes of humanism

---

[18] Karl Marx, *Zur Kritik der Hegelschen Rechtsphilosophie. Die Frühschriften*, ed. S. Landshut, Stuttgart 1964, 208. Engl. *Introduction to A Contribution to the Critique of Hegel's Philosophy of Right*. Cambridge 1970.

against God: you declare the healthy to be sick and the sick to be criminals.

What they want is for everything Christian that forms the basis of our image of man and our world view and which permeates and shapes our individual and social thinking and acting to be supplanted by a universal counter-paradigm with man himself as its ground, norm and goal. The intention is that Christianity as it manifests itself in public in the Creed and sacramentality of the Church, in worship and liturgy, in ethics, mysticism and asceticism will not only become a purely private matter but will also be completely ousted from people's consciousness by means of permanent brainwashing. The marginalization of Church and religion (in the *Kulturkampf* in Germany and Italy) or even their physical destruction (in the Reign of Terror of the French Revolution, in National Socialism and Bolshevism) is celebrated as an act of liberation, freeing the people from the power of the priests who kept them in ignorance and dependency. With Voltaire's mantra, *Ecrasez l'infâme*, (referring very much to the Catholic Church) ringing in their ears, the murderers of tens and hundreds of thousands of priests and lay faithful have known themselves to be borne by a higher legitimacy.

At its heart, the Enlightenment is a materialism that leads logically to atheism and in its milder form indulges complacently and with genteel aloofness in cultured skepticism and agnosticism. From the high horse of proud reason, its exponents condescended to allow the simple people to retain a residue of religious feeling and symbolic worship for the sake of their mental health and on socio-political grounds. They used "traditional, outdated and medieval Christianity" merely as a negative foil for the self-determined, autonomous, tolerant and pluralist modern man. This not only casts doubt on the truth of faith, which is the response to God's free self-disclosure in his Word, and together with this the witness to revelation in the shape of the Church. It also endangers the unity of the faith community, which reacts to this challenging of its right to exist with either total resistance or partial accommodation.

Since the epoch-making project of a humanism without God arises from the insight that the process of the infinite self-perfection of the human race is inevitable according to natural law, this in principle leaves no room for a religion of redemption by God and the perfection of man in God.

Christian theology, as the scientific interpretation of God's historical self-revelation in Jesus Christ, is faced with the alternative of re-interpreting its teachings naturalistically, placing its worship and morals at the disposal of a natural and rational "religion," or of setting itself supranaturalistically against progress, science and modern culture, which will result in its being felt to be a foreign body and being more or less violently shaken off.

Right up to the 18th century, the majority of the population of Europe regarded Christianity as the intellectually and morally unsurpassable apogee of human history since there can be no deeper knowledge of our origins and future or the meaning of existence altogether beyond God's eschatological self-revelation in His Incarnate Word. The split in western Christianity that accompanied the coexistence side by side of the Catholic Church and the Protestant denominations did not substantially change this fundamental insight since the controversy mainly concerned the ecclesial-sacramental mediation of redemption. Nevertheless one must not, of course, forget the shift in the image of man that resulted from the teaching of the total depravity of human nature as a result of Original Sin as opposed to its merely being wounded, which led to a divergence into a more pessimistic or a more optimistic view of mankind.

In the 16th and 17th centuries the disputes about the contentious doctrines were so closely linked to the interests of the ruling powers and employed in support of existing social conditions that Enlightenment humanism proclaimed its grand visions of freedom and autonomy, of progress and a society with equal rights and opportunities in opposition to the political and spiritual power of the Church.

The Cardinal

We cannot make revealed religion per se into the opposite or complement of the sum and system of the natural knowledge acquired in the natural, historical and social sciences or the worldly wisdom derived from everyday experience. But it is also true that the two spheres of knowledge are not unrelated. Grace and faith presuppose nature and reason. If I can see farther with a telescope than with my natural vision, I still see the object through my own eyes. So if, enlightened by the Holy Spirit, I know God in the Word of His revelation, I still know Him through the natural cognitive faculty of my own reason. But the will is also involved since the innermost essence of faith is love of God above all else and of one's neighbor as oneself. And if I love God above all else through the Holy Spirit that has been poured out into my heart (cf. Rom 5:5), I love with the natural intentionality of my will and its longing for union with the Beloved. Hence natural and supernatural knowledge of God do not exclude self-knowledge and knowledge of the structures of the natural world; rather, these can be mutually dependent and promote and augment one another. For God cannot be known by us in and of Himself but only through the world as its Creator (cf. Rom 1:20) and through the conscience as its judge (cf. Rom 2:14-16) and finally through the human words of Christ as the medium of the divine Word, Who is Himself God (cf. Jn 1:1-3).

The two dimensions come together subjectively in the consciousness of the perceiving and believing individual, meaning that that person must reflect on the difference between them with respect to the various sources, principles and methods involved. But the individual must also be capable of constructing a tension-free synthesis in his mental conception of God, the world and man. And that is a task that theology must fulfill anew in every epoch. It is not the findings and new methods beginning to flourish in the natural sciences, historical criticism of the Bible and of Church and world history that are antithetical to revealed theology but rather their reduction to a single metaphysical principle. Knowledge of the ontological status of the human intellect does not necessarily lead to rationalism and idealism accompanied by the assumption that matter possesses a lower status. Conversely, the empirical observation that matter is the prerequisite for all human knowledge does not lead to empiricism and to sensualism, which debases the intellect to nothing more than an epiphenomenon of matter. The fact that human knowledge is always linked to the senses does not mean that it cannot extend beyond them. The limited scope of human reason does not necessarily exclude the possibility of any supernatural revelation: for God revealed Himself to the People of Israel through sensory and intellectual means and, in Christ, spoke the Word of God, "words of eternal life" (Jn 6:68), to the apostles. I certainly cannot reach the other side of the river in one jump if it is 100 meters away. But if someone has the will to save me and the power to build a bridge over to me from the unattainable other side, then I shall be rescued and reach the saving shore through that person's affection.

The totally justified criticism directed by the Enlightenment philosophers—who cannot claim a monopoly of it, though—at the absolutist monarchy and the feudal system, at the inhuman punishments of the justice system, the lack of understanding of educators, and at the stagnation of scientific and technological progress is in no way an obstacle to the principles of the concept of the person and the shared responsibility of all for social, political and cultural life. A differentiated look at the socio-cultural conditions in pre-revolutionary France is beneficial in the controversial discussion of the achievements and limitations of the philosophy of the time.

Despite great achievements in producing historical editions of the most important patristic sources and of Church history, the France of the Enlightenment did not display sufficient theological involvement with the new findings and methods of the natural sciences or social and economic developments for it to keep pace in foresight and intellectual energy with the creative syntheses between philosophy and the sciences in patristics and Scholasticism. In France, the religious energies were spent in the bloody conflict between the denominations. Christianity as the religion of love of God and neighbor appeared fundamentally compromised by the atrocities of the Huguenot Wars. The Christian denominations, which wanted to assert their absolute claim to truth not with hearts and minds but rather with brute force and the help of the State themselves undermined the credibility of the Church. Supernatural faith, which we can only have with the aid of the Spirit, is either promoted or obscured by the credibility of the visible Church in Her witnesses and teachers.

Within Catholicism the Jansenist controversy, the battle with the Jesuit Order and the massive subordination of the Catholic faith to the interests of the State (king, crown cardinals, parliament, etc.) were counterproductive to the true mission of the Church. When the clergy saw their raison d'être as lying in their social rank as the first of the three estates in the Kingdom of France and in the acquisition of benefices through the King's favor and not in the proclamation of the gospel and in pastoral care for the salvation of souls, then the contradiction inherent in this was clearly apparent to the well-disposed, and even more so to the enemies of the Church.

A *Spring Evening at the German Embassy*

In political Gallicanism and the Catholic State Church (for example, in Austrian Josephinism), the outward institution of the Church was instrumentalized to serve the interests of the State (*ius circa sacra*). In the period of enlightened absolutism, the State authority in Josephinism and Febronianism even attempted to intervene in doctrine and liturgy (*ius in sacra*).

The French cultural historian

In the course of the French Revolution, the parties came into being as political-ideological power groups with a tendency towards claiming totalitarian power (Girondists, Jacobins). As part of the belief in progress and an exclusively this-worldly definition of the goal and purpose of human history and in view of the ideals of a complete new beginning after the fall of the Ancien Régime (of Church and monarchy, clergy and nobility), intellectual life and society split into ideological parties whose aim it was, however, to lay claim to total power over people's hearts and lives. Some were satisfied with what had already been achieved while others regarded the present as being merely a transition towards the real goal. This led to the formation of conservative and progressive (liberal, socialist) tendencies which each dismissed the other as reactionary or revolutionary (anarchistic).

Even in constitutional democracies, which recognize fundamental human rights and make no totalitarian claims over the religion and moral consciences of their citizens, the seating arrangements in freely elected parliaments (right, left and center) still bear traces of an ideological division of society.

This ideological alien infiltration of intellect and morals is the outcome of relinquishing the transcendence of human reason and freedom. For if man's finite reason is its own origin, measure and goal, then in the end it is merely the power of leadership figures or parties that determines the direction in which everyone has to go. Liberation from ideological tutelage switches dialectically to being the ideological tutelage of the liberated. The Church must offer humanity today Her support in overcoming the ideological contradictions and totalitarian tendencies of the ideologies with their own programs of self-redemption. What monsters have emerged from of this morass! I am thinking of Robespierre with his loyal assistant Saint Just, the president of the Committee of Public Safety, the *Comité de salut public*, and the Public Prosecutor Fouquier de Tinville or also of canaille like Fouché who together sent thousands of innocent people to be executed. All totalitarian systems produce such criminal cliques. Hitler was flanked by Heydrich and Himmler and found in Roland Freisler a willing judicial murderer at the People's Court. In Stalin's Soviet Union, even his bloodiest henchmen in the NKVD from Yezhov to Beria, who had millions of human lives on their consciences, themselves fell prey to the executioner. Doesn't *The Black Book of Communism* speak of hundreds of millions of people who met violent deaths because of this ideology?

The history of humanism without God is the narrative of its historical and thus empirical self-refutation. Maybe Robespierre did just misunderstand his master Rousseau and maybe Lenin and Stalin were no more than epigones of Marx and Engels, or maybe Hitler just took from Nietzsche what suited him. But every thinker is responsible not just for his good intentions but also for the practical consequences of his theory. Belief in a progressive humanization of the world without a morality that owes itself to a transcendent power has lost its innocence.

The thing with political ideologies is that they are by no means just side effects of revolutions involving a bit of regrettable collateral damage that could after all be justified with the "achievements of socialism" and the "great leaps forward." In nationalistic imperialism and colonialism, the ideological distortion of the true task of politics has led to whole continents being exploited and subjugated. Then came Fascism and Communism with two world wars and genocides of unimaginable barbarity. And the confrontation between the West and the socialist regimes brought the world to the brink of the nuclear suicide of the whole human race. All war is fratricide. No terror can invoke God to justify it. The essence of all ideology is self-redemption and its root is atheism.

The Catholic journalist

Since the French Revolution and the consequent ideological split in western societies, the Catholic Church and theology, too, have always been faced with the choice between joining either the conservative or the liberal wing, of positioning themselves between Maistre and Loisy, Lefebvre and Küng, *Action française* and Christians for Socialism. Internally, this leads to a disintegration of unity in the revealed faith. Liberal and conservative tendencies arise, or whatever variations there are of this pattern: left — right, progressive — reactionary, dialogical — dogmatic, open-minded — hardliner, etc., etc.

The Creed, which is the Church's response to revelation and the way She makes this present in the world as a defined profession of faith, is overlaid or even replaced by prior ideological decisions. The fraternal community of the Church, which is based on shared participation in grace and the one hope of eternal life, is invaded by partisan friend-foe thinking. This is inevitably combined with unscrupulousness regarding the means employed in jockeying for the power to interpret the faith and to fill influential posts.

The Church no longer fights "the good fight of the faith" (1 Tim 6:12) by trying to convince every human being of Jesus Christ, the Savior of the world. Nowadays people fight against each other, trying to persuade one another of their own view and, if need be, even imposing it on them by force. Looking at the present dreadful disunity, you get the impression that the unethical principle of "the end justifies the means" has become the law dictating behavior in the Church, too.

The loss of unity in the faith inevitably brings with it an erosion of solidarity among the faithful. In order to achieve their goals, people will even join forces with anticlerical groups. And they imagine they are serving the unity of the Church when their own faction dominates everything and they have neutralized or silenced the others, be they conservatives or progressives.

The height of "desolidarization" in the Church is reached when the "St. Gallen Group" shamelessly boasts of having got one of its own through as Pope at the conclave because he is working his way through a liberal agenda and thus breaking down the deadlock in reform. The concept of reform has a good ring to it in the Catholic Church because it has always been about fighting the secularization of the Church; take, for example, the Gregorian Reform, the Cluniac and Hirsau Reforms of religious orders and those of St. Teresa of Avila and St. John of the Cross, or the Tridentine Reforms, etc. Here, both the impulse and the criterion for the renewal was to orientate themselves more deeply to Christ and the ideals of the early Church. However, under the influence of the ideology of man's self-redemption, which makes man, instead of God, his own origin, measure and goal, the purpose of ecclesial reform shifted to being one of adaptation to the world. The term "Church reform" has taken on the meaning not of "conformity to Christ" but of "conformism with the world." The aim of these reforms is the survival of the Church as an institution and its benefices, not a renewal in the Spirit of Christ so that the Church "as the universal sacrament of salvation" (*LG* 48) mediates the life of God to all people.

The Cardinal

Someone who does not believe in the existence of a personal God in accordance with revelation is certainly not automatically amoral.

A Spring Evening at the German Embassy

We have always recognized natural ethics. That follows from the Catholic teaching on the consequences of Original Sin and the personal, social and material effects of Original Sin. Despite the loss of supernatural grace and community of life with God, there remains a certain facility to perceive what is true, to do good and to recognize a moral responsibility towards a higher authority. That is the fundamental difference between Catholic and Protestant anthropology, the effects of which extend right down to attitudes towards the breadth and depth of redemption.

The denial of Original Sin by Jean-Jacques Rousseau and his Jacobin disciples does not lie in the concept of man's being created in a state of natural goodness which was, however, corrupted by the social conditions on his transition from a natural to a cultural being, but rather in the fact that he denies grace as the necessary condition of nature reaching its perfection in its supernatural goal. Nor is there, incidentally, any social contract at the beginning of history. Before people approach each other as legal contractual partners and conclude a contract, they are already linked to one another by natural bonds. They are husband and wife, parents and children, brothers and sisters, relatives, contemporaries and friends to one another. The social and political organization is there for the people and not vice versa. Sociology cannot be the leading science; only philosophical and theological anthropology can. The awareness of solidarity and responsibility for each other, in short love, means that humanity shares a common destiny long before, on a secondary level, the administrative association of the State comes to be organized. Ideally, in both, everyone shares responsibility for the whole, each according to his or her particular talents.

Sin comes from free will, not from flaws in human nature and the social development of mankind. A spiritual and physical nature never exists that would not be worn by the individual person with a sense of responsibility towards fellow individuals and towards the Creator and Father in heaven. The human being is personally responsible for the good and the bad that he or she does. The individual's moral autonomy lies in not being at the mercy of a fateful failure, of his or her own innate frailty. Autonomy means precisely not being able to do what I want, what suits and serves me, but rather being capable of wishing to do good for its own sake. The crucial difference between Christian anthropology and the naturalistic images of modern man, including in Marxism, lies in the recognition of man's personhood. Man is an ontologically and ethically indivisible unit and not, for example, the ensemble of his impressions, his social circumstances and his unconscious spiritual experiences. Under the power of Original Sin and his own personal sins, the individual has not lost his original nature but rather cannot employ it in such a way as to serve his person's intention with respect to truth and love. It is similar to the paralytic at the pool at Bethesda with its five covered walkways. He would drag himself to the healing water but never managed to enter it because others were always there first and got in before him. At that moment Jesus, the divine Word of truth and love, addresses him: "Stand up! Pick up your mat and walk" (Jn 5:8). And at once the wounded nature is healed. And he starts walking around freely and with peace in his heart.

Both Catholic and Reformed theology say that the inherently integral and perfect state of man at the beginning of his history was disintegrated by free will. He can neither recreate himself nor redeem himself with his own powers. He remains captive in all the evil consequences of this for his self-understanding and his relationship to the material world and his social environment. But God's grace and love in Christ redeems, lifts up and liberates man, giving him a new identity in fellowship with God and his fellow human beings. Unlike in the liberal and socialist anthropologies since the Enlightenment, man is not the ensemble of the biological and social conditions of his existence but rather a person. Neither is society to blame for everything, nor can even the best society redeem man. In a state of grace, conditions no longer enslave man by leaving him at the mercy of a blind evolution of the animate world or depersonalizing him as an exemplar of a social class. Through his dignity as being made in the image of God, a person knows that the positive and negative conditions of his historical existence are merely a medium through which to achieve his supreme self-realization in the love that "never ends" (1 Cor 13:8). Love perfects man in God, who in his very essence and life "is love" (1 Jn 4:8.16).

Anyone who says: "Whatever serves me, my people or my class is good" cannot develop an ethic of responsibility. Morality is always universal because all human beings are alike in nature and each one is linked to the fate of the whole of humanity. A radical atheism à la Lenin, Stalin, Hitler and their thousands of henchmen was not just a hiccup in the history of atheism and certainly cannot be accused of going against its own principles. Hence people cannot point the finger at the Crusades, the Inquisition, and the Renaissance Popes in Christian countries because these are not true parallels. What matters is whether the conclusions you draw from your own principles comply with them or contradict them. In an intellectual debate, everything ultimately depends on your image of man.

The journalist

May I quote from Gerd Koenen's book *Die Farbe Rot. Ursprünge und Geschichte des Kommunismus* [*The Colour Red. Origins and History of Communism*] (Munich 2017, p. 821), which I can see here on your reading table?

In the middle of the civil war between the Red Army and the White Guards with its millions of dead, Lenin wrote in a letter on 19 March 1922: "Now and only now, when people are being eaten in famine-stricken areas, and hundreds, if not thousands, of corpses lie on the roads, we can (and therefore must) pursue the removal of church property with the most frenzied and ruthless energy.... Therefore, I come to the indisputable conclusion that we must precisely now smash the Black Hundreds [meaning counter-revolutionaries, pre-fascists] clergy most decisively and ruthlessly and put down all resistance with such brutality that they will not forget it for several decades." And these were the victims: "in 1922 alone, just under 2,700 secular priests, just under 200 monks and 3,500 nuns were liquidated."

The spiritual descendants of the Jacobins, the liberal proponents of the *Kulturkampf*, the Nazis and the Marxists, the Freemasons in Mexico and Spain have actually never been heard to apologize for the misdeeds of their icons in the fight against the "obscurantism of religion," which they hold to be "opium of the people." They probably imagine themselves justified by the slogan: no tolerance for the intolerance of revealed religion. Of civil religion, Rousseau states: "Its negative dogmas I confine to one, intolerance, which is a part of the cults we have rejected" (*Social Contract* Chap. VIII). Karl Popper was of a considerably different opinion in his book *The Open Society and Its Enemies* (1945) in not wanting to extend the principle of tolerance to those who wish to use it to destroy the foundations of the democratic state by recognizing religious freedom. It is also a human right for a citizen to be convinced that God revealed Himself as truth and life in Jesus Christ. For this religious belief requires an individual's free assent and neither can nor wants to be forced on citizens by the State against their convictions and with the use of coercion.

The actual contents of revelation cannot be grounded outside the faith, otherwise they would descend to being natural truths of reason. The truth contained in them can only be revealed and rationally comprehended by the believer in the light of the Holy Spirit and in accordance with the free assent of the will. They are neither rationally deducible nor refutable from reason. But nor can man's capacity for transcendence, his fundamental openness towards the word of a possible self-revelation by God be either apodictically or hypothetically ruled out with the help of reason as empiricism and criticism wish to do. Nor must the social implementation of a transcendentally open or immanentistically restricted epistemology be employed by the State in order to force someone to faith and religious praxis or to impede someone's faith and the expression of it in worship, way of life and social commitment. The State and public life must be ideologically neutral towards its religious or agnostic citizens and their associations. The State must maintain the same distance to them all and should promote their contributions to society. The basis for everyone must be the recognition of the fundamental universal human rights that are grounded in the nature of reason and free will. The unbelievers' contemptuous sense of being superior to believers, imagining themselves able to see through the latter's obsessive thinking and themselves to have direct access to unobstructed reality, is totally incompatible with tolerance. For the mainspring of tolerance is respect for others.

I am familiar with the tremolo in the voices of anti-clerical and ecclesially progressive authors when they intone No. 80 of the Syllabus of Errors (1864): "The Roman Pontiff can, and ought to, reconcile himself, and come to terms with progress, liberalism and modern civilization"—a proposition that Pope Pius IX had rejected. But what lies behind the sounding slogans?

The Pope and the Church are not at all faced with a need to be reconciled with progress in science and technology and medicine or with the programme of a society based on the principles of social justice and peace between nations because the faith's responsibility for the world is derived from its understanding that man is made in the image of God and possesses an inviolable dignity. Even irrespective of faith, the natural moral law in the conscience of nonbelievers, too, voices the decree to do good and eschew evil (cf. Rom 2:14). One of the original meanings of the word "liberal" in the Latin *liberalis* is "generous and bountiful," which explains why Thomas Aquinas was able to say that God is most perfectly liberal in the generosity of his grace—*maxime liberalis Deus.*

"To act from need belongs only to an imperfect agent, which by its nature is both agent and patient. But this does not belong to God, and therefore He alone is the most perfectly liberal giver, because He does not act for His own profit, but only for His own goodness" (*S.th.* I q.44 a.4 ad 1). Every Christian is liberal in accordance with Jesus' command: "You received without payment; give without payment" (Mt 10:8). And with this he certainly did not mean being "liberal" in the ideological sense of rejecting a supernatural revelation; instead, he meant precisely showing gratitude for God's turning to us in truth and love. Being makes sense even when man merely participates in it in his existence and cannot, like God, himself be it in his nature. But this leads to insight into the meaning of being. In the light of this, man knows that he is "being-towards-life" and not "being-towards-death." "For God created us for incorruption, and made us in the image of his own eternity [or: nature]" (Wis 2:23). All attempts to unmask religion as originating in alienation from oneself, to expose it sociologically and according to depth-psychology as a utopia and wishful thinking, and to make "clerical deceit" and superstition responsible for its "power over souls" are just a childish game with one single rule: what should not be, cannot be. In the criticism of religion, the Enlightenment has remained infantile.

Instead of calling on the Pope to reconcile himself with the modern age, try it the other way round. The Enlightenment only avoids the dialectical transformation of emancipation from God into the total control of man over man if it allows itself to be reconciled to a humanism with God. Only the child of God is truly free (cf. Gal 4:7). Because in Christ we are sons and daughters of God, we accept one another as brothers and sisters. Without a transcendent anchoring, the ideals of "liberty, equality, fraternity" have no clear meaning. They are a gift and commission for others and not a war cry against others, otherwise they do not build up but instead bring about the opposite. The problem with the 1789 Declaration of the Rights of Man was that it was not sufficiently well argued, a deficit the Church was the first to point out, especially regarding Article III, according to which all sovereignty emanates from the people. The latter can only extend to State institutions and not also to innate human rights or freedom of religion and association and thus also the Church, which according to the faith of Her members is a foundation established by God.

In France, the Revolution did not bring the end of Gallicanism but rather its most extreme form of state church in which priests and bishops are employees of the State who teach, govern and sanctify the Church, the People of God, in the name of the people constituting the State. If later on the Popes and particularly also Vatican II defended religious freedom and universal human rights against totalitarian states, this was not a late concession to democracy and the constitutional state; rather, it came about as a result of deeper anthropological reflection while retaining the fundamental difference between the State's right to regulate public welfare and the Church's understanding of mankind's divine calling and the justification of man's freedom of faith and conscience with reference to God and not to some fictitious "Supreme Being." The latter is what was done by the National Assembly in its "Declaration of the Rights of Man and the Citizen" on 26 August 1789.

The standard accusation intended to convict the Church of being pre-modern and repeated ad nauseam is that She relies on authority, tradition and dogma. Man should, they say, liberate himself from this self-imposed immaturity by using his own understanding without the guidance of others. "The motto of enlightenment is therefore: *Sapere aude*! Have courage to use your own understanding!"[19] — and this they hold to have dispersed the fog of Church superstition. And with the irrefutable authority of Kant behind him, every arrogant scoffer imagines himself to be a bold and independent thinker.

Dogma in Catholic theology implies neither a mathematical axiom nor an apodictic statement of rationalist philosophy without empirical verification but rather expresses the certainty of the knowledge of a revealed truth. Compared to Sacred Scripture, Tradition, in the proper meaning of the term, is a different form of mediating the word of God in the Christ event. And the authority of the Church's Magisterium is not the reason for the obedience of faith towards God but merely the form in which this is authoritatively mediated by witnesses, namely, the apostles.

The capitalist or socialist materialist, the tragic and heroic nihilist, the naïve progressive who has his body frozen after death in the hope that science might one day be able to thaw it out to eternal life on earth — these are, after all, poor answers to the deepest questions relating not to external circumstances but to man's real existence: what is man? What is the sense of pain, evil and death — all things that continue to exist despite so much (intraworldly) progress? Why these victories when they have had to be paid for so dearly? What can man offer to society, what can he expect from it? What follows this earthly life? (cf. GS 10).

---

[19] I. Kant, *Beantwortung der Frage: Was ist Aufkärung?* (1783). Immanuel Kant, *Werke in zehn Bänden* 9, ed. W. Weichedel, Darmstadt 1968, 53. Engl. Immanual Kant, *An Answer to the Question: What is Enlightenment?* Translated by Ted Humphrey Hackett Publishing, Indianapolis 1992, 1.

Some people may have reasons for not relating to the answer offered by the Christian faith community, but no one can dismiss it as irrational or illusory when the Church justifies Her existence not with a claim to power but with the commission to bear witness to Jesus the Son of God and Savior of the world. "The Church firmly believes that Christ, who died and was raised up for all, can through His Spirit offer man the light and the strength to measure up to his supreme destiny. Nor has any other name under the heaven been given to man by which it is fitting for him to be saved" (ibid.).

The Cardinal

I can see my edition of Newman standing there and recall the pivotal distinction he made between liberal and dogmatic thinking. I mean his Biglietto Speech when he was raised to the rank of cardinal (1879).

In it, John Henry Newman explains the distinction between the "liberal" rejection of supernatural revelation on the part of Enlightenment naturalism, which will only allow empirical-material verification, and the "dogmatic" acceptance of it as truth: "Liberalism in religion is the doctrine that there is no positive truth in religion, but that one creed is as good as another.... Revealed religion is not a truth, but a sentiment and a taste; not an objective fact." Thinking that is grounded in faith (*ratio fide illustrata*) recognizes the fact of God's historical self-communication in Jesus Christ as truth and love. Whereas pantheism perceives a divine ultimate origin of the world to be intrinsic to all its phenomena and postulatory theism turns God either into a hypothesis with which to explain the material world or into a moral postulate, in the teaching of Christ and the Church, on the other hand, the Incarnate Word gives us a reasonable and clear knowledge of the goal of man in God's plan of salvation. Man's infinite perfectibility cannot lie in the progressive improvement of the material and social conditions in which he lives or in the refinement of culture. Man strives after perfection in the knowledge of the first and innermost principles of his being and of acting morally for the sake of good (cf. Aristotle, Met. 982b). Knowing God as truth and love is the purpose and goal of man's intellectual and moral existence. "And this is eternal life, that they may know you, the only true God, and Jesus Christ whom you have sent" (Jn 17:3).

Joy on earth is but transitory; the joy of the love of God is everlasting. It cannot be unreasonable that reason strives to know the ultimate truth and that it reflects on the principle of its own intelligibility. Only if the conditions of intellectual cognition, which begins with sensory experience (*intellectus possibilis*), are declared to be both cognition's criterion and the limit of its scope, instead of being understood as its medium for mediating insight into the real ground of the existence of all that is (*intellectus agens*), the reasonable inference of the originator and mediator of being (*actus essendi*) — from that which is, whose being is its thinking and living — must seem groundless. A reason that is not enlightened about the precondition for its enactment lying in the self-transcendence of the intellect, meaning that it is essentially referenced to God (*Verwiesenheit auf Gott*), cannot deny that natural reason's knowledge of God is rational. The naturalistic fallacy is rarely avoided in the polemics and agitation that have been directed since the 18th century against the rationality of the Christian faith or even of philosophical theology, metaphysics. If the existence of God and the intellect's transcendental reference (*Verwiesenheit*) are denied a priori, then it is an easy thing to debunk faith as false consciousness as it "is nothing else but ..."

And so in the Introduction to his *Das Wesen des Christentums* (1841) Feuerbach sets himself the task "to show that the antithesis of divine and human is altogether illusory ...; that, consequently, the object and contents of the Christian religion are altogether human.

"Religion, at least for the Christian, is the relation of man to himself, or more correctly to his own nature ... but a relation to it viewed as a nature apart from his own. The divine being is nothing else than the human being.... All the attributes of the divine nature are, therefore, attributes of the human nature" (Frankfurt 1976, 32). And according to this schema, all the mysteries of Christianity can be explained as projections to an imaginary hereafter and denounced as alienations of man from himself. For Karl Marx "The critique of religion ends in the doctrine that man is the supreme being for man; thus it ends with the categorical imperative to overthrow all conditions in which man is a debased, enslaved, neglected, contemptible being."[20]

In this radical atheist anthropology there can be no compromise with a Church that derives a Catholic Social Teaching from its image of man. In fact, the latter is even more critical towards Capitalism than Marxism since these two opponents both have the same parentage in materialism and the idea of man as his own Creator and Redeemer. And the apple does not fall far from the tree. Lenin and Stalin understood Marx very well when they glorified the eradication of religion as rendering a service to mankind. Humanism without God is always inhuman because its protagonists are inevitably bound to act like lords over life and death towards their own faithful as well as their opponents. All kinds of humanist unions and societies of militant atheists outbid one another in sickening vainglory when defaming people who believe in God as stupid, backward and dependent. That's not exactly what you imagine intellectual self-assurance and the equanimity of reason to look like, do you?

---

[20] *Zur Kritik der Hegelschen Rechtsphilosophie* (1834/1844). Karl Marx, *Die Frühschriften*, ed. S. Landshut, Stuttgart 1964, 216. Engl. *Critique of Hegel's "Philosophy of Right."* Cambridge 1970 (2009), 137

Roman Encounters

French cultural historian

The political dialectic between revolutionary and reactionary ideologies, conservative and progressive parties, left and right wings
in parliaments and the ideological oppositions in intellectual life
is reflected in the development of the Church and theology, too.
This results in phases of restoration and reform, stasis and new
departures. It is often bound up with how closely one of the wings
of the Church is linked to political and ideological constellations
to the logic of whose power it subordinates itself. But the Church
is united in the revealed faith. She only claims moral influence
in order to give orientation to politics and culture with respect to
the common good and so as to raise a prophetic voice on behalf
of human rights and social justice.

In France, since the Revolution we have always had a vacillation
between restoration and adapting to the liberals. And I don't need
to mention the great crisis of Modernism, which seems to me only
to have been overcome with Vatican II. But perhaps it has merely
been superficially covered over. When I look at how the Council
has been received, I can see the two extremes in Traditionalism
on the one hand and the Progressives on the other who want to
go beyond it. One side views it as a betrayal of the Catholic faith
and liturgy. The other accuses it of stopping half way in the process
of reconciliation with the modern age.

But an ecumenical council is an assembly of the universal
Church in the Holy Spirit whose task it is to uphold in the teaching and life of the salvific community God's self-revelation given
once and for all in Christ as the truth and life of mankind and to
update the understanding of the faith. Anyone who brings the
political categories of restoration and revolution into play here
merely shows that his faith has degenerated into an ideology. If
Vatican II, in a spirit of ecumenism, takes up justified concerns
of Protestant theology, this has nothing to do with catching up

on the Reformation on Catholic soil any more than the positive evaluation of beneficial developments in science and technology, legal culture and democracy means subjecting her understanding of revelation to the naturalism of the Enlightenment.

The Cardinal

I, too, am worried about the path the Church is taking, but no less so about the people of today and tomorrow as well. We are not experiencing a crisis of the Church and the faith faced on the other side with a perfect brave new world. However much they speak in theory of people today also being happy and contented without God, in practice the opposite is true. How many young people ask themselves in all seriousness what sense there is in life? It is one thing to be given whatever you want by your parents, but to be given caring personal attention and affection is another. People may boast of having thrown off the shackles of the Church's sexual morality, but they are still left with the wretchedness of eros without love. It is the polarizing thinking and agitation in the Church that is itself the problem that must be overcome.

Synthetic thinking and synodal action are what offer a way out of the crisis. Faith is the opposite of ideology. It unites us in the Word and Spirit of God. An ideology is incapable of doing anything else but impose the narrow viewpoint of its inventor on the rest of humanity through propaganda and the use of force. Faith convinces people — ideology catches them off their guard.

But I am not going to attempt a third way between the two camps. The task is rather to overcome thinking in camps at all.

Fidelity to the faith of the Church and service of mankind today are not alternatives between which we have to choose. They are in themselves already a synthesis. To understand that we only have to study Vatican II's Dogmatic Constitution on Divine Revelation *Dei Verbum*. According to the principle that grace presupposes nature and that faith is not the opposite but rather the perfection of reason in the perception of truth, the contradiction played up by the Enlightenment between naturalism and supernaturalism collapses. The Pastoral Constitution on the Church in the Modern World *Gaudium et Spes* not only points out the principles governing the relationship between Church and world but also reflects on the positive developments and dangers in the development of society since the Enlightenment. That removes the obstacles of ideologies. It pulls the rug from under the formation of ideological camps in the Church that undermine Her unity. Let's take a more in-depth look at the Council.

Gaudium et Spes by no means represents a capitulation to the modern world on the part of the Church. Nor is it naïve optimism that allows itself to be ensnared by the utopias of an intraworldly belief in progress. Rather, a convincing synthesis is developed between supernatural revelation and a positive unfolding of all man's natural abilities in creation.

What is normative here is the primal principle of Catholic theology: grace presupposes nature, purifies, develops and perfects it — *gratia praesupponit naturam*. We do not acknowledge the autonomy of the earthly realities and thereby also the achievements of recent developments in science, technology, in constitutional-democratic social orders and a humane justice system because we are forced to but rather because they accord with the intrinsic reality, activity and value belonging to created things (cf. GS 36). From the fact of man's having been created in the image and likeness of God follow the dignity of his reason, the direction of his intellect towards truth and his free will towards good (cf. GS 15). Nevertheless, the Council does not overlook the destructive power of Original Sin and the personal sins of the individual. The Original Sin against the transcendental of man's historical existence, which goes beyond its empirical beginning in time, results neither from human nature's being ill-equipped nor from a primitive mental state of mythical confusion but rather from the will. Therein the person constitutes her relationship to the transcendent God and in so doing categorially also to herself, to other people and to the world. Furthermore, this means that humanity shares a common destiny in both good and evil. This applies to man's comprehensive relationship to God as the origin and goal of all being and also to people's relationship with one another in marriage, family, tribe, nation and world history. The personal freedom or the moral-intellectual autonomy of the individual is realized through the conditions of his embodied, social and material state. This takes place in such a way that he himself and the community with him are either built up or else obstruct and ultimately destroy one another. The example of the symbolic story of Cain and Abel (Gen 4) by no means justifies the social Darwinist principle of the right of the stronger. Since we all proceed from the one creative will of God which unites us and therefore have God as our Father, we are all brothers and sisters to each other.

Infinitely long before the French enlighteners discovered them in the 18th century, the Creator had already engraved the qualities and relationships of equality, liberty and fraternity on man's intellectual and social nature. All forms of violence, subjection, exploitation, terror and war are nothing other than fratricide. Every terrorist who invokes God, the Creator of all things, will be called to account by God Himself. For creation does not mean just the artifact produced by a craftsman. God's holiness and glory shine out in creation because everything created is an expression of and participation in God's goodness. And man is distinguished by being able with his free will to recognize and worship the good God in the good of creation — but also to deny him. All evil that is committed is directed at God and is therefore not merely a falling

Roman Encounters

short and a failure but also a sin for which we shall be brought before God's judgement. God alone judges us and is Lord over life and death. Even of the murderer Cain we are told: "And the Lord put a mark on Cain, so that no one who came upon him would kill him" (Gen 4:15). That means that God reserves the right to call people to account for their sins. The modern state guarantees the legal system, but it is not permitted to claim the right over the life and death of offenders.

Redemption in Christ brings about a new community of life with God and thus also a new creatureliness of the baptized. Man's comprehensive orientation towards God as his origin and goal, his truth and salvation, results of inner necessity in the Christian's responsibility for every sphere of life. What is presented here as a socio-ethical imperative is formulated in the theology of grace as follows: good works are necessary in order to reach the goal of the way of salvation, namely, the full community of life with God that has begun in faith and Baptism and which has always been accompanied by grace.

The French cultural theorist

We must begin once more with the old topic of the *praeambula fidei*. Let me summarize a book by M.J. Marmann that has recently been published in Italian, which is a doctoral thesis written under the supervision of Joseph Ratzinger. I quote: "The existence of God and all the other truths that, according to Rom 1:19, we can know about God are not articles of faith but the *praeambula fidei*. Faith presupposes natural knowledge in the same way as grace presupposes nature and perfection presupposes something that can be perfected—*sic enim fides praesupponit cognitionem naturalem, sicut gratia naturam, et ut perfectio perfectibile (S.th. I q.2 a.1 ad 1)*." Or put differently: "*gratuita praesupponunt naturalia, si proportionabiliter utraque accipiantur*" (*Verit.* q.27 a.6 ad 3).

With this famous statement at the beginning of the *Summa theologiae*, St. Thomas Aquinas conceptualizes the material and cognitive principle (*Real- und Erkenntnisprinzip*) of Catholic thinking. The natural cognitive faculty of human reason constitutes the prerequisite for a knowledge of God, who communicates Himself and reveals Himself in His Word and Spirit. And if man's spiritual nature were not accompanied by free will, the result of the bestowal of divine grace could not be the union of God and man in love. In his existence, with his spiritual and moral predispositions, man owes himself totally to God, the *causa prima et universalis*. But God created man in such a way that he is neither an accident of a higher substance nor God's mode of existence or appearance (Spinoza). Nor is his free will an empty word, so that man, in the imagery that Luther used in his response to Erasmus *De servo arbitrio* (1525), resembles a will-less beast, the donkey, blindly obeying the command of its rider, whether God or Satan. He is so constituted as a creature by God that his participation in being mediates him to himself. He has a reality of his own. For that reason he can also become a partner to God in the covenant of a relationship between the divine I and the human I (of the baptized person) and We (of the Church). In his *Eigensein* (being himself) and by virtue of his intellectual and moral power of judgement, man is also endowed with the right to act on his own as his own cause—*causa sui ipsius in movendo et iudicando est et liberii iudicii de agendo et non agendo* (*Verit.* q.24 a.1). Man as a rational being knows the purpose of his actions and must choose the means appropriate for them, also weighing up their moral pros and cons.

The Reformers' formal and material principles (*solus Christus, sola fide et gratia, sola scriptura*) conceive of the relationship between God and man dialectically as a unity of opposites. Catholic theology proceeds from an analogous mediation, so that reason and faith, nature and grace, human receptivity and divine gift are thought of more as a synthesis which is based on and supported by the fact that the Divine Word took on human nature. The *analogia entis* is the prerequisite for *the analogia fidei*. This results in the Catholic *et-et*—but in the irreversible sequence of Christ *and* the Church, faith *and* reason, grace *and* sacraments, love of God *and* love of neighbor (good works). Pope John Paul II developed this basic principle of Catholic faith comprehensively in his encyclical *Fides et ratio* (1998).

It is all about God and His turning to mankind in Creation and Redemption, in salvation history and final perfection. And it is about the dignity of man, who does not shut himself off autarchically from God or take possession of him, but who is instead called to "the freedom of the glory of the children of God" (Rom 8:21). It is only in this way that Catholic theology can arrive at a differentiated answer to the challenges posed by the Reformed theology of grace, the naturalism of the Enlightenment ("*etsi Deus non daretur*") and the criticism of religion (God as a dangerous or useful illusion) without itself falling into the opposite extremes, namely, the self-redemption of a humanism without God or a positivist supranaturalism in which revelation constitutes an arbitrary adjunct to a "pure nature" that is in itself incapable of perfection (two-storey thinking).

The Cardinal

Gaudium et Spes, the Second Vatican Council defined the position of Church and the gospel in the world of an "autonomy of earthly affairs" (GS 36). The theocentricity of the believer and his full responsibility for the world as God's creation are not mutually exclusive in the way of alternatives. In Christ, the God-Man, they are interreferenced, so that "The truth is that only in the mystery of the incarnate Word does the mystery of man take on light"

(GS 22). In revelation, God the Creator, Redeemer and Perfecter revealed Himself to mankind as its origin and goal. Man is, in the unity of his person, an image and likeness of the perfection of God (*perfectio formae*). But he finds the end that perfects him (*perfectio finis*) in the supernatural community with the Triune God who dwells in man, that is, in the *visio beatifica* and the *communio sanctorum*. Because man is person, he can only find his salvation and perfection in a successful personal relation to God and the created persons (angels and human beings). A spiritual nature always transcends itself towards truth and carries within itself the longing for the good that God is in Himself. How often have the words of St. Augustine at the beginning of his Confessions been quoted in sermons: "Great art Thou, O Lord, and greatly to be praised; great is Thy power, and Thy wisdom infinite. And Thee would man praise; man, but a particle of Thy creation; ... Thou awakest us to delight in Thy praise; for Thou madest us for Thyself, and our heart is restless, until it repose in Thee — *Tu excitas, ut laudere te delectat, quia fecisti nos ad te et inquietum est cor nostrum, donec requiescat in te*" (Conf. I, 1).

Man's being his own and his own cause as a person, albeit one orientated towards the Creator and Perfecter for its freedom and self-transcendence, does not stand in the way of grace but instead constitutes the reason why grace reaches man and is accepted by him. But this has always been the subject of Catholic theology. In Christ, the Son of God, the history of revelation achieved its historical fullness and became definitively present. The Risen Lord promises His Church: "And remember, I *am* with you always, to the end of the age" (Mt 28:20). He is the Son of God, the God who himself once revealed his name to Moses for all time: "I AM WHO I AM" (Ex 3:14).

The whole faith of the Church is an expression and communication of its reasonableness and knowability in the Logos, the

Verbum incarnatum. The understanding of faith, the *intellectus fidei*, is grounded in the hearing of faith, in which man freely acknowledges God in faith and, with the help of reason, recognizes him as the originator of nature and perfecter of man in grace. For the finite reason of the theologian, God remains inexhaustible as a mystery; but he is also not alien to it for he came into what was his own. He imparted to the children of God the light of truth and the fullness of his grace (cf. Jn 1:9.18).

Thus the history of Catholic theology is not a series of the closed systems of isolated thinkers but rather a coherent overall understanding of the one mystery in its totality and in the structure of its individual constituents, the articles of the Creed or, as Vatican II's Dogmatic Constitution on Divine Revelation *Dei verbum* puts it, the *nexus mysteriorum* (*DV* 8). Furthermore, this is an understanding that enriches and corrects itself, progresses and grows. It is a matter of a progressive acquisition of revelation in the articulation of faithful thinking. Even with the emergence of scientific theology in Scholasticism, Patristics by no means recedes into the role of being no more than just past history but remains constantly present as a witness to the original apostolic tradition.

Hence, for example, Augustine can never be eclipsed by Thomas or a contemporary theologian. Rather, every Christian and theologian should be a student of both the "existential" and the "speculative" theologians and learn something from all of them about the inexhaustible nature of God's mysteries in truth and love. The great insights of faith given to us by the Fathers of the Church remain valid. But the qualitative leap in Thomas is that, with the aid of Aristotelean ontological and cognitive realism, he overcomes the limitations that result from their thinking being couched in Platonism and Neoplatonism. By unreservedly taking created realities seriously in their existence (*Da-sein*) and nature (*So-sein*), the believer is not led away from God and the Redemption but instead led precisely towards a fuller knowledge and love of God in His works of nature and grace. Only in this way is it possible to overcome the Manichaeism that is latent in all heresies. Neither is man's matter and corporeality the reason for and cause of sin nor must sin be exaggerated by the idea of man's total depravity to such an extent that in the end sin is projected into God. Somehow God would then become the cause of sin by permitting it or, despite His goodness, by not preventing it. Even in the Neoplatonic hierarchical structure of created being, there can easily be a confounding of created finitude with moral imperfection and even sin. But redemption does not constitute a subsequent rectification of an imperfect act of creation but rather the liberation of the will from its self-enclosure (*Selbstverschlossenheit*) so that it can reach its goal of loving God above all else and one's neighbor as oneself. God is in Himself good and everything He has created is an expression of and participation in His goodness. It is not that there is something sinful and contrary to God in our finitude, but rather that sin comes from the free will's decision against God and what is good. Grace presupposes nature. With respect to redemption, grace does not destroy nature but rather heals it and raises it to being a child of God "created according to the likeness of God in true righteousness and holiness" (Eph 4:24).

The journalist

Let me return once more to the book by Hans Joas with the programmatic title *The Power of the Sacred (Die Macht des Heiligen)*. What he attempts with it is nothing less than to offer "An Alternative to the Narrative of Disenchantment." As is well known, the term "disenchantment" stems from Max Weber, who thought he had discovered in it the ultimate paradigm of modernity. According to Weber, the long process of the history of religion over thousands of years leads, of inner necessity, to the secularization of all spheres of life and of the whole cultural awareness. This then, he argues, definitively invalidates the truth of all religious doctrine and the meaning of cult and ritual in which the transcendental reference is symbolized and represented.

Hans Joas naturally does not wish to go back behind the 18th-century Enlightenment and the 19th-century criticism of religion, but wants rather to move beyond the fruitless antithesis of religion and science. But there is not the least contradiction between, on the one side, religion as experience of the sacred and philosophy as thinking of being (*Denken des Seins*) (with its transcendentals of the *unum et verum*, the *bonum et pulchrum*) and, on the other side, empirical science's analysis of the structure of the material world and of man from sociological and psychological perspectives. At the same time though, because of their methodological limitations, the empirical sciences are not capable of providing information on the real ground of man's relation to transcendence. Beyond the fruitless dialectic of rationalism and empiricism in the new philosophy, Blaise Pascal—with the Jansenist undertone of exaggerating the consequences of Original Sin—points correctly to God's hiddenness and presence as follows: "All appearance indicates neither a total exclusion nor a manifest presence of divinity, but the presence of a God who hides Himself. Everything bears this character."[21] And in the following fragment of the *Pensées* he states: "But it is at the same time true that He hides Himself from those who tempt Him, and that He reveals Himself to those who seek Him, because men are both unworthy and capable of God; unworthy by their corruption, capable by their original nature."[22]

---

[21] *Pensées* VIII, as quoted in English from: Pascal's *Pensées*, New York (Dutton) 1958 = frag. 555.
[22] Ibid. frag. 556.

A Spring Evening at the German Embassy

The religious experience of the "power of the sacred" undoubtedly constitutes an anthropological constant in our awareness of our existence in the world. The modern age is not in the true sense characterized by secularization as the necessary goal of a disenchantment of the world but rather by the alternative it offers between authentic religion and its alienation in all kinds of substitute forms of religion with their personality cults in various kinds of political totalitarianism.

The Cardinal

As you know, the Christian faith does not begin with a general experience of the sacred but with God's self-revelation as a person in His Word, in which He speaks to us. Jesus, the Incarnate Word, Who was with God and is God (cf. Jn 1:1.3.14), prays to the Father: "I have made your name known to those whom you gave me from the world.... Holy Father, protect them in your name that you have given me, so that they may be one, as we are one" (Jn 17:6,11). The God of Abraham, Isaac, and Jacob, the Father of Jesus Christ, in no way represents a culturally determined personification of cosmic forces, as is the case in polytheistic myths and in religions that conceive of the divine nonpersonally. Nor is it another variety of philosophical theism that thinks of the absolute as the supreme spirit.

Faith is, rather, the reaction to an initiative coming from the sphere of the sacred if and when God reveals Himself in His absolutely holy name. God is holy because He shows Himself not to be at man's disposal (*unverfügbar*). However, in revealing His name, He also begins a relationship with us, so that we are related to Him and are in communion with Holy God. God is holy and He sanctifies us. Being addressed by God in this way makes us aware of our own dignity, too. We know ourselves reflexively as persons as a result of being called by God. Man is revealed as "the only creature on earth which God willed for itself" (GS 24).

In the wilderness, Moses sees the puzzling phenomenon of the thorn bush burning yet not being consumed—an image for the non-disposable (*unverfügbar*) power of the sacred, of the sacred mystery in and above the world. God Himself calls Moses by name out of the burning bush. Yet Moses does not react with horror and the reflex of flight but rather presents himself, saying without any sense of either arrogance or inferiority: "Here I am" (Ex 3:4). On this holy ground of revelation, God discloses His name to him, making Himself identifiable and addressable as the God of Abraham, Isaac and Jacob. Jesus says later that this God of promise is not a God of the dead, but of the living (cf. Mt 22:32). The God of the Fathers is for Israel the "I am there"—always and everywhere.

So it is not that Israel imagines the sacred personified as its God. On the contrary, it is God who responds freely to the misery and cries of an enslaved people and actively approaches it. The Israelites' question to Moses is totally legitimate: "What is his name?"

And Moses does not tell the people of his mystical experiences, which cannot possibly be of general interest, but fulfills his commission and informs them: "I am has sent me to you" (Ex 3:14).

This also displays the unique combination of the predicate of holiness with God's self-revelation as a person in relation to the people of his covenant. It remains without any analogy in the history of religion and nor can it be derived from the concepts of the Sacred or Absolute and the Universal One. Words from the First Letter of Peter can be cited as a summary of the total self-revelation of our holy God as grace and life: "Set all your hope on the grace that Jesus Christ will bring you when he is revealed.... as he who called you is holy, be holy yourselves in all your conduct; for it is written, 'You shall be holy, for I am holy' (Lev 19:2)" (1 Pet 1:13-16).

Furtive glances at iWatches signal that it's time to depart. The participants express their thanks and appreciation to one another.

A Spring Evening at the German Embassy

The Cardinal

So now we've spent the whole morning talking to each other. But it has been worthwhile. Now I have to prepare a talk I am giving this afternoon at a Pontifical University. It's not about the Church and Her future but about God as our future. God bless you, gentlemen.

The Cardinal prints out his manuscript and reads through again what he is going to be expecting of his academic audience.

3

God in a Secular Age
A Talk at the Pontifical University

Dear confreres,
Ladies and gentlemen,

An eminent contemporary philosopher at Berlin's Humboldt University, Volker Gerhardt, has recently presented the project of a "rational theology." His book bears the significant title *Der Sinn des Sinns. Versuch über das Göttliche* (The Sense of Sense. An Essay on the Divine).[23]

The aim is to show philosophically the rationality of a natural belief in the existence of God even prior to revealed religion. Starting with an analysis of self-awareness, which cannot be separated from awareness of the world, he comes to the remarkable conclusion: "As long as the individual understands himself as a person, he comprehends the world that makes him and his kind possible. It is his self-understanding that makes him rely on the understanding of the world. As long as he does not overestimate himself in this, he has every reason to designate as 'divine' the world surrounding both him and everything else when he recognizes its immense variety and size, its beauty and terror as well as the possibilities it contains, which are made use of with every word and every deed.

[23] Berlin, 2nd ed. 2015.

Anyone who is not afraid under these circumstances to believe in himself in spite of everything has a good reason to believe in the divine in God."[24]

In the Introduction to his book, Gerhardt relates somewhat sardonically that the leading professor of philosophy at a major German university used to expound to his first-semester students in an authoritative and apodictic manner that God is *today* no longer a subject for philosophy. He used Nietzsche's phrase about the "death of God" in order to prove definitively that it is impossible to deal rationally with a non-existent being. During his grand performance, however, our respected colleague seems not to have been aware that Nietzsche's talk of the death of God was not a statement of the findings of neutral research. Instead, it actually reflected the convulsion caused by nihilism, which robs our existence of all support and direction. Meanwhile the aforementioned professor is said to have recognized that the question of God will live on as long as, in their fragile existence, people occupy themselves with the meaning of their individual existences and that of the whole of humanity, to which I belong.

So God is both a worthwhile and an inescapable topic, one that is linked to the question of who and what I am whether or not I believe in Him, deny His existence atheistically or doubt skeptically that God has any interest in me.

It would be completely erroneous from the start to wish to use the methods of natural science, i.e., *more geometrico*, in order to prove or disprove the existence of a thing or living being lying beyond the sensory and phenomenal world as a part of precisely this world. For God by definition does not belong to the universe. He is neither a part of the empirical and phenomenal world nor an immanent effective force in it but rather its transcendent ground.

[24] Ibid. 340.

So what is needed instead is to show that because the human spirit is related to the One and Whole of the world, it is *sensible* (*sinn-voll*—full of meaning) and hence *reasonable* to pose the question of the transcendental origin and end of both mankind and the world.

Discovering the meaning of the whole in its transcendent ground does not mean being condemned to having to invent it. How should we transient beings be capable of this?

Another consequence follows from belief in God: we do not have to justify the fact that we exist at all and that we take space away from others by being a burden to them as children or when we are sick and old. It is instead God who justifies that I exist and am who I am. Apologizing for one's existence is therefore an insult to God. Believing in the good and merciful God dispels the feeling that everything is senseless and in vain. The apostle expresses this as follows: "But when the goodness and loving-kindness of God our Savior appeared, he saved us, not because of any works of righteousness that we had done, but according to his mercy, through the water of rebirth and renewal by the Holy Spirit" (Titus 3:4f.).

The atheist conviction that intellectual history and the breathtaking progress in science and technology, as well as in the digitalization of knowledge, leads, of inner necessity, to total immanentism and secularism is inconsistent with the fact that man both must and wishes to continually confront the existential questions of his Whence and Whither anew. For that reason the question of the meaning of being and the goal of our existence cannot be rejected as meaningless by Positivism and can therefore never be silenced.[25]

The philosopher Robert Spaemann declares in his book *Der letzte Gottesbeweis* (The Final Proof of God): "The sciences have

---

[25] A seminal analysis of the contemporary intellectual and religious situation is provided in: Charles Taylor, *A Secular Age*. Cambridge, Mass., 2007.

to date failed to produce a single serious argument against the rumor of God; this has only been done by the so-called scientific weltanschauung, Scientism, i.e., what Wittgenstein called the superstition of the modern age. Modern science is research into conditions (*Bedingungsforschung*). It does not ask what something is and why but rather what the conditions were of its coming into being. But being, being self (*Selbstsein*) is emancipation from the conditions of one's coming into being. And, like the projector in a film, the Unconditional, i.e., God, can by definition not occur in intra-world research into conditions.... Thus the alternative is not: scientific explicability of the world or belief in God; it can only be: foregoing understanding of the world, resignation or belief in God.... Belief in God is belief in a ground of the world that is itself not groundless, i.e., irrational, but rather 'light', transparent to itself and thus its own ground."[26]

This is not a matter of the technical philosophical question of whether the transcendental or the ontological approach should take precedence or whether, in view of the indivisibility of self-transcendence and world-transcendence, a synthesis of both points of departure recommends itself to reason in the act of cognition. These two approaches lead either to God as Absolute Spirit, the infinite awareness of Himself, or to a being that exists through itself and has no need of any other ground in order to be realized (*ipsum esse per se subsistens*). When we speak in philosophical theology of reason as the locus of opening the question of God, we are not referring to instrumental reason or sheer intelligence as a survival strategy, which according to Nietzsche makes us essentially indistinguishable from "inventive animals." What is meant here by the term "reason" is "the capacity by means of which man goes beyond himself and the world around him and is able to relate to a reality

[26] Munich 2007, 11.

that is transcendent to him.... To believe that God is means that God is not our idea, but that we are his idea."[27]

By way of clarification, I would like to point out here that despite all the interreferentiality of the philosophical and the theological knowledge of God there is an essential difference between them. On the basis of God's revelation, we do not say merely that God is Absolute Spirit and being in and for Himself (*ipsum esse per se subsistens*). For the Christian believer, the supreme insight is that God is love (1 Jn 4:8, 16) in the community of Father and Son and Spirit. With the help of reason we can get as far as understanding that God is a mystery and the One unknown to us, but that in His self-revelation He can, when He wishes, disclose His identity to us in the Word and give Himself to us to love in the Spirit.[28]

The modern alienation from God, ranging from the initial depersonalizing of God in Pantheism and Deism via resigned agnosticism to aggressive neo-atheism, which regards every religion as harmful and worth fighting,[29] ultimately has two roots.

The first is *philosophical epistemology*, which, above all in Kant, limits the scope of metaphysical reason in such a way that all that remains of God is as an ideal of pure reason or as a postulate of practical, i.e., moral reason. This renders theology obsolete as a science.

The second, and linked to the first, is the so-called *scientific world view*. This begins with modern science, which, although restricting itself methodologically to what is empirically quantifiable and mathematically describable, i.e., to the logical structure of matter, then, in conjunction with a monistic materialism, reduces everything that exists and is perceptible to what is objectively and

[27] Robert Spaemann, *Der letzte Gottesbeweis*, Munich 2007, 20.

[28] Thomas Aquinas, *De pot.*

[29] Cf. on this the pertinent analysis in: Alexander Kissler, *Der aufgeklärte Gott. Wie die Religion zur Vernunft kam* (The Enlightened God. How Religion Discovered Reason), Munich 2008.

sensorily given. Knowledge (*Wissen*) as cognizance (*Kenntnis*) of the objective is set against faith as a meaning-disclosing perceiving (*Erkennen*) of God. The paradoxical result of this is that knowledge (*Wissen*) becomes a belief (as in belief in science and in progress) and faith, which is by its very nature a personal, cognizing and free ship to God, is reduced to objective knowledge (*Wissen*). In this way God would become a necessary or superfluous hypothesis for explaining the existence and appropriateness of natural processes (God as the engineer of the world clock, an intelligent designer of nature or a programmer of evolution).

Positivism as a so-called scientific world view brings with it the reductionist consequence for the determination of man's essence that man is *nothing but* matter, a machine, an animal. His brain is just a computer, which will one day be surpassed by artificial intelligence. He is one species among others, with a typical propensity to raise himself up above other species. For this reason, its better performance as far as intelligence is concerned makes an animal, for example, superior to someone who is mentally ill, to an embryo or to a small child who has not yet learnt to count.

It is obvious that in ethics the difference between good and evil was then replaced by the category of the useful and expedient and what is empirically verifiable. In his *Système de la nature* (1770), Paul Henri Thiery d'Holbach attributes empirical naturalism to a matter existing eternally from itself. According to him, it is solely according to mechanical—and today one must add, biological and chemical—laws that, by means of the evolution of living things, matter shapes itself into the individual species and living beings. Man's life and consciousness would then be just higher forms of self-organizing matter. The ideal contents of consciousness, like the idea of God and moral imperatives, are, he contends, merely products of sensibility and projections of the will to survive. Hence there is nothing in reality that corresponds to the ideas of our minds except matter and evolution. Either they are development-psychologically determined relics from our childhood phase as individuals or as a species, or they are — read with a socio-political slant — instruments of domination on the part of Church and State. It is only when the blocks constituted by metaphysics and revealed religion, namely, Christianity, are overcome that man has unimpeded insight into his situation. Then he is freed of the superstition and religious fanaticism with which the clergy hold the people captive in a state of immaturity. Tolerance based on agnosticism and relativism must, Holbach concludes, sweep away the Church's rigid belief in dogmas. And a pleasure-oriented life liberates us from Christianity's law-based moral code with its hostility to both life and the pleasures of the body.

In an Enlightenment that had turned radically critical of religion, people were convinced that only a sociologically and pedagogically implemented atheism would free mankind of all its ills and prepare the way for a bright future. Instead of theonomy, autonomy was called for; instead of theocentricity they wanted anthropocentricity. Similar consequences result from the findings of neurology when interpreted in terms of monistic materialism. If all, even the most abstract, achievements of the human brain's thinking are based on measurable material energy, then, they argue, the brain is nothing more than a computer that processes information. The mind would thus be merely an epiphenomenon of matter. Combined with evolutionary biology, neurophysiology would prove, as it were empirically, that man possesses neither a faculty of reason that is capable of transcendence and can distinguish truth from falsehood nor a will that can freely and spontaneously aim at good and abhor evil. What is true and good will be decided for those who are still immature by the majority, or even by the minority, of enlightened citizens. Here, they contend, Rousseau must be followed in distinguishing between the *volonté générale* and the *volonté de tous*: Here it is the

Party, which is always right, or its leaders that set the direction of travel into a happy future — if necessary, against the will of the yet to be 'educated' majority.

In response to this one can ask: if there is no mind, to whom is this theory supposed to make sense then? For all cognition pre-supposes the ontological distinction between the subject and the object of cognition; nor is this a distinction that can be removed in self-reflection. I can see myself in the mirror, but the mirror cannot see itself.

The positivism in the natural, social and historical sciences as well as critical rationalism make obsolete the philosophical and theological reflection of the fundamental existential questions of the Whence and Wherefore of human existence. But with such an image of man, people's hearts are filled with a collective depression instead of the joy of the gospel. Bertrand Russell (1872-1970), one of the fathers of analytical philosophy, expressed the transcendence-less sense of time that is typical of monistic naturalism by speaking of the world as "a flash in the pan" and "a stage in the decay of the solar system."[30] Appealing to the emotion that might overcome one at the findings of astrophysics and evolutionary research, Jacques Monod formulated humanity's harrowing forlornness in the infinite space and time of the cosmos as follows: "The ancient covenant is in pieces; man knows at last that he is alone in the universe's unfeeling immensity, out of which he emerged only by chance."[31]

---

[30] *Why I Am Not a Christian*, London 1957. Quoted from Routledge Classics 2004, 10. The "flash in the pan" is missing there but is to be found in Russell on *Religion: Selections from the Writings of Bertrand Russell*, eds. Louis Greenspan and Stefan Andersson. London/New York 1999, 82.

[31] *Chance and Necessity: An Essay on the Natural Philosophy of Modern Biology*, New York 1971, 180. Original title: *Le Hasard et la Nécessité: Essai sur la philosophie naturelle de la biologie moderne*. 1970.

The only escape is to make the best of oneself in this short earthly existence before passing on into eternal oblivion. The feeling of God's absence in the desolate expanse of space and time on our tiny planet is echoed when man resigns himself to giving up his tragic existence as lost or numbs the pain of his transience with drugs.

The nameless burial of the dead that is unfortunately already being chosen by some is merely the distressing consequence of this existential nihilism. While using my ashes as humus in the cycle of nature is not an act of love, sinking into eternal anonymity represents an absurd renunciation of my dignity as a son or daughter of our loving Father in heaven. By contrast, the biblical experience with the God of Israel, who protects and liberates his people, expresses a comforting certainty: "Do not fear, for ... I have called you by name, you are mine" (Isa 43:1).

It must be conceded that Christians were themselves — seen from an historical perspective — partly responsible for the loss of the credibility of revelation by associating their religion with the interests of society and the State, as in the case of the Gallican Church in the Ancien Régime, or attempting to uphold the contents of their faith with outdated scientific world views. Nevertheless this still leaves a theoretical complex of the radical immanentization of our conception of reality as a whole.

The inner core of specific atheism as it emerged against the background of western Christianity but in strict contradiction to it seems to me to lie in the opposition between grace and freedom, which is felt to be insuperable. Is there any scope left for human freedom if God is everything and does alone, or does man first have to fight for his freedom in the face of an overpowering God?

A paradigmatic example of western criticism of religion out of the spirit of empiricism and sensualism from David Hume to Ludwig Feuerbach is the opinion of Bertrand Russell that religion, particularly Christianity, is the result of an sickness resulting from fear. He calls Judaism, Christianity and Islam slave religions because they demand unconditional submission. "The whole conception of God is a conception derived from the ancient Oriental despotisms. It is a conception quite unworthy of free men."[32]

Ladies and gentlemen,

With all due respect, we have every right to expect a better knowledge of the Bible of anyone making such steep statements. What happened to the memory of the God of Israel's revealing Himself as having freed His people from Egypt, the house of bondage, and from their captivity in Babylon? In the New Testament, the fruit of Christ's salvific deed on the Cross is "that the creation itself will be set free from its bondage to decay and will obtain the freedom of the glory of the children of God" (Rom 8:21). The content of the salvific deed is liberation from the material and spiritual need caused by sin, and the freedom of the sons and daughters of God. The God who is rejected above is merely a hypothesis of idealistic speculation or of a false soteriological approach or else the stop-gap of scientific research—but it is *not* the living and merciful God of Abraham, Isaac and Jacob and the Father of Jesus Christ, who gives us our being and wishes to perfect us in His love. As a Catholic and a theologian one asks oneself how the Enlightenment philosophers, living as they did in such a magnificent Catholic culture, could arrive at such a grotesquely distorted notion of the Christian faith. Deism alone is already a miserable caricature of the God and Father of Jesus Christ. Ultimately, the hatred of God, the faith and the faith community displayed by all the modern atheisms can only be explained with disappointed love.

In its Pastoral Constitution on the Church in the Modern World, Vatican II offers a depiction of atheism as it exists in reality

---

[32] Bertrand Russell, op.cit., 19.

in its varieties and outgrowths along the following lines. Atheism counters the belief that God is the origin and purpose of mankind and the world with the contention that man himself is the origin and purpose. Man must and can create and redeem himself. Therefore he must free himself from all creaturely givens, at least condition himself mentally and psychologically like a demiurge and also model himself physically and socially. Religion, that is, a relationship to God in whatever form, is regarded by atheism to be the expression of man's alienation from himself or as a means to keep him immature. Religion is the opium of the people. Instead of redemption through God's glorious grace, atheism offers a paradise on earth created by man himself, albeit one that humanity has up to now experienced only as a hell on earth. So it is better to be with Mother Teresa in a slum than with "Papa Stalin" in the Kremlin.

Postulatory atheism is actually attacking a phantom when it fails to recognize that divine grace establishes, promotes and perfects human freedom since God's nature is not pure power that contains itself but rather love that gives itself away.

For God's omnipotence expresses itself and is experienced as a gift of being through which we participate in his life and his knowledge. God gains nothing and loses nothing when He calls us into being and when He awakens a longing in our hearts for union with Him. For God is love. It may be that modern man was profoundly unsettled in his belief in the God of love by the intense upset caused by the schism within western Christianity and the terrible wars of religion in England, France, Germany, Switzerland and elsewhere. But alongside the offence it gives with its false notion that grace is an impediment to freedom and self-determination, postulatory atheism also displays an underlying tendency to a "will to power," which is combined with an authorization to make itself its own law of being and of good. The atheistic political ideologies from the French Revolution to the present fascinate the masses because they claim to exert absolute power over nature, history and society, right down to the most intimate thoughts and the consciences of every individual (hence the control mania of the secret services and their frantic bugging and phone tapping).

Ladies and gentlemen,

The Church does not confront militant atheism, with its frequent contempt for humanity and the power it wields in the State, the media and academia, with the same means as it employs itself. Since we are convinced that God also loves those who do not yet know Him or who even deny Him, we have to seek the right means in order to grant mankind access to the mystery of His being and the love that has been communicated to us in God the Creator, Redeemer and Perfecter.... It is, as the Council, said: "The remedy which must be applied to atheism, however, is to be sought in a proper presentation of the Church's teaching as well as in the integral life of the Church and her members."[33]

With respect to the prejudices and false judgements of modern atheism, Vatican II declares: "The Church holds that the recognition of God is in no way hostile to man's dignity, since this dignity is rooted and perfected in God. For man was made an intelligent and free member of society by God who created him, but even more important, he is called as a son to commune with God and share in his happiness. She further teaches that a hope related to the end of time does not diminish the importance of intervening duties but rather undergirds the acquittal of them with fresh incentives. By contrast, when a divine instruction and the hope of life eternal are wanting, man's dignity is most grievously lacerated, as current events often attest; riddles of life and death, of guilt and of grief go unsolved with the frequent result that men succumb to despair.

[33] *Gaudium et Spes* 21.

"Meanwhile every man remains to himself an unsolved puzzle, however obscurely he may perceive it. For on certain occasions no one can entirely escape the kind of self-questioning mentioned earlier, especially when life's major events take place. To this questioning only God fully and most certainly provides an answer as he summons man to higher knowledge and humbler probing."[34]

This is the only way out of the "Dialectic of Enlightenment" (1944)[35] with its rapid change into the despotism of totalitarian ideologies and the tragedy of "Atheistic Humanism" (1950).[36]

It is only possible to close one's mind to this insight if one fails to recognize the dramatic crisis in which the world finds itself today. Pope Francis frequently says that we already find ourselves in something like a third world war. By that he means "a globalization of indifference."[37] This global battle of everyone against everyone else is not conducted with military weapons alone, but also with psychological warfare (fake news, smear campaigns in the social media). We just have to think in a global context of the civil wars, the genocides, the degradation of children, women and men as slave labor or sex slaves, the mass flight and migration of millions, the hunger and poverty of half of humanity, the countless numbers of children growing up without human warmth, a compassionate upbringing and career prospects, the children of divorced parents, the

---

[34] Ibid.

[35] Max Horkheimer/Theodor W. Adorno, *Dialektik der Aufklärung*, Frankfurt a.M. 1969. Engl. transl. (based on the definitive text from Horkheimer's collected works) by Edmund Jephcott (Stanford: Stanford University Press, 2002).

[36] Henri de Lubac, *Le drame de l'humanisme athée*, Paris 1944, translated as *The Drama of Atheist Humanism*, trans. Riley, M., Nash, A. & Sebanc, M. (San Francisco: Ignatius Press, 1995 — translation of the 1983 edition including chapters omitted from the 1949 translation).

[37] Apost. Exhort. *Evangelii Gaudium* 54, cf. 52-75 for the wider context.

unbridled capitalism that subjects everything and everyone to the dictatorship of economic benefit and profit, the terrorism operating worldwide in criminal gangs and states, the organized crime, the intentional destabilization of the legal system and the subordination of the common good to group interests. Not even the established democracies are immune to all this. And how the life of the Church, the harmonious togetherness of the members of the Body of Christ, is being thrown into disarray by partisanship and thinking in stereotypes. That is the Adversary, the *diabolos*, the destroyer of unity.

In our technically efficient civilization, the crisis of modernity and postmodernity is there staring anyone in the face who has eyes to see.[38]

On account of its lack of a relationship to the transcendent, post-modernism is essentially based on a deficient image of man, the dire consequence of which is above all a loss of both solidarity and socialization. If man is reduced to a product of matter playing with itself or a construct of society or if he is only worth anything as a participant in social networks or for paying pensions, then he is robbed of his being a subject, of his personality. For he has been instrumentalized as a means of industrial production, political power or as biomatter for research. Behind the shiny façade of a brave new world, the whole extent of the misery manifests itself: loneliness, isolation, mental illness, increasing violence and brutality, self-centerdness, egomaniacal self-fulfillment and looking out first and foremost for one's own advantage, the witholding of primary communication within families.

Ladies and gentleman, a further comment on the dictatorship of relativism:

---

[38] Cf. the profound study by Matthew Fforde, *Desocialisation: The Crisis of Post-modernity*, Cheadle Hulme 2009.

Despite their many mutual contradictions, all models that deny man's irreducible *Eigensein* (own-being, self-being) as a person—i.e., the spiritual nature and immortality of the soul as a substantial form of his spiritual-corporeal nature and its unfolding in history and culture—and cut him off from his essential relation to the transcendent God, thus delivering him up to man's absolute dominion over man, all agree on one thing: the relativism of the question of truth. The denial of objective truth does not lead to freedom, for the opposite of truth is falsehood. The truth is no more the cause of intolerance than promoting social justice unleashes class warfare. Nor is relativism the basis for tolerance and for freely establishing a relationship between the perceiving individual and the truth of reality and being; rather, as has been rightly stated, it leads to the dictatorship of those who claim to understand the big picture or who regard themselves as the only good people. Relativism contradicts itself by apodictically claiming absolute validity for itself and at the same time denying the existence and cognizability of any truth outside its own.

Certainly, there are many interpretations of the world and of existence without God, as is stated in Vatican II's Pastoral Constitution on the Church in the Modern World. Nevertheless, in the face of the global political, economic, moral and religious crisis, "the number constantly swells of the people who raise the most basic questions or recognize them with a new sharpness: what is man? What is this sense of sorrow, of evil, of death [...]? What can man offer to society, what can he expect from it? What follows this earthly life?"[39]

The Church advocates an image of man that does indeed draw its essential contents from Judaeo-Christian tradition but it is one which, in its positive and constructive orientation, also comes

[39] *Gaudium et Spes* 10.

together into a community of action with many people of good will and from other religious and ethical traditions.

All the findings of the modern natural and historical sciences can be brought into a rational synthesis with what is known from revelation without a Christian and his contemporaries having to live in two different intellectual worlds. But beyond this, the Christian message is the gospel of love. The truth of truth is not power but love. Power without service, riches without generosity, eros without agape can never satisfy man's heart. What matters is for people to accept themselves and love their neighbors because each one of them is already accepted and loved unconditionally by God.

The experience of God as man's sense and purpose means an end to the dialectic of negativity and all the non-sense in world history. Only belief in God can take account of the whole of reality because it is a sharing in the infinite mystery of God, which for now only reveals itself "in a mirror, dimly" (1 Cor 13:12). For God's mystery does not stand before us like an impenetrable thicket, a black hole or a nihilating (*nichtend*) nothingness. It is luminous superabundance and pure goodness. We see the world in his light. But we cannot look directly into the sun even though we see everything through its light.

In his Letter to the Romans, Paul insists that in their "ungodliness and wickedness" and when they "suppress the truth," people cannot make the excuse of not knowing of the existence of God (1:18). "For ever since the creation of the world his eternal power and divine nature, invisible though they are, have been understood and seen through the things he has made" (1:20). Even the Gentiles, to whom the commandments were not revealed on Mount Sinai as they were to the Jews, know the natural moral law, i.e., that which is accessible to reason, because it "is written on their hearts" (2:15) and their own conscience also bears witness to it (cf. 2:14f.).

God remains the mystery above us. He is the subject of His revelation of His glory in the works of nature and history. Through the prophets, and finally and unsurpassably in His Son, God speaks *to us* from person to person. We can speak *to Him* in prayer and in professing our faith. The Church can speak *of Him* and bear witness *to Him* in dialogical preaching.

It is precisely in professing the trinitarian God that the *proprium* is manifested. Belief in the Trinity is what distinguishes Christianity from the monotheism of the Old Testament, Judaism and the Qur'an as well as of speculative monotheism.

Unitarian monotheism cannot deny the logic of trinitarian monotheism. For its consistency lies in the divine logic of love which effects God's essence in the relations of the three Divine Persons to each other, doing so without dividing the divine essence but rather eternally actualizing it. This is beyond human understanding. But the latter is nevertheless raised up through God's self-revelation so as to participate analogously in God's self-knowledge in His Word, which assumed our flesh, and to be united with Him in the love of the Holy Spirit.

Being children of God in Christ and friends of God in the Holy Spirit are the essential points of reference for the Christian image of man. The Church believes that the magnitude of the Christian mystery of man can only be fully understood in the light of Christ, and that it is only in Him that the enigma of pain and death does not overwhelm us.

The question of God is certainly an intellectual challenge for people today, but it is even more an existential one. In the face of death, faith comes face to face with its ultimate test.

The camp doctor who accompanied the then 39-year-old Dietrich Bonhoeffer on his way to be executed at the Flossenbürg concentration camp on 9 April 1945 relates: "Through the half-open door in one room of the huts I saw Pastor Bonhoeffer, before taking off his prison garb, kneeling on the floor praying fervently to his God. I was most deeply moved by the way this lovable man prayed, so devout and so certain that God heard his prayer. At the place of execution, he again said a short prayer and then climbed the few steps to the gallows, brave and composed."[40]

And his last words in the face of death were: "This is the end — for me the beginning of life."[41]

The Rector

Your Eminence, I would like to thank you in the name of everyone present for your committed contribution to an anthropology which only becomes coherent when viewed in the light of the philosophical and theological question of God. Rather than break up the overall impression with individual questions, I would recommend, ladies and gentlemen, that you read it again at home. We have put it on our home page. It is in the nature of the speculative sciences that they do not just present factual information about objects and their functional connection which, if you have a good memory, you can easily remember and make your own. They are not concerned with knowledge alone but rather with understanding. *Intelligere* means to read from inside. That is the *intellectus principiorum*, which is also so significant for the understanding of revealed faith (*intellectus fidei*). "*Le cœur a ses raisons que la raison ne connaît point* — The heart has its reasons whereof reason knows nothing."[42] With this Pascal was not wanting to place warm emotionality alongside cold rationality. The heart belongs in reason, so that in philosophy we think with a love of wisdom and in theology with a love of God. The greatest commandment is: "You shall love the Lord your God with all your

---

[40] Eberhard Bethge, *Dietrich Bonhoeffer: Theologian, Christian, Man for His Times. A Biography*, rev. ed. Minneapolis 2000, 927f.

[41] Ibid. 927.

[42] *Pensées* IV, frag. 277.

heart, and with all your soul, and with all your mind" (Mt 22:37). Mind (*dianoia*) refers to the capacity for thinking, to the intellect, and to the power of the human spirit. But, alongside God, it is also necessary to know man in all his greatness and wretchedness. Only then is reason freed from the temptation, in its pride, to deny God or to declare Him to be irrelevant. Religion, to quote Pascal again, "teaches men these two truths; that there is a God whom men can know, and that there is a corruption in their nature which renders them unworthy of Him.... It is equally dangerous for man to know God without knowing his own wretchedness, and to know his own wretchedness without knowing the Redeemer who can free him from it. The knowledge of only one of these points gives rise either to the pride of philosophers, who have known God, and not their own wretchedness, or to the despair of atheists, who know their own wretchedness, but not the Redeemer."[43]

The Apostle to the Gentiles did not shrink from laying himself open to the criticism and irony of the Areopagites in Athens. He appeals to the philosophers with the knowledge of God in reason, then wanting to bring them to a knowledge of man's redemption in the Cross and Resurrection of Christ. To the friends of wisdom Paul proclaims the unknown god whom they worship without knowing Him to be the one God who created heaven and earth. He it was who created mankind so that man "would search for God and perhaps grope for him and find him—through indeed he is not far from each one of us. For 'In him we live and move and have our being'" (Acts 17:27f.). And this "God who is above us and in us"—as the great Jesuit philosopher Erich Przywara put it[44]—"now ... commands all people everywhere to repent" by recognizing God in Jesus Christ, "a man whom he has appointed,

---

[43] *Pensées* VII, frag. 556.
[44] Cf. Erich Przywara, *Gott: Schriften II*, Einsiedeln 1962 245-372.

and of this he has given assurance to all by raising him from the dead" (Acts 17:30f.).

But I am already beginning to embark on a talk of my own in spite of preventing you from asking questions so as not to blur the overall impression.

May I ask the Cardinal for his blessing and wish you all a safe way home.

4

The Church in a Secular Age

In the Rome studio of the International Press Agency. The Cardinal arrives at the studio for a press interview with critical journalists. He patiently allows himself to be questioned for two to three hours. He thinks to himself: "What you don't do for the Church!"

Question 1: *In our secular age, things seem to be going downhill not just for belief in God but also for Church life. Your Eminence, do you see any signs of hope for the Church?*

I am not a politician who lets sociological and market analyses make him worry about the chances of the institution he represents. During the life-threatening crisis of the Roman Empire, during the Great Migration and the collapse of the culture of Ancient Rome, St. Augustine developed his magnificent theology of history and published it under the title *De civitate Dei*. The fact that God's work of redemption will not fail does not depend on worldly factors and power constellations but rather on His promise that the gates of Hades will not prevail against the Church. He made Simon the First of the Apostles and named him Peter, the Rock. And on this Rock the Lord wanted to build His Church. But it is not on the inconstant character of this man or of his successors on the Chair of St. Peter in Rome that the Church is built but rather on his office. Christ's promise refers to the stability of his commission.

Even with a sinful priest, it is still Christ who baptizes. And with a bad Pope it is Christ who teaches infallibly through him when it comes to the definitive interpretation of the revelation that God has entrusted to His Church.

Hope is a theological virtue that is infused into our hearts by God. "Hope does not disappoint us, because God's love has been poured into our hearts through the Holy Spirit that has been given to us" (Rom 5:5). I see signs of hope in the priests and lay people who accept faith in Jesus Christ and are prepared to walk the Way of the Cross with Him to the Resurrection. "Now faith is the assurance of things hoped for, the conviction of things not seen" (Heb 11:1). Hope is not linked to the Church's acceptance in the media, to Her usefulness for a civil religion or to the securing of Her continued institutional existence with concordats but rather "to Jesus the pioneer and perfecter of our faith.... Consider him who endured such hostility against himself from sinners, so that you may not grow weary or lose heart" (Heb 12:2f.).

Question 2: *What will the Church in the West look like in future? A collection of small communities amid a sea of unbelievers? Or will there be a revival of Christianity as a cultural and social reality after all?*

That's hard to say. Theologically speaking, we are always a "little flock." But Christ exhorted us not to fear the powers and the powerful of this world. He said to His disciples: "'Do not be afraid, little flock, for it is your Father's good pleasure to give you the kingdom" (Lk 12:32). But we also want to lead the societies and nations to their inner calling, i.e., to knowing Christ as the salvation of the world.

Question 3: *What values are generally recognized to enable us to live decently together as befits our human dignity? What basic principles should be applied in education and in bringing up children, and what are the principles that govern international law?*

The Church can make an essential contribution here to the humanization of mankind. What She wants above all, however, is to proclaim to everyone the message of their redemption in Christ, the Son of God, and offer them the opportunity of a life as disciples of Christ. A society without any spiritual orientation or any ethical foundation is doomed to fail. I don't know of a single case of a purely secular ethic's ever having been successful.

Question 4: *How are we to understand the words of Pope Francis that inside the Holy Trinity they're all arguing behind closed doors, too, whereas on the outside they present a picture of unity. Is the inner unity of the Triune God just a facade?*

The Most Holy Trinity is the profoundest mystery of our faith. Outside revelation, we have no knowledge of it, "… no one knows who the Son is except the Father, or who the Father is except the Son and anyone to whom the Son chooses to reveal him" (Lk 10:22). The three Divine Persons are not, as in the human sphere, three personalities who are in harmony or argue with one another. The unity of the three Divine Persons is not a moral community that can also be destroyed, but rather a unity of essence as a triad of love.

We believe in the one God. And between the Father, Son and Holy Spirit there is only the opposition of their relationship to one another. The Son is one with the Father. And this unity of God in the essence and love of the Divine Persons should become the measure of the unity of Jesus' disciples in the community of Father and Son in love. "The glory that you have given me I have given them, so that they may be one, as we are one, I in them and you in me, that they may become completely one" (Jn 17:22f.). The hallmark of Satan's rule is inner disunity. "If a kingdom is divided against itself, that kingdom cannot stand. And if a house is divided against itself, that house will not be able to stand. And if Satan has risen up against himself and is divided, he cannot stand, but his end has come" (Mk 3:24ff.).

Question 5: *There are theologians who say that Catholics, too, should take a greater interest in reincarnation. Is it possible to reconcile belief in the existence of one human soul with the idea of reincarnation?*

The idea that the human soul materializes over and over again in a new body after death is completely incompatible with the Catholic faith. Furthermore, the term "reincarnation" is inappropriate for some sort of transmigration of souls. The human being is—metaphysically speaking—created from nothing at conception and a person's identity consists in the unity of soul and body. There is no pre-existent soul that could migrate from body to body. God's becoming man in Christ (cf. Jn 1:14) is called "the Incarnation," which is a one-off event. Here the person of the Eternal Son of the Father assumes a human nature, so that Christ is true God and true man. His individual human nature consists of the body, the formative principle of which is its spiritual soul. We Christians believe in the uniqueness of each individual human being in their spiritual-corporeal nature and the unrepeatability of their history: "… it is appointed for mortals to die once, and after that the judgement" (Heb 9:27). Unlike pre-Christian speculations as to man's fate after death, the Christian faith professes that—after the separation of the immortal soul from its body in death—man rises again with Christ to eternal life and that he does so with his soul in its restored and glorified body. For man is not only one in body and soul but also *one individual person* in his or her spiritual-corporeal nature.

Question 6: *You could sometimes get the impression that what people today call mercy is more akin to radical indulgence. And, vice versa, that divine justice is nothing but cruelty. Isn't it true that many people confuse God's mercy with the right to sin with impunity?*

Any right-minded person used to know in the past, and still does so today, that you have to answer to a higher authority for what you do. Those who blithely ignore their consciences will nevertheless have to face judgement on them one day. Paul speaks of the Gentiles' having the law distinguishing good from evil written on their hearts in the same way as the Jews, who know God's same commandments through revelation (cf. Rom 2:15f.).

It only gets really bad if God's mercy and justice are played off against each other in the Church in an attempt to gain popularity among people today. God's justice is His mercy, and through it He puts us into a right relationship with His essential goodness. That relationship means overcoming the sin through which we destroy ourselves and distance ourselves from God's truth and goodness. The punishment for it is not meted out on us externally; rather, it follows inwardly hard on the heels of the evil deed. Those who have behaved cruelly towards themselves or their neighbors cannot blame God for the curse of the evil deed that weighs them down and then dismiss repentance, penance and restitution as a dreadful imposition! If people have grown rich through exploiting others and then have to return the stolen money, they cannot call the end of their life of luxury an act of cruelty. The punishment is actually the great opportunity to become an inwardly good person again. Egoism kills; love builds up.

Question 7: *The old teaching of the Church used to be that whoever presumptuously sins hoping for divine mercy is guilty of a sin against the Holy Spirit. Is that still true? The theologians today are saying that God always accepts me and that He loves me as I am.*

There is no such thing as an old teaching of the Church that could be exchanged for a new one by this or that theologian. Apostasy from the faith is quite the opposite of interpreting it wisely for those with whom we share an epoch and culture. And in any case, where does it say that God loves me as I am? The "dear old grandad in his armchair" that they are talking about here is not the God of Abraham, Isaac and Jacob and the Father of Jesus Christ. The image rather calls to mind the reflection Narcissus was gazing upon before he fell into the pool. Paul states clearly that "all have sinned and fall short of the glory of God" (Rom 3:23). We cannot justify ourselves before God if we are "Fornicators, idolaters, adulterers, male prostitutes, sodomites, thieves, the greedy, drunkards, revilers, robbers" (1 Cor 6:9f.) and then presume to lay claim to the Kingdom of God and His mercy. Sinning in the hope of God's mercy is nothing less than mocking God by accusing Him of being incapable of doing anything but forgive. God loves us in the good that we are in our created nature and that we do with the talents and potential of our personalities. Thus we live out of the grace of forgiveness and being raised to the friendship with God that we have received from him in Christ. More gratitude than self-pity would do us all good.

Question 8: *According to Benedict XVI, since the 1950s we have been experiencing a "profound evolution of dogma" (discussion with Jacques Servais) as far as the salvation of non-Catholics is concerned. But what does "evolution of dogma" mean? The First Vatican Council after all stated: "Hence also that meaning of the sacred dogmas is perpetually to be retained which our Holy Mother Church has once declared, and there must never be a deviation from that meaning on the specious ground and title of a more profound understanding" (DH 3020).*

In Jesus Christ, God revealed Himself in the "fullness of time" (Gal 4:4) as the truth and life of every human being. Therefore there cannot be any further new revelation beyond Christ. The Son of God is after all the Logos who was and is with God. All things came into being in and through Him, and everything through which we know God. The fullness of all wisdom and life is known in the Word that became flesh (cf. Jn 1:14). The many individual teachings and "the words of eternal life" (Jn 6:68), which Jesus as a human being unfolded in the vocabulary, syntax and grammar of human language and expressed in the articulation of the finite spirit, couching the plurality of ideas and concepts in a sequence of space and time, are summed up in the one uncreated Word that he is in his divine nature and proceed from it (cf. Jn 1:1ff.). The one divine Word expresses itself in Jesus' many human words, uniting human perception with divine reason, in which he knows and loves himself in the Logos and the Pneuma.

God's truth is inexhaustible for us. And this does not just mean the mystery of God before revelation, that is, as we know God in His eternal might and divinity through the works of His creation, i.e., in His existence as the Creator of the world, without our being able to grasp His essence. It also refers to the fact that even after revelation and this revelation's being fully present in the Incarnate Word and the Spirit poured out upon all flesh (cf. Acts 2:17), we are still incapable of grasping God like an object of our natural, empirically bound knowledge (i.e., of empirically proving or disproving his necessary existence). He remains a mystery, though not one of darkness but rather one of a superabundance of light. Only through the humanity of Jesus and its presence in the Church and the sacraments can we share in the truth and life of God in Jesus Christ.

In order always to "be ready to make your defense [*apologia*] to anyone who demands from you an account of the hope that is in you" (1 Pet 3:15) we must also reflect on our faith. We do not have a positivistic understanding of revelation. The word of God was not dictated in Hebrew or Arabic in heaven to an angel who entrusted it to a chosen prophet to repeat mechanically. God meets us in the life and preaching of the Son of God as the Word made flesh. If the Word of God took on human form in Jesus, the way the faith community of the Church makes this Word its own as dogma must also have a history of how the understanding of it is communicated linguistically, historically and socially, but in itself definitively. This does not mean that new things are constantly being understood but rather that, in the course of the history of the Church and of dogma, we comprehend the unsurpassably new, the *Verbum incarnatum*, ever more deeply in all its richness and unparalleled newness.

Christ entrusted the apostles with bearing witness to His salvific work. And so the apostle Paul thanks the Thessalonians for having accepted his preaching not just as human words about God, but as God's word in human words (1 Thess 2:13). Belief in the Divine Logos is already intelligible in itself. We must on no account reduce it to blind faith. It is risking self-giving, but not recklessly jumping over a dark abyss.

Faith is always also perceiving because it is a sharing in the mutual knowledge of the Father and the Son in the Holy Spirit. That is why the Church's faith has rational structures. Her teaching can be communicated dialogically because it is in itself dialogical and thus logical, albeit not one-dimensionally and self-reflectively but in a relational-dialogical-sociological manner (i.e., the *logos* of the *societas* of the Church). In rejecting fideism, let us not fall into the opposite extreme of reducing faith rationalistically to what the created mind can grasp or even of making this the criterion of what we accept or reject as being rationally and scientifically provable. Faith does not have to justify itself before the forum of fallible human reason but only before the forum of infallible divine reason, in which the infallibility of the Church participates in matters of faith and doctrine. Truth is reason, and reason is truth.

All belief in the God of truth is a sharing in God's reason. This was expressed by Aristotle as follows: "The intellect thinks itself in grasping the intelligible, since in the act of touching and knowing its object it becomes intelligible. Therefore the intellect and the intelligible are the same. For that which can receive the intelligible and essence is the intellect, and its operation lies in possessing the intelligible. It follows that the object rather than the power of thought is that which is divine in the intellect, and that the contemplation thereof is supremely pleasurable and good. If, then, that happiness which is ours sometimes is God's always, it is a marvellous thing; if a greater happiness, it is still more marvellous. And this is the case. Life also is his, for the operation of the intellect is life, and he is that operation; and this operation of reason in and for itself is life supremely good and eternal. We say, then, that God is living, eternal, supremely good. Hence life and existence continuous and eternal are God's, for God is these things" (Met. 1072b). One must wholeheartedly agree with Enrico Betti: "In my opinion, this is the preeminent conception of God to be developed outside the biblical tradition, without the help of revelation but with the intellect alone. Furthermore, it deserves to be appreciated from the Christian point of view, too, if it is true that the few established divine attributes in the New Testament identify God as life and intellect (thinking substance) as well as being."[45]

The *lumen naturale* of human reason transcends itself in the *lumen fidei* when reason allows itself to be illumined by the Holy Spirit. As a result of the inner unity of faith and reason, the need arises for a "rational" (1 Pet 3:15 λόγον; Vulg. *rationem*) reflection of faith. Faith is neither deduced from the natural cognitive principles of reason nor reduced to them. But Catholic theology, as a function of the Church

---

[45] Enrico Betti, *Der Begriff der Wirklichkeit in der Metaphysik des Aristoteles: Metaphysik.* Die Substanzbücher, ed. C. Rapp, Berlin 1996, 289-309, here 308.

and Her proclamation, understands Her cognitive principle to be *fides quaerens intellectum* (Anselm of Canterbury).

The dogmas of the Church's faith do not express our own mutable personal and collective views. Rather, in them the Church merely recognizes—reflexively and conceptually mediated—what is definitively contained in revelation itself. A certain progression does take place in the deeper spiritual and theological understanding of revelation on the part of the believing subject, the Church, over the course of history. The great English theologian Cardinal John Henry Newman (1801-1890) developed a comprehensive theory of how it is possible to uphold the completedness of revelation in Christ at the same time as a growing understanding of it in the Church. The reason for this is that the word of God communicates itself via the words and comprehension of man. But this does not refer to individual thinkers wanting to force their private opinions on the Church; rather, it refers to the Church, which also corrects the individual theologian and incorporates his or her ideas into the overall structure of Sacred Scripture, Apostolic Tradition and the decision-making competence of the Magisterium.

Question 9: *Benedict XVI showed that without the belief in the need to belong to the Church, Christianity would be unnecessary. He outlined two consequences of such thinking: on the one hand, it means an end to mission; on the other hand, it is also the end of Catholic morals within the Church. How can this logic be overcome?*

The Church and the sacraments are necessary means of salvation in which the Christian believer receives the grace of Christ. Christ brought about redemption for all people. The Church does not originate the grace of the sacraments; rather, She mediates the sacraments of grace. It is necessary for someone first to come to a personal faith in Christ, the universal Mediator of salvation between God and man, and to accept the Church's profession of faith in Baptism before becoming a member of the Body of Christ in the visible Church and being able to receive other sacraments and participate in the life of the Church. In our missionary work, we do not force our religious opinions and practices on other people in the way of political and ideological propaganda and we certainly do not manipulate and seduce them with spiritual and material promises. Jesus was sent by the Father, and the Church has the commission from Him to continue His mission on His authority. Faith comes from hearing, and hearing results from the proclamation of those who were sent by Christ and authorized by Him to preach the gospel (cf. Rom 10:14f.).

Question 10: *If faith and salvation are no longer interdependent, faith itself becomes senseless—so Benedict added. The Pope formulates this conflict and then attempts to resolve it. The first solution, that of Karl Rahner, is rejected by Benedict. According to Rahner, it is sufficient for a man to accept himself and in so doing he is already a Christian no matter whether he knows it or not. That is the theory of anonymous Christianity. According to Benedict, this theory casts doubt on the seriousness of existence. He believes that the approach of Henri de Lubac comes closer to the truth. According to de Lubac, the nonbelievers are healed as members of humanity. Because the whole of humanity will be redeemed, nonbelievers, too, will be healed as members of the whole. So where is human freedom? And doesn't this then make salvation automatic?*

What we have here is, on the one hand, the Catholic belief that God has redeemed all people in Christ and that both an explicit belief in Him and a concrete making present of salvation through the Church and the sacraments become necessary for salvation—in accordance with both Christ's command and the means ordained (*de necessitate medii et praecepti*). On the other hand we have the question of the theological communication of these two revealed truths. However, even though there are differences between them on the level of theological reflection, neither Joseph Ratzinger nor Hans Urs von Balthasar, neither Karl Rahner nor Henri de Lubac calls these truths into question. The ambiguous term "anonymous Christian" does not imply that one is already saved merely through a natural acceptance of oneself. That would be self-redemption, which is completely at odds with the mystery of Christ. What Rahner in fact meant was rather that on account of the Christ event, human nature has always been under the influence of Christ's grace. This means that in everything good a person does and in everything in which he cognizes what is true, that person is incapable of doing these things using the powers of his own nature but already has the help of Christ's grace, the grace for which he is created and towards which he is orientated. But this grace must then be visibly and concretely realized in the sacramental and ecclesial life of the believing and confessing Christian. So it is not good will alone that allows a person to partake of the grace of Christ's redemption unless he or she explicitly recognizes Christ in faith and professes Him in the Creed. It is rather the grace of the sole Mediator between God and man that opens heaven to a person. This does not render the proclamation of the faith and the receiving of grace through the sacraments superfluous because these are as Christ intended them to be and accord with man's corporeal and social nature. And a person who expressly recognizes Christ in this life is illumined by his light and lives in the joy of the gospel that the world needs.

Question 11: *Pope Francis supports the immigration of Muslims to Europe. But is this migration not a new form of conquest of Europe? Is the immigration of Muslims an invasion, a conquest or an opportunity?*

On the one hand we have the help that we owe to anyone in need. But then there is a politics that uses human need for its own purposes. You cannot promote a mass migration of people who are not in need into Europe simply in order to marginalize Christian culture. In any event, we owe it to Christians, and even more so to non-Christians, to go to them, to proclaim the faith to them and, if they accept Christ, to baptize them in the name of the Father and of the Son and of the Holy Spirit, and to teach them to obey everything that Jesus commanded the disciples (cf. Mt 28:19f.).

Question 12: *Jihad is for Muslims a principle that means they have to spread out. The aim is to extend the dar al-Islam over most of the globe and introduce Sharia law. Is that a real danger? A warlike and violent expansion of a religion, so that there is no room left for others, at most tolerating them as third-class citizens, is incompatible with the human right to freedom of religion.*

Here the State has to protect the rights of its citizens. Islamic legal systems cannot be made the basis for public law, not even for citizens who follow the religion of Islam. We make a strict distinction between civil and canon law.

Question 13: *The Pope has called on Catholics to go into mosques and pray with Muslims on Fridays. Is this invitation wise?*

No ecclesial authority can invite or urge us to visit the house of prayer of another religion. Moreover, we cannot share in prayer with Muslims, either in a building or in the open air. We pray through Christ in the Holy Spirit to God our Father.

And we do not have a common abstract God alongside or above the Triune God. The God of philosophical theology is simply the expression of reason's ability to convince itself quite generally of God's existence without anticipating the more profound knowledge of God acquired through his self-revelation. In this respect we have a point of reference to everyone who is convinced of God's existence, including the Muslims. But we do not share with them the understanding of God that they draw from the revelation that Mohammed claims to have received. We share the belief that God exists, but we do not believe in the same God of revelation. Hence it is a merely theoretical statement to say that Jews, Christians and Muslims believe in one God. For the God whom the Muslims worship and the God and Father of Jesus Christ who is worshipped by believers in Christ are not the same God. If it were so, the Trinity would be for us Christians merely an adjunct that could be dispensed with in certain circumstances and out of consideration. That would be a betrayal of the supreme mystery of the Christian belief in the Father, the Son and the Holy Spirit. For the unity and trinity of God is, along with the Incarnation, the essential mystery of the Christian faith. We are baptized in the name of the Trinity. In Christ we are sons and daughters of God. Changing this would not be just changing an abstract theory; it would mean losing the "grace and truth [that] came through Jesus Christ" (Jn 1:17).

Question 14: *How can anyone make such a sweeping statement as to claim that Islam is a religion of peace? There are verses in the Qur'an that clearly and unambiguously recommend the killing of infidels.*

On the one hand we have the self-delusion of many people in the West; on the other is the reality of the many perpetrators of violence who invoke the Qur'an as the will of God. When the most brutal murders and the most heinous acts of violence are purported to be the will of God, then this God cannot be the true God, the Creator of all mankind. In his 2006 Regensburg lecture, Pope Benedict XVI demonstrated clearly that any act of destructive violence claiming to be committed in the name of God is contrary to our God-given reason. God Himself is the most perfect reason, indeed His essence is reason and will to Himself as love. Many Islamic scholars have concurred with Pope Benedict on this. Unfortunately, however, they have not been listened to by the terrorists acting in the name of Islam. Those who have themselves baptized have had bad experiences with Islam in their own countries and they rejoice in the freedom to which Christ has liberated them (cf. Gal 5:1). I can well understand the concern of our brothers and sisters in the Christian faith and share their fears and anxiety.

Question 15: *Your Eminence, there is a great deal of talk about the Church and faith right now. Often it is lamenting the decline of both. Do you share this view? Or have there been positive developments in the last few decades, too?*

It's hard to weigh this up. You see, you have to ask what criteria are to be used in making a judgement. We Christians have an eschatological understanding of history. God's action in the Cross and Resurrection of Jesus Christ is the ground and measure of everything. That is why, right from the start, we expect there to be dramatic ups and downs in history rather than a harmonious upward movement or a tragic downward one. Undoubtedly, we do have positive signs to report in the Church with, in particular, the liturgical and biblical movements and ecumenism. Nevertheless, it certainly troubles us when people attend worship less often, when the baptized are turning their backs on the Church, their Mother, and when many young people are no longer rooted in the Christian faith at all. But instead of just resigning ourselves to this, we should regard it as a call to take courage and see ourselves a missionary Church. Being a Christian is something that is communicated — hopefully convincingly — by both parents and Church, but it is still then up to the individual to make the contents of the faith his or her own. The gospel as such is unsurpassably new. But every single person sets out right at the very beginning of the path of discipleship in his or her life with Christ. That is why it is never too late. Now is the time of grace. Today is the day of salvation.

Question 16: *Were the Fifties, when it was taken for granted that most of the population belonged to one of the national churches, a better time? Or is there a greater honesty inside the Church today as well?*

Certainly it was better that more people went to church fifty years ago. All the same, you can't ultimately judge this accurately: when everything around them is socialized by Catholicism, many people just get carried along by it, too. Being borne along by a Catholic milieu does have an advantage, but it also has the possible disadvantage that people's faith just drifts along and won't stand up to being tested. But whenever you select a particular time in the past and declare it to be the norm, you trip yourself up. There were times in the *Kulturkampf* and National Socialism when Christianity was sorely oppressed. At those times, too, there was a rapid rise in the number of people exiting the Church, which was written off as antiquated. Certainly, Christians may no longer be bloodily persecuted in Europe, but their faith is challenged or it can happen that they are dragged before a court if someone sees their faith as a threat and claims to have been defamed by it. Nor can you always hope for an impartial judge. They, too, are children of their times and sometimes not immune to ideological contagion. It is difficult for young people in particular if they are exposed to public malice and mockery as Christians. What is called for here is not just to hark back to a Golden Age but to recall the roots of our faith. We, too, must allow ourselves to be told by Jesus: Cast out your nets again!

Question 17: *From the very beginning, Francis has performed actions that relativize the papal office.* Evangelii Gaudium *speaks expressly of a "sound 'decentralization.'" To what extent is the theological profile of the papal office changing with Francis, not least of all as a result of his style?*

The doctrine of the papacy as a divine institution cannot be altered by anyone; this would mean trying to correct God. According to Vatican II, the successor of Peter is in his person the perpetual principle of the unity of the Church in faith and in the community of Christ. But for 2,000 years different epochs have had different styles of exercising the Petrine office. It is quite a different matter when you live under the rule of ancient Rome or in a feudal society compared to living in a global world community with all the possibilities offered by the Internet and social networks. In addition, there are also individual personal styles. Pope Francis tries to get beyond everything that smacks of formality or distance and to break down fears of coming into close contact. In pursuing this he crosses conventional boundaries.

Decentralization is a difficult word to interpret. It presupposes a duality of center and periphery. Rome is not in the secular sense the center of power and the control center of a global organization. The universal Church consists in and of the local churches. Within the community of local churches, the particular church of Rome with the Pope at its head continues to have a quite specific significance, one given to it by the apostle Peter, for the unity of the Church and Her remaining in the truth of the gospel. Some time ago, there were people being peddled in certain tendentious media as close advisers of the Pope who claimed that the seat of the papacy could be moved to Medellin or that the curial offices could be shared out among the local churches. That is fundamentally wrong and even heretical. You only have to read Vatican II's Dogmatic Constitution *Lumen Gentium* in order to recognize the ecclesiological absurdity of such fantasy scenarios.

The seat of the Pontiff is the church of St. Peter in Rome. All Jesus' promises to Peter and his commission to feed his flock as the Supreme Pastor devolved upon the Roman church and thus to its bishop, the Pope. This is not just organizational juggling; rather, it is a matter of maintaining the Church's God-given unity. It would also be a misunderstanding to view the Curia as the Pope's central

administrative apparatus. The paranoia being cultivated about organized resistance in curial circles not wishing to be reformed by Pope
Francis simply provides a countercheck to the misunderstanding
that the Roman Curia is an apparatus of political power. Its real
function is rather to be the representation of the leading clergy
(cardinals) of the Roman Church, who share in upholding the Papal
primacy and, within the framework of the Roman church already,
lend the primacy the synodal character that is inherent in it.

Synodality does not begin with the collaboration between
bishops and Pope at the level of the universal Church. After all,
the Pope is not some kind of super-bishop who does not belong
anywhere in particular but just happens to be in Rome by chance
and from habit; no, he is the Bishop of Rome and as such also the
Pastor of the universal Church. The ancient documents from the
patristic period speak of the primacy of the Roman church with the
Pontiff at its head. This was later reduced, not entirely correctly, to
speaking of the primacy of the Pope as one would of an ecclesially
isolated individual. But the papacy is located, i.e., has its locus in
Rome. In this sense, the Roman church is the *mater et magistra* of
all the churches around the globe.

Question 18: *How can it be possible to show off to advantage the
diversity of the universal Church while striving for unity?*

By appointing bishops and priests from different continents
and cultures to head the congregations and pontifical councils.
They must be spiritually and theologically well qualified and have
pastoral experience of leading a diocese. This makes it possible to
avoid a career ladder within the Curia which, with the way things
are, could draw on just one nation. Depending on the task in question, those appointed must have the appropriate qualifications. The
Congregation for the Doctrine of the Faith, for example, must, since
Cardinal Ratzinger, who completely reshaped it, be led by a Prefect

and a Secretary who are at home in systematic theology — and not by someone who might be particularly skilled in diplomacy or administration. On the other hand, the Pontifical Council for the Interpretation of Legislative Texts must rely on highly competent specialists in Canon Law. Any attempts to indulge in the power play of allocating posts on the basis of friendship or dependence must be constantly thwarted — in defiance the woundedness of our nature as a result of Original Sin. That constitutes reform of the Church in the spirit of serving the Kingdom of God, the Church and the Holy Father.

Question 19: *How are we to understand Pope Francis' statement in* Amoris Laetitia *that the Church's teaching should not be hurled at the faithful like "dead stones"?*

Theologically there is not much to say about that. Perhaps this turn of phrase arose from a specific feeling. Such images are meant more to be used paranaetically rather than dogmatically. I do not believe that God gave us the commandments for us to use them as weapons against others; no, it was for us to achieve salvation by keeping them. "Blessed rather are those who hear the word of God and obey it!" (Lk 11:28). With this in mind, let me say quite frankly and in all humility, that I would not be happy if anyone invoked the Pope in order to denigrate our faithful and diligent theologians as "teachers of the law." Theology and theologians are indispensable for the Church's proclamation. For we are supposed to make our defense to anyone who asks us about the *rationality* of the hope and the faith that we have (cf. 1 Pet 3:15). It is not education that is the tinder of arrogance, but rather pride, which has its seat in the heart, not in the head but can, of course, go to one's head.

Question 20: *But hasn't the Church — sometimes more, sometimes less — actually run into this danger?*

Well, that's probably in everyone's human nature. Even those whom others denounce as cold teachers of the law are themselves at risk of it. This is not particularly Christian: then the image is taken of picking up stones to hurl at others. That is why I am not really convinced that images are always happily chosen. We should all unite in the aim of overcoming both legalism and laxism in the interpretation and application of God's commandments. If we quarrel with each other, strike victorious poses and fling bitter reproaches at one another, then there's something we've misunderstood. To play truth and love off against each other is the Devil's game.

Question 21: *Against this background, how significant do you find the Apostolic Exhortation* Amoris Laetitia *with respect to the burning issues surrounding marriage and the family? Does it constitute a new approach in papal doctrinal teaching?*

In its type and style, as compared to other doctrinal documents, it does indeed strike a new note. But it is not a change from one extreme to the other. For doctrinal documents have up to now also fulfilled their task of explaining the faith and promoting a life in Christ. After all, separating the doctrine from the praxis of the faith would be just as disastrous for the Church as wanting to set Christ the Teacher of the truth against Christ the Good Shepherd who gave His life for His sheep. There is only one Christ. What is special about *Amoris Laetitia* is that the Pope casts the net wide so as to take into account the subjective situation of the individual as well. He goes even more into concrete situations because the content of the gospel we have been given has to be internalized. What is new is the way in which this is now pastorally mediated in personal dialogue, in the most sacred space of the conscience and in the Sacrament of Reconciliation and linked to the concrete reality of life. The opposite extreme would be to dissolve everything in a postmodern subjectivism according to the motto: everyone is a law unto himself and acts as his own judge.

Question 22: *Isn't that one of those examples of a teaching's becoming ossified, where you need to take a look at how this interpretation of the words of the Bible came about historically and in what context Jesus demanded the indissolubility of marriage?*

There is no such thing as an "ossified" or a "softened up" doctrine. We have different ways of thinking and speaking. The Word of God is truth and life for all mankind in every age. The way of discipleship of the unjustly condemned, suffering and risen Christ is, in his own words, both "narrow and steep." But with His help the burden He lays on us is light to bear. In Christianity there is no stoical fulfilling of duty and no keeping of the commandments for their own sake. The commandments are signposts pointing the way to the life and the freedom of children of God. Christ brought something completely new, something that was beyond the comprehension of the people of His day and always will be; for Romans and Jews were familiar with divorce as a simple means of getting out of one marriage and embarking on another. When Jesus spoke of the indissolubility of marriage, the disciples, as we all know, opposed Him, thinking that such a thing was not humanly possible. The Church must both remain faithful to the word of Jesus, which can only be profoundly understood and lived in faith, and at the same time press for the natural preconditions for a successful marriage and family to be improved in education, politics, and society.

Question 23: *Since the Second Vatican Council, people have spoken of "aggiornamento," that is, an adapting of doctrine to humanity's journey. The Pope speaks of a "cammino insieme," a journeying together, a way on which the Church wishes to accompany the believer in the practical reality of his or her life. But how can this happen if you don't want to adapt it at all?*

Roman Encounters

The Church has been journeying in different cultures and epochs for 2,000 years. But Her message has always been the one identical gospel of man's redemption in Jesus Christ, Who unites all in the community of faith and love, namely, His Church. But the Church is not a business that wants to sell something and switches from producing bicycles yesterday to sports cars today. The faithful are children of God on the way of salvation, not customers to be enticed with good offers and on no account to be alienated. We human beings should change the way we think and act. There would be no need of revelation, doctrine or faith if we were to say that Christianity is no more than a civil religion which dresses up what goes on in everyday life in a little religion so that, for example, Christmas can be celebrated without believing that God was made man. It is just not enough for the Christmas tree to glitter and the mince pies to waft so enticingly.

We must not acquiesce when the mystery of Christmas is adapted to economic reality and sentimental needs. Faith is not self-reassurance and a poetic idealization of life; it wants to open up new horizons. With the Kingdom of God, something completely new begins, something that is more than the old parts being put together differently. The old has passed, and through Baptism we become a new creation in Christ. We are children of God and brothers and sisters to each other. That is something utterly different from one of the many programs for self-redemption and world improvement that are condemned to failure from the outset since they far exceed our powers.

Question 24: *Has Amoris Laetitia brought with it an upgrading of decisions of conscience?*

The decision of conscience cannot be upgraded because the conscience is the God-given supreme authority where I deliver myself up directly and in person to the will of God, who always desires my salvation. Our Catholic understanding of conscience does not, however, dispense with the mediation through the message of the gospel and the Church that is necessary for salvation. For although we as Catholics are in a direct personal relationship to God and by no means only indirectly related to Him through the means of grace of the Church, this relationship does not occur alongside or even contrary to the Church, the Body of Christ, whose members we are through Baptism. For in his humanity Jesus is the Mediator of the immediacy of God. And He realizes this mediation through the Church and particularly through the sacraments.

You cannot juxtapose the autonomy of the conscience and obedience to God and the Church as alternatives without already having given up the Catholic faith. By its very nature, the conscience is never self-referential; it is relationally determined as a relationship to the personal God. It is clear here that the ecclesial authority can never prescribe or permit anything that contradicts the revealed faith or the natural moral law. A conscience cannot simply decide for itself, for instance, that in a particular case the Fifth Commandment does not apply. If in the case of self-defense the attacker ended up dead, one would have to speak not of an exception to the prohibition of killing but rather of the absence of an objective and subjective culpability for a person's death. It is a matter of applying the teaching on faith and morals to the concrete situation — mediated by a conscience formed by the word of God in the profession of the Church.

Question 25: *But* Amoris Laetitia *also contains the implied criticism that the aspect of the need for the formation of conscience has been so overemphasized that it rendered the individual decision of conscience obsolete.*

My conscience can never dispense me from fulfilling the divine commandments because God does not deny us the grace to know and fulfill them if we honestly request it. It is a matter of interior decisions in accordance with my conscience, where in my knowledge and will I am confronted with the holiness and truth of God. I cannot justify myself in my conscience if I act against the perceived will of God, who always desires my salvation, and instead make my own interests my yardstick, thus compromising my salvation. I cannot circumvent the basic demands of morality. Always and in all circumstances, good is to be done and evil avoided. "Good" and "evil" are not the legitimation of a system of rules and sanctions invented by us. All created good reveals the goodness of God. And in all moral evils man does not transgress against abstract norms but against God's goodness, against love of neighbor and against the necessary acceptance of himself as being in the image and likeness of God, his Creator. The individual does not always have the level of knowledge that he actually should or could have. And there is an ignorance that can actually endanger salvation, for example a lack of marriage preparation or an inadequate introduction to Christian teaching and the life of the Church. The indissolubility of marriage is rooted in its sacramentality. If that is not understood, the Catholic teaching on marriage seems like an insurmountable hurdle, remote from life — and yet it is precisely the sacraments that lead to a fullness of life in Christ.

Question 26: *During the latest synod of bishops, the Pope made some extraordinary statements concerning synodality as a structural principle within the Church. Has the Pope given the bishops and episcopal conferences greater scope in his latest document?*

The complete body of bishops together form one unit with the Pope. The episcopal conference is a sensible structural principle, but it exists by virtue of human and not divine ecclesial law. It is certainly to be treated with skepticism if someone says that the Pope is giving, perhaps even giving back, certain powers to the episcopal conferences as if he had previously taken something away from them. The Pope cannot give the bishops more than what has already been given them through ordination and thus by Christ in the Holy Spirit. Nor can he take an episcopal ordination away from anyone.

Nor, though, can the power of primacy be shared—notwithstanding the fact that the Roman church (in the organizational form of the Curia) plays its own special part in supporting the exercise of it. The Pope—let alone "the Vatican"—is not the employer or boss of the bishops. They are not dependent on him, or even on his secretariat or the secular authorities of the Vatican State, in the manner of employees of a firm. For a bishop to be removed from office must remain an absolute last resort. Problems should be solved in fraternal dialogue between the Pope, or the relevant members of his staff, and the bishop in question. The quasi-automatic resignation of a bishop on his 75th birthday and the possibility of his term's extension at the Pope's personal discretion are both very much on the borderline from a dogmatic point of view. There is, of course, the pragmatic element of declining powers, but there is nevertheless a need for an adjustment of Canon Law here so as to prevent there from being any secularization of the episcopal office.

The situation is anyway different in the case of diocesan and titular bishops. The prime concern here must be to see how the fundamental theological relationship of the Pope to the local churches and the bishops in communion with him can be implemented for the good of the Church and with due regard for the conditions prevailing in the individual nations and cultural spheres. It is here that the episcopal conferences play a legitimate and important role in ensuring that an individual bishop in, say, Germany or Thailand does not settle things on his own that need to be shouldered by all. They must agree on joint solutions regarding, for instance, relations with the respective state or shared standards in catechesis and sacramental preparation. The faith, however, is universally one and the same. It unites peoples and languages in the Holy Spirit and resists nations going their own ways in a manner that has over and over again threatened the catholicity of the Church. Anyone who obscures the Church's catholicity also relativizes Christ's universal mediation of salvation and the unity of all the members of His Body, the Church.

Question 27: *But there are various approaches within theology, aren't there? The really exciting questions arise when theologians ask what the priorities are from the perspective of certain cultural contexts. Wouldn't it be important for the Catholic Magisterium to listen more to the variety of theological voices, to acknowledge them and to use this plurality as a basis for dialogue to seek out common ways or, as the case may be, to concede that there are also different ways?*

In spite of there being various theological schools and different interpretations and explanations, in Her decisions the Church is definitively committed to revelation. That is something that can never be revoked. We cannot say that the Council of Trent defined seven sacraments back then, but we here in Germany manage quite well with just five. Admission to the sacraments is part of the sacrament, so you cannot go allowing Catholics in a state of mortal sin to receive Holy Communion in one place and refuse it to them in another according to the regulations set out by different episcopal conferences. The Church cannot interfere with the substance of the sacraments. But how a sacrament is then concretely translated into the praxis of the respective cultural sphere can quite easily differ, for example in the case of First Communion or preparation for Confirmation.

We have always had variety in theology. But there is also a hypocritical way of citing of the variety to be found within theology so as to, as it were, favor the centrifugal forces and render the universal Church incapable of acting. The fact that for a long time theology in Germany played a leading role should be regarded as a commission rather than as flattering our arrogance. In the face of such temptations, St. Paul comes to my aid with his counter-question: "What do you have that you did not receive?" (1 Cor 4:7). But the Church cannot split up into national churches and different theological schools playing incompatible programs. There is, then, a great danger of tearing apart the Body of Christ. Plurality must not shatter the unity of faith but must instead enrich it. The unity of the Church is an object and content of faith, so that a merely loose world federation of Catholic-minded national churches with a papal honorary president would be the diametrical opposite of the Pentecost event, from which sprang the one Church in the many nations.

Question 28: *The Secretary of the Commission "Ecclesia Dei" has spoken of the possibility of members of the Society of St. Pius X being readmitted to the Church without any further conditions. Has something changed in the way of looking at things as a result of the present Pope?*

If you want to be completely Catholic you must acknowledge the Pope in his teaching office (not in all of his private statements) and also recognize the Second Vatican Council as what it was, namely, an ecumenical council assembled in the Holy Spirit, a gathering of all Catholic bishops with and under the Pope, the head of the college of bishops. Naturally, the constitutions, decrees and declarations vary in their relative weight and importance. We have two dogmatic constitutions and other important texts that, for instance, apply the natural right of freedom of religion to our present circumstances. But these are statements by the Catholic Magisterium. Freedom of religion as a fundamental human right and the freedom to adhere to the true religion as applied to the supernatural revelation in Jesus Christ are to be acknowledged without reservation by every Catholic. You do not have to be enthralled by every single sermon preached by a bishop or by the Pope. They can differ in quality, too. But the Magisterium as such, which provides an explanation of the faith, is to be accepted and received as an element of the revealed faith itself. I must follow what it teaches with religious obedience and inner assent. I cannot accept one thing but reject another. For example, the Resurrection of Christ is not in a formal sense a dogma as it has never been proclaimed ex cathedra by a Pope. But it is central to the Creed, indeed foundational. So even if they have not been proclaimed ex cathedra, central statements of the faith are nevertheless integral for us Catholics. That is why Vatican II cannot be written off as a council that was just a pastoral talking-shop simply because it did not define any dogmas in the technical sense of the word. Pope Francis does not differ in any way from Benedict XVI in his relationship to the Society of St. Pius X. He regards these and similar groupings as Catholics, but ones who are still journeying towards full Catholic unity. Hence recognition of the Second Vatican Council is not an inappropriately high hurdle to jump but rather an appropriate medicine to enable them to enter into full communion with the Pope and the bishops who are in communion with him.

Question 27: *Here, too, Vatican II proves to be a further development of tradition, doesn't it?*

In a way, the Second Vatican Council made a new method possible for the Magisterium. The Council rethought many resolutions and justified them in a new way. But this does not mean that you can just come along and say that it is not valid because it was not all formulated word for word the same in earlier documents of the Magisterium. The ecumenical endeavour, for example, results from the nature of revelation and the nature of the Church. Hence it is necessary not merely to consent to the content of the Catholic faith if one wishes to be a Catholic; one must also recognize the fundamental hermeneutic or interpretive key of the Catholic faith, or as the Second Vatican Council put it: "that sacred tradition, Sacred Scripture and the teaching authority of the Church, in accord with God's most wise design, are so linked and joined together that one cannot stand without the others, and that all together and each in its own way under the action of the one Holy Spirit contribute effectively to the salvation of souls" (*DV* 10).

Question 28: *And now one more question on what is certainly a growing antagonism between traditionalists and modernists—or whatever you want to call these two extremes. Why is the unity of the Church seen as so dangerous, and how should a possible schism be averted in this phase of weak Roman leadership?*

What is needed in this hour of the Church is prudence and circumspection. Just don't add fuel to the fire! And don't all crowd on one side and make the Barque of Peter keel over. When the extremists block each other, I always think of Paul and the advice he gave to Timothy, his quick-learning pupil: "Whoever teaches otherwise and does not agree with the sound words of our Lord Jesus Christ and the teaching that is in accordance with godliness, is conceited, understanding nothing, and has a morbid craving for controversy and for disputes about words. From these come envy, dissension, slander, base suspicions, and wrangling among those who are depraved in mind and bereft of the truth.... But as for you, man of God, shun all this; pursue righteousness, godliness, faith, love, endurance, gentleness. Fight the good fight of the faith; take hold of the eternal life, to which you were called and for which you made the good confession in the presence of many witnesses.... I charge you to keep the commandment without spot or blame until the manifestation of our Lord Jesus Christ" (1 Tim 6:3-5, 11-14).

Roman Encounters

Question 29: A question on the 500th anniversary of the Reformation. Should Catholics join in the celebrations or mourn the schism of Christendom? After all, it's possible to laugh or cry about the same thing. It's a matter of what sentiments the cue prompts.

Strictly speaking, we Catholics cannot celebrate 31 October 1517, the date taken to mark the beginning of the Reformation, which led to the schism of western Christendom. If we are convinced that the hierarchical constitution of the Church—grounded as it is in doctrine and in the sacraments, including that of Orders—is of divine law and that the one revelation (in Scripture and apostolic Tradition) has been preserved complete and unfalsified by the Church, then we cannot accept any reason to separate ourselves from Her. The Protestants view the event of the Reformation with different eyes. And that is why they celebrate the rediscovery of the unadulterated word of God, which to their way of thinking had been corrupted by purely human traditions. The Reformers had become convinced that it was not just that a number of high-ranking representatives of the Church had grown morally corrupt but that they had adulterated the true gospel, thus blocking the way to salvation in Christ for the faithful. Their idea that the Pope, i.e., the head of this system, was the Antichrist was their justification for the separation. When a tension arises between the unity of the Church and the truth of the "gospel of grace alone," it is the truth that must tip the balance. That is why a reunification is also only possible in the truth. A prominent present-day theologian says that relativizing the question of truth and unthinkingly adopting fashionable ideologies actually blocks the way to unity in the truth. In this spirit, a Protestantization of the Catholic Church would neither reconcile us with a secularist way of thinking that lacked transcendence nor make it possible to meet in the mystery of Christ. In Christ we have a supernatural revelation to which we owe "full submission of intellect and will"

(*DV* 5). The Catholic principles of ecumenism as they are set out in Vatican II's Decree on Ecumenism still remain valid (cf. *UR* 2-4). The document *Dominus Jesus* published by the Congregation for the Doctrine of the Faith in the Holy Year 2000, which was not understood by some and wrongly opposed by others, is the Magna Carta against the christological and ecclesiological relativization of post-modernity.

Question 30: *You have recently spoken about the publication in German of King Henry VIII of England's* Defence of the Seven Sacraments *against Martin Luther (1521). What can we learn from it?*

Even those who did not want to believe it were forced, at the latest with the publication of his reformist tracts in 1520, to concede that it was not the spiritual and moral reform of Christians in the Catholic Church that Martin Luther (1483-1546) sought but rather that what he instigated was a break with "the Catholic Church, which is governed by the successor of Peter and by the bishops in communion with him" (*LG* 8). In particular his treatise *On the Babylonian Captivity of the Church* (1520) shows that he held a completely opposing opinion on the crucial questions of salvation and the ecclesial and sacramental mediation of salvation for in it he announced and wished to bring about the liberation of the Church as it had hitherto existed from its "Babylonian captivity" under the Church's hierarchy and from what he considered to be the false concept of grace in the Catholic teaching on the seven sacraments. This intention was immediately clear and comprehensible even to his contemporaries. Proof of this is offered by the King of England—a highly educated Catholic, secure in his knowledge of the faith but not a specialist theologian—whose polemical treatise against Luther just a year later shows that the question of the sacraments touches the nerve of just how different Luther's understanding of the Church is. By way of thanks and confirmation for his *Assertio Septem Sacramentorum adversus Martinum Lutherum* (1521), the *Defence of the Seven Sacraments*,[46] Henry received the title of "Defensor fidei" from the Pope, a title that English monarchs have retained to this day. This paradoxically confirms how the Anglican Church, which dates back to Henry's schismatic severance from the Holy See (1534), remains indissolubly connected with the Church of Rome that had a thousand years earlier planted Christianity in England. In 2017 we are looking back on the secession of a large part of Western Christianity from the *ecclesia principalis* that was set off five hundred years ago. It is the Church of Rome that was founded and organized by the Princes of the Apostles, Peter and Paul, so "it is a matter of necessity that every Church should agree with this Church, on account of its pre-eminent authority" (Irenaeus of Lyon, *Adv. Haer.* III, 3,2), and it is only thanks to being in communion with Her that they belong to the Catholic Church. The separation from Rome and the disunity among Christians in communities that differ considerably in their creeds, sacramental life, and recognition of the bishops as successors of the apostles and as pastors legitimately instituted by Christ goes against Christ's will for His Church. He founded the Church in Her unity, sanctity, catholicity, and apostolicity on St. Peter and his successors, the Bishops of Rome, so that they should be in their person "a permanent and visible source and foundation of unity of faith and communion" of the episcopate and all the churches (*LG* 18).

In retrospect, the year 1517 cannot be a cause of rejoicing over the anniversary of the Reformation breakthrough to evangelical freedom and to "liberation from the rule of the pope, the Antichrist, over the true church," which allowed Christianity to appear in its

---

[46] Henry VIII, *Defence of the Seven Sacraments*, ed. by Raymond de Souza, 2007.

true form and achieve a right understanding of itself. Instead, this historic date should be an occasion for repentance and renewal in Christ for all Christians. The separation can be overcome with the help of the Holy Spirit if we recall the ground and center of our faith. At a time when all signs of Christian culture are being eliminated in Europe and the "inner man" is being removed from the love of Christ with a tragic ignorance of the great salvific mysteries of the revealed faith, we must find ourselves again in the knowledge of the great treasure that Christ bequeathed to His Church in the celebration of the sacred sacraments. King Henry VIII, who ruled England from 1509-1547, did not scorn the help of great scholars in writing his defense of the sacraments against Luther. Of particular note among them is St. Thomas More, who was martyred under Henry for standing up for papal primacy and the indissolubility of every sacramental marriage. This treatise, with its knowledge of the Bible as well as patristic tradition and the beginnings of scholastic sacramental teaching—citing particularly the work of Hugh of St. Victor—is a noteworthy testimony to Catholic tradition. Anyone who might have imagined that it was only as a result of the Protestant challenge that the Church arrived at her dogmatically binding teaching on the sacraments will be disabused of the idea by this. Quite apart from that, you only need to look at the magisterially binding definitions on the number, nature and efficacy of the sacraments *ex opere operato* (in contrast to the subjective confidence found in Luther's fiducial faith) promulgated by the Fourth Lateran Council (1215) and the Council of Florence (1439).

King Henry stresses frequently that his main concern is not to produce a strictly academic treatise and a purely technical theological dispute. Luther's 1,520 tracts, particularly his denial of five of the sacraments—of which penance was initially still disputed—and among these especially his denial of the sacrificial nature of the

Mass and the objective Real Presence of Christ (in the sacrificial signs and not merely in the subjective faith) were themselves populistically and polemically calculated to appeal to the "common people." Henry's reply is not intended as an arena for scholars to compete with and outdo one another in their knowledge of the sources, their astute arguments and their polished formulations. Its aim is to reassure Christians of the reliability of their faith and of the sacramental mediation of salvation as had been taught and lived by the Church since the time of the apostles.

In a postscript that is remarkable from the point of view of Church history, the King stresses that both the Pope and he personally have always only been interested in converting Luther, who, however, could not be brought to his senses either by Holy Scripture or by reason to see that his position is inconsistent with the Church's entire tradition. Luther's concern was not, King Henry contended, to reform the Church, since the Holy Father would certainly have been grateful for suggestions. Everyone would, he argued, have had to make a concerted effort to help renew the Church "in head and members," as the late-medieval demand put it. But with his subversion of the "Church of the living God," which is "the ground and pillar of truth" (1 Tim 3:15), Luther had founded a "new Church" (*Assertio septem sacramentorum*; or *Defence of the Seven Sacraments* [NY 1908], 408).

Studying the writings of the 16th-century Protestant Reformers and the Catholic Reform theologians should not cast us back into the days of confessionalistic polemics. Nevertheless, it can preserve us from superficial euphemisms in the ecumenical movement and increase our awareness of the real differences that still remain to be overcome and the challenges we face in our own day. Today humanity needs and demands the common witness of all Christians to God in Christ and in His holy, catholic, and apostolic Church united in the Holy Spirit.

5

Reform or Reformation of the Church?

The Cardinal is speaking at a joint Catholic-Protestant symposium and puts forward the thesis that, alongside the legitimate political and cultural categories, it is the theological perspective that is crucial for an understanding of what began with Luther's theses on 31 October 1517.

Ladies and gentlemen,

In a comprehensive study by the Oxford Church historian Diarmaid MacCullough, the "Reformation" is the name given to the period between 1490 and 1700, the result of which can be seen today in the political and religious fragmentation of western Christianity.[47] Depending on one's point of view, how these historical events are assessed will be different, even contradictory. Some people completely disregard the content of the Christian faith and interpret the Protestant Reformation together with Catholic Reform and the Counter-Reformation as a pluralization process at the transition from the Middle Ages to the modern era. Viewed in terms of a belief in linear progress, the historical Reformation becomes a precursor and generator of ideas for a development that will be completed in the Enlightenment and the Modern Age. But what is the essence of the Modern Age: man without God or man in free encounter

---

[47] Diarmaid MacCullough, *The Reformation: A History*. London 2003.

with God? From this perspective, the Reformation, abandoning its true religious concern, ultimately leads to a secular view of the world in which the religious option in general and the Christian one in particular is just one among many.[48] This would make the Reformation merely the first step on the way to a self-relativization of the truth and salvation that have come into the world once and for all with God's eschatological self-revelation. But the Reformers did not intend to pave the way for a de-Christianization of society and a de-Churching of the Christian community. What they sought was a renewal of the Church in accordance with the gospel as they understood it. Although this brought them into opposition to the Catholic view of gospel and Church, they did not form a coalition with the secular culture that had begun with the Renaissance, which is what cultural Protestantism's interpretation of the historical event of the Protestant Reformation and the revolution against the Catholic Church actually wished to happen.

This makes obsolete in substance the old contrary, polemical characterizations derived from a superficial interpretation of justification by faith or works that contrast a Protestant church of the gospel, freedom, conscience and the Word with the Catholic Church of the law, obedience, authority and the sacraments.

Despite all their controversies over the doctrine, life and constitution of the Church, Christians of all denominations are one in their belief in God's final and unsurpassable self-revelation in His Word, the Son of the Father, Who took on our flesh and through His death on the Cross and His Resurrection from the dead established the Kingdom of God for all time. Seen in this light, their common profession of Christ as the Son of God and sole Mediator of salvation unites Catholic and Protestant Christianity and does not divide the Church into a supposedly medieval, backward form of

---

[48] Cf. on this Charles Taylor, *A Secular Age*, Cambridge, Mass. 2007.

its historical realization and one that is supposedly compatible with the Modern Age. The Church as the sacramental sign and instrument of the rule of God that has come and that will be fulfilled in Christ coming again, cannot be overcome by the powers of death and evil. This is what Jesus once promised to His disciples, with Simon Peter at their head, in Caesarea Philippi (cf. Mt 16:18). If the fullness of time has arrived in Christ, there can be nothing new beyond Him that surpasses Him or makes His message outdated. But the Church is so closely linked to Her Head that She always shares in His life and is led by His Spirit, so that She can never be completely separated from Him and need to be, as it were, reborn or refounded. "Christ loved the church and gave himself up for her, in order to make her holy by cleansing her with the washing of water by the word" (Eph 2:25f.). Just as the marriage between a man and a woman is indissoluble in Christ and, despite possible crises, is always renewed from the wellspring of love, so Christ does not turn away from the Church in spite of the sins and transgressions of Her members. And just as the husband is one body with his wife, so it is true of Christ, the Head of the Church, that "no one ever hates his own body, but he nourishes and tenderly cares for it, ... because we are members of his body" (Eph 5:29f.). Reform does not mean changing the way of conducting Her life in *martyria*, *leiturgia*, and *diakonia* that Christ established in the Church at Her foundation, but rather the renewal of the members of the Body of Christ in the life that passes from the Head to the Body of His Church. Reform is not a return *ad fontes* in the way that humanism and the Renaissance perceived it with a sense of superiority at being better able to gain a philological understanding of the original Greek, Hebrew and Latin texts of the Bible, the Church Fathers and the pagan authors of Classical Antiquity than their professorial predecessors, let alone the common people. Renewal in Christ is a going forward towards the coming Lord so that, like the wise virgins, we may be able to go to meet the bridegroom with our lamps burning and be ready to go with Him into the wedding banquet (cf. Mt 25:10).

Reform in a theological sense has nothing to do with the myth of a Golden Age in the dim and distant past that people want to restore. Any interpretation of Church history according to the model of its being either a falling off from a pure origin or a wholly positive forward development founders on our belief in the eschatological presence of salvation in Christ and on our knowledge of the drama of world and Church history held between the *civitas Dei* and the *civitas terrena*. Christ is the undying light of God in the world. But the history of the Church moves between light and shade. "The Church, 'like a stranger in a foreign land, presses forward amid the persecutions of the world and the consolations of God,' announcing the cross and death of the Lord until he comes' (cf. 1 Cor 11:26). By the power of the risen Lord, she is given strength that she might, in patience and in love, overcome her sorrows and her challenges, both within herself and from without, and that she might reveal to the world, faithfully though darkly, the mystery of its Lord until, in the end, it will be manifested in full light" (*LG* 8). To the Gnostics' question as to what was unsurpassably new that had come with Christ, Irenaeus of Lyon replied in the 2nd century: "Know ye that He brought all [possible] novelty, by bringing Himself who had been announced. For this very thing was proclaimed beforehand, that a novelty should come to renew and quicken mankind—*Omnem novitatem attulit semetipsum afferens . . . quoniam novitas veniet innovatura et vivificatura hominem.*"[49]

Christ can be neither outdone nor equalled by this-worldly progress in science, technology and the social order. The fullness of salvation and truth has been mediated to all people for ever in Christ by God His Father. In the Holy Spirit, the Church is led to an ever

---

[49] Irenaeus, *Adv. haer.* IV, 34,1.

deeper understanding of the revealed truth. That is why, despite the fullness of time's having been realized in Christ, there is such a thing as collective and individual progress and there are different forms of the inculturation of Christianity proper to the given context, which thus lead to new cultural forms of Christianity. It is — in conformity with the incarnational and sacramental presence of truth and salvation — not about passing on the faith mechanically, but rather it is the living tradition of the apostolic teaching, one that is vigorous and kindles spiritual and religious life. The Church's teaching authority therefore has neither a conservative nor an innovative function if each is taken separately. It is instead the two working together that displays fidelity to the definitiveness of revelation and the growth of the Church in the living faith of Her members. The Second Vatican Council sums up this tension when it states in the Dogmatic Constitution on Divine Revelation *Dei Verbum*:

> But in order to keep the gospel forever whole and alive within the Church, the apostles left bishops as their successors, "handing over" to them "the authority to teach in their own place" (Irenaeus of Lyon, *Adv. haer.* III, 3, 1).... This tradition which comes from the apostles develops in the Church with the help of the Holy Spirit. For there is a growth in the understanding of the realities and the words that have been handed down. This happens through the contemplation and study made by believers, who treasure these things in their hearts (cf. Lk 2:19. 51) through a penetrating understanding of the spiritual realities they experience, and through the preaching of those who have received through episcopal succession the sure gift of truth. For as the centuries succeed one another, the Church constantly moves forward toward the fullness of divine truth until the words of God reach their complete fulfillment in her (*DV* 7f.).

According to Catholic belief, which is founded on the words of Jesus, a plurality of opposing denominations contradicts the unity of the Church as contained in revealed truth. Since the Church is the Body of Christ, which is held together in its many members by Christ Himself as the Head of this Body, there can be only one Church in faith and sacramental life. The Church is "one body and one Spirit" and "one Lord, one faith, one baptism, one God and Father of all, who is above all and through all and in all" (Eph 4:4ff.).

Nor did Martin Luther, Huldrych Zwingli and John Calvin, who had a crucial influence on the historical epoch of the Reformation and were the ones who set it in motion (hence they are referred to as "Reformers"), by any means intend to relinquish the unity of the Church in favor of a plurality. Their aim was to reform and renew the existing Church that had been founded by Christ in history, and to do so in the Spirit of Her divine founder and living Head. Their method was to cleanse the Church of Christ of those dogmatic errors which they held to have resulted in abuses and malpractices that jeopardized salvation. The separation of the followers of Luther, Zwingli and Calvin from the Church gathered around the Pope and bishops was not the result of a desire to improve moral and spiritual life, to modernize the Church's human institutions (universities, care for the poor, the selection and training of suitable candidates for religious office) and to battle against the secularization of the Church; rather, it was the assertion that the Church had committed serious errors of faith and had, through a false understanding of the sacraments, severely endangered the faith of believers that marked the turning point from a reform of the Church to a Reformation that produced a new church.

Here we have reached the point at which Catholic and Protestant understandings of Church reform diverge. If it is possible for the Church to depart from revelation and leave Sacred Scripture alone as the criterion for correct teaching and praxis, then it is necessary to cleanse and reform the Church in Her teaching, life and constitution in accordance with the Word of God. If, however, as the Catholic Church teaches, She cannot depart from revelation, then there can only be reform in the shape of renewal and deepening. For Protestantism there is a *reformation of the Church*, that is, a profound reforming of the Church according to the Word of God. For Catholics, on the other hand, there is a reform in the Church in which Pope and bishops, priests and religious and all the laity are called upon to fulfill their vocations better. Because the Reformers were convinced that in Her central teaching on redemption and the justification of the sinner the Church, with the Pope and bishops at Her head, had diverged from the gospel of Christ, they became convinced of the need for a reformation and substantial transformation of the Church that belonged to a completely different category of reform from those had taken place up to then.

So let us recall some of the reforms that occurred in the Catholic Church. There was, for example, the Carolingian Renaissance, which was essentially a reform of the theological educational institutions. Then the Gregorian Reforms aimed at liberating the Church from the straightjacket of feudal society and the system of proprietary churches. Their goals were to combat simony and lay investiture and to support priestly celibacy. There were the great monastic reforms (Gorze, Cluny, Hirsau, Windsheim, Melk) and the new orders coming into being with their own specific charisms and responding to particular challenges posed by processes of change taking place in Church and society. We are all familiar with the reforms to regulations, curricula and seminaries that followed the Council of Trent. We know, too, which bishops strove with apostolic zeal to fulfill the Tridentine ideal of the pastor (Cardinal Charles Borromeo of Milan, Archbishop Toribio of Mogrovejo, Cardinal Gregorio Barbarigo of Padua).

The great orders founded by St. Dominic and St. Francis were concerned with a renewal of apostolic preaching and with pastoral care suited to the rising urban culture and for students, pursuing alongside this the ideal of a life of evangelical poverty and humility. In the 19th and 20th centuries, the Church provided magnificent examples of Her adaptability in mentality and structure by establishing new religious orders and developing Her social teaching.

The 15th-century reform councils endeavoured, albeit largely in vain, to bring about a reform of the Church "in head and members." Characteristic of the incipient anti-Roman sentiment and the ever-increasing doubts about the visible Church and Her sacramental mediation of grace are, among other things, the *gravamina germanicae nationis* that were frequently raised at the Diets and which together prepared the ground for the ecclesial revolution of the 16th century.

The Catholic reform based on the Council of Trent is essentially different from the Reformation that gave rise to the various Protestant denominational associations (*Konfessionsverbände*) because the Catholic Church retained Her identity in Her teaching and sacramental constitution. But connections do also exist with the communities that came out of the Reformation in that the concern of both Catholics and Protestants is to deepen their piety and seriously pursue a moral life as followers of Christ.

But Christianity as a whole lost credibility as a result of the religious wars in England, France, Switzerland and Germany as well as the inhuman and unchristian persecution and oppression of members of the respective other denominations, as it had even before that due to its violent behavior toward Christian heretics as well as its treatment of Jewish fellow citizens and those belonging to non-Christian religions. The Enlightenment confronted Christianity and all religions orientated towards transcendence with an interpretation of existence that saw the goal of humanity as lying no longer in God but rather in this-worldly happiness. From now on, belief in progress begins to move in the direction of self-perfection by means of science and the construction of an ideal society. This was meant to replace belief in redemption through the grace of God. Theonomy based on God's word and commandment is played off against the moral autonomy of the human subject. However, they overlooked the fact that God's grace does not condemn us to passivity but rather makes the free will capable of participating actively in the coming of the Kingdom of God. For grace presupposes nature in reason and freedom and perfects it, yet without destroying it, as Thomas Aquinas already explains the relationship of the creature to his Lord and Creator.[50] In the various forms of cultural Christianity, attempts were made to resolve the tension between, on the one hand, belief in revelation and grace as the ground of salvation of all and, on the other hand, the this-worldly liberal and socialist programs of self-redemption.

On the Catholic side, too, the tension was felt that existed between the traditional faith and the so-called modern world. Here the "modern world" is not understood to mean just a few technological achievements that make practical life easier. Modern culture is rather the embodiment of all the guiding principles and concepts that appear to be antithetical to the Catholic faith and its ecclesial form: subjectivity, freedom, autonomy of conscience, and in general the metaphysics-free view of the world propounded by empiricism and positivism. The Syllabus of Errors (1864) containing the eighty errors condemned by Pope Pius IX was for a long time regarded by friend and foe alike as a synonym for and evidence of the irreconcilable incompatibility of the Catholic faith and the modern world. The final proposition condemned in this document reads: "The Roman pontiff can and should reconcile and adapt himself to progress, liberalism, and the modern culture" (DH 2980).

---

[50] *S.th.* I q.1 a.8 ad 2.

It is necessary here to reflect on what is actually meant by this modern liberal dominant culture to which the Pope as the supreme representative of revealed Christian religion is supposed to adapt himself. It refers to the liberalism that permits at most an immanence religion in the form of cultural Christianity and otherwise uses the omnipotence of the State to bring all its citizens into line and subject them to its own cognitive paradigm. The so-called culture wars and the struggles between Church and State directed against us in the 19th and 20th centuries offer enough instances of what kind of tolerance and freedom of conscience the Church can expect from the representatives of a scientific world view and ideology.

At the beginning of the 20th century, Albert Erhard, an important representative of so-called Reform Catholicism, countered Adolf von Harnack's theory that modern culture was incompatible with the Catholic Church and even that the Church was an opponent of and obstacle to progress by convincingly proving the cultural significance of Catholicism.[51]

Precisely with its Pastoral Constitution *Gaudium et Spes*, the Second Vatican Council presents the positive and constructive relationship of the Church to the world in its immanent development and in man's transcendent goal in God, thus giving the lie to the hostile juxtaposition of Church and world posited by the ideological liberalism of the 19th century and the political ideologies of the 20th. No one has played a more crucial role in setting the course for the progress of mankind for the better than the Catholic Church with Her unwavering adherence to the inalienable nature of human dignity, with Her social teaching since Pope Leo XIII,

---

[51] Albert Erhard, *Der Katholizismus und das zwanzigste Jahrhundert im Lichte der kirchlichen Entwicklung der Neuzeit*, Stuttgart and Vienna 1902.

and now with Pope Francis' encyclical *Laudato Si'* on ecology from the viewpoint of a theology of creation.

Faced with an inner-worldly ideology of progress and self-redemption, the Church must always maintain Her identity as the sacrament of the salvation of the world instituted by God; and in view of the profound transformation of our scientific and historical image of man She must also come up with ever new theological syntheses of faith and reason, grace and freedom that can be applied to practical life. But over the past two decades this has led to a polarization and factionalization within the Church into so-called liberals and progressives on the one side and so-called conservatives and integralists on the other. This has devastating consequences for the mission and global commission of the Church.

It has also led to a reshaping of the content and aim of the concept of reform within the Catholic Church.

In all the historical forms of Church reform the aims have been a renewal of Christian living and Church life, a deepening of faith and a renewal in Christ. The term "reform" enters the Church's terminology via the Vulgate translation of the Letter to the Romans. The apostle urges the faithful in Rome not to be conformed to this world (*nolite conformari huic saeculo*) but to be transformed by the renewing of their minds (*sed reformamini in novitate sensus vestri*) "so that you may discern what is the will of God—what is good and acceptable and perfect" (Rom 12:2).

What is currently understood by reforms that are held to be necessary is much more a secularization of the Church. The divine commandments that are not liveable are to be reduced to ideals that everyone can, but by no means must, strive after in all good conscience in order to make peace with themselves or to feel happy in a worldly sense. The Church no longer serves the world on its journey to God but rather offers Her services to it so as to make Herself useful as one of many social initiatives, thus proving Her right to exist. The Church is then no more than an ideology for mastering contingency and an agency for social outreach.

But the Church cannot adopt a political and ideological concept of reform that is alien to Her because She is a divine foundation and not a finite and transient reality created by human beings. Everything that comes from man can and must be adapted to changing circumstances in order to better serve human beings in their families and nations as well as in the social and economic spheres. The yardstick is the realization and preservation of human dignity. Attentiveness to the "signs of the times" and an analysis of the contemporary cultural and social situation of mankind with the aid of the empirical sciences are the prerequisites for the Church to be able to fulfill Her mission. She is sent by Christ into the whole world and to all people so that She might, in the light of Christ and the power of God's Spirit, bring home to every human being their divine calling to know God and to live from grace and compassion. This is described by the Second Vatican Council in *Gaudium et Spes* (GS 4-10).

The Church as a creation of God cannot, of course, be the object of human reforming endeavours. We cannot reform and refashion the Church at our own discretion and as we see fit. God is the subject of the covenant people whom he calls. God founds the Church in Christ. He Himself leads Her as the Good Shepherd and fills Her with His Spirit and life. It is not we who reform the Church of God and reshape Her according to our own image and likeness; rather, it is God Who reforms us when we allow ourselves to be renewed in Christ in our thoughts and actions and become conformed to Him. The result of this is that the Church is brought alive in performing Her fundamental tasks in proclamation and pastoral care, in liturgy and caritas, and in Her social services. It is the spirit that brings life, not the letter; in other words, the renewal of life in Christ also gives a positive direction to any structural and organizational reforms. Which is why the term "backlog of reform," coming as it does from politics, cannot be applied to the Church without politicizing and secularizing Her. There is a widespread opinion that we would only have to "abolish" priestly celibacy or introduce *viri probati* and then there would be no numerical lack of priests any more. If the Church would only admit women to holy orders, the debate on "women and the Church" would instantly calm down. You would simply have to invite Protestants to share Holy Communion and it would immediately bring about unity in faith, even though the doctrinal differences would remain and the still separate churches—visibly contradicting Christ's will in their separateness—would bear counterwitness to full communion in the one Church of Christ. You would just need to appeal to Jesus' mercy and we would immediately be rid of the indissolubility of sacramental marriage—thereby debasing it to a human ideal and thus denying its origin in God's covenant activity.

These are all operations and options that by calling themselves reforms claim a positive connotation for themselves but which have nothing to do with the historical ecclesial and monastic reforms or with reform as renewal in the everlasting novelty of Christ.

The formulation "*ecclesia semper reformanda*" does not, as is frequently supposed, come from St. Augustine but rather from the milieu of 17th century Reformed theology—more specifically from the Dutch theologian Jodocus van Lodenstein in his *Beschouwinge van Zion* (Contemplation of Zion), Amsterdam 1674-1678—and was popularized by Karl Barth. The Catholic view is that because of apostolic succession the Church cannot in Her episcopal and papal teaching office fall into contradicting the truth as revealed in Sacred Scripture and the Apostolic Tradition. While the Church is holy and can always be certain of the support of the Holy Spirit in the sacramental means of sanctification, She also embraces sinners in Her bosom, from the lay person to the Pope. These can incur guilt before God through personal sin, through failure in their allotted tasks or through failure to take urgently needed measures. For this reason, the Church is "at the same time holy and always in need of being purified, [and] always follows the way of penance and renewal" (*LG* 8), as Vatican II puts it in the Dogmatic Constitution *Lumen Gentium*.

Here the connection between reform of the Church and ecumenism becomes manifest. Looking retrospectively at the deplorable fragmentation of western Christianity, we must ask ourselves to what extent human beings are at fault for the disruption of the ecumenical process and how far a lack of love, a convenient hardening of old prejudices and the prioritizing of political over theological thinking in dealing with controversial issues are to blame for this. In its Decree on Ecumenism, the Second Vatican Council states that a "change of heart and holiness of life ... should be regarded as the soul of the whole ecumenical movement" (*UR* 8). It is only in such a context that theology is able to offer important assistance in seeking convergence on weighty dogmatic differences.

And it is only in this way that the historical Reformation of 1517 can go beyond purely historical issues and make an important contribution to the challenge to all Christians to renew ourselves in Christ and reform our thoughts and actions so as to bear witness convincingly to the redemption of the world through Jesus' vicarious atoning death on the Cross and the Resurrection of Jesus Christ.

When people today talk about reform of the Church or reforms in the Church, the question immediately arises of what we can and should do. We arrange a process of dialogue, we employ a consultancy firm that has performed brilliantly in business and banking and whose advice is quite literally "near and dear." We organize some initiative or other in the parish and diocese and set up a further commission. The religious orders draw up new statutes and the professors of theology organize lists of signatures in support of fiery manifestoes and ineffective appeals. All this is Pelagian thinking. It runs: first we have to do something in order to get somewhere with the people and in order that in the end the Holy Spirit will give it his blessing.

Because of his teaching of the primacy of grace before deeds, the apostle Paul approaches it the other way round. It is not that we should be assimilated to the world. Quite the opposite: through Baptism we are conformed to Christ, which means that we can subsequently live our lives as a way of constant discipleship of Christ. From this new being there results a new way of thinking and acting. For we should examine and reform our thinking so as to know God's will and achieve goodness and perfection by obeying it.

This must also apply to the controversial concept of the Church as a *creatura verbi* or as the *sacramentum mundi*.

The hitherto irreconcilable conflict between Protestants and Catholics does not actually manifest itself in the concept of justification by grace alone but rather in the concept of Church. For it is utterly clear from the sources of the Christian faith in the Sacred Scriptures we share that redemption cannot be bestowed on any human being subjectively in justification through his or her own actions, which would, as it were, then make the sinner his or her own redeemer. But objective belief in the reality of salvation in Christ must also not be reduced to the subjective assurance of being justified as this would make my state of being personally convinced more important than the fact of real redemption in Christ. For faith as trust also includes the knowledge of God and His revelation in the teaching of the Church, hope as the abiding grace to continue on *the way* that is *Christ* to the *goal* that is likewise *Christ*, and love as the inmost essence and the achieved goal in one's relationship to God.

But the still-unresolved conflict lies not in the existence and nature of the Church but rather in the significance of Her sacramental form and in the need for salvation to be mediated. From this the questions of the sacraments, the priesthood and the teaching authority follow logically.

For Luther, the Church is, in a nutshell, a *creatura verbi*: "But the Church owes its life to the word of promise through faith, and is nourished and preserved by this same word. That is to say, the promises of God make the Church, not the Church the promise of God. For the Word of God is incomparably superior to the Church, and in this Word, the Church, being a creature, has nothing to decree, ordain or make, but only to be decreed, ordained and made."[52]

This says, then, that the inner Church as the congregation of saints, the justified whom God alone knows, is formed through the word of promise in faith but is only present and manifests itself where word and sacrament are preached and administered in accordance with their foundation (*Confessio Augustana* 7). It is a different matter if the external Church order is regulated by the secular authorities or by the members of an organization. This institutional belonging to a corporate body has no salvific relevance for justification and thus for membership of the Church in the true and proper sense, namely, of the Church as the *communio sanctorum*, i.e., those truly justified in faith who are known to God alone.

The Catholic view of the Church proceeds from the opposite understanding, namely, that we can only achieve salvific community through the Church with Her authoritative teaching and sacramental means of salvation and by recognizing Her apostolic constitution and order as established by Christ in the Holy Spirit.

Johann Adam Möhler sums up the difference in his *Symbolik*: "The Catholics teach: the visible Church is first, then comes the invisible one: it is the former that produces the latter. The Lutherans, however, say the opposite: the visible comes out of the invisible,

---

[52] Martin Luther, *De captivitate babylonica* : WA 6,560.

and the latter is the reason for the former. This seemingly extremely insignificant antithesis expresses an enormous difference."[53]

According to Möhler, Luther's understanding of the Church is not utterly wrong, just one-sided. It does not have to be rejected in toto, and it can also be deemed a corrective to a Catholic ecclesiology committed one-sidedly to the visible shape of the Church. In order not to make assurance of salvation dependent on created things and people in the Church, Luther rejects the salvific efficacy of the sacraments *ex opere operato*, the binding nature and infallibility of the decisions of Church councils, and the spiritual authority of the priest consecrated in his ordination (*character indelebilis*) to offer the Sacrifice of the Mass. For in all of them he sees the danger of man putting himself in a right relationship to God through human works and institutions instead of through faith. But for him nothing created can ever be the ground of the justification of a sinner; it can only be the cause of the place and space in which it is manifested in keeping with man's physical nature. The visible serves only as a reassurance of what takes place on the level of the immediacy between God and man in the correlation of God's promise and grace-effected faith. However, Luther underestimates the fundamental law of the mediation of grace, one grounded in the Incarnation, which says that on account of our physical, social and historical constitution we can only reach the invisible via the visible, *per visibilia ad invisibilia*. If, however, the visible and the invisible Church, divine salvation and the mediation of it entrusted to man are not seen as diametrical opposites but as analogously related to one another — in both what connects and what distinguishes them — in the light of the mystery of the Incarnation, then it is possible to take up Luther's concern and nevertheless express the

---

[53] Johann Adam Möhler, *Symbolik*, Mainz 1832, §48. Engl. transl. *Symbolism, or Exposition of the Doctrinal Differences*, New York 1844.

Catholic faith without any pointedly controversial theology as Vatican II does in the following passage:

> Christ, the one Mediator, established and continually sustains here on earth his holy Church, the community of faith, hope and charity, as an entity with visible delineation through which he communicated truth and grace to all. But, the society structured with hierarchical organs and the Mystical Body of Christ are not to be considered as two realities, nor are the visible assembly and the spiritual community, nor the earthly Church and the Church enriched with heavenly things; rather they form one complex reality which coalesces from a divine and a human element.
>
> For this reason, by no weak analogy, it is compared to the mystery of the incarnate Word. As the assumed nature inseparably united to him, serves the divine Word as a living organ of salvation, so, in a similar way, does the visible social structure of the Church serve the Spirit of Christ, who vivifies it, in the building up of the body (cf. Eph 4:16).
>
> This is the one Church of Christ that in the Creed is professed as one, holy, catholic and apostolic, which our Saviour, after his Resurrection, commissioned Peter to shepherd (Jn 21:17) and him and the other apostles to extend and direct with authority (cf. Mt 28:18-20), which he erected for all ages as "the pillar and mainstay of the truth" (1 Tim 3:15).
>
> ... This Church constituted and organized in the world as a society, subsists in the Catholic Church, which is governed by the successor of Peter and by the bishops in communion with him, although many elements of sanctification and of truth are found outside of her visible structure. These elements, as gifts belonging to the Church of Christ, are forces impelling toward catholic unity. (*LG* 8)

In the precise Evangelical-Lutheran sense, the Catholic Church cannot be recognized as *the* Church but only as *one* ecclesial community among others. An all-embracing unity of all Christians, united in a Church that is visibly one like that which, in Catholic terms, results from her sacramental nature, which in turn comes from the incarnational nature of her foundation, is in Lutheran eyes not necessary for salvation even though it may be for pragmatic reasons desirable ("the Pope as the spokesman for Christendom" but not as the witness of Christ and hence the everlasting principle of the Church's unity in Christ).[54] For this reason it is maintained that despite the disparities in the creeds and order of the manifest ecclesial communities, "reconciled differences" could continue to exist if only unity with Christ and hence communion of the saints were displayed through community in preaching, Baptism and the Lord's Supper.

In our Catholic understanding, "church" is not a general term that can be granted by definition to concrete ecclesial communities or denied them. Church is always the community existing continuously in history that is identifiable by Her characteristic marks and traces Her origin back to Christ, the Word made flesh. Her badge of historical identity and continuity belongs to Her essence and therefore constitutes "Church" in the proper meaning of the word.

This is also the basis on which She defines Her relationship to other episcopal and non-episcopal ecclesial communities. And She seeks full communion through the restoration of unity in the profession of faith, in the essential sacramental forms of worshipping God and mediating the sacraments and in the apostolic foundation of Her teaching authority. The Second Vatican Council expressly

---

[54] Cf. CA 7, where what is understood by human traditions is not secondary manifestations; rather, the means of salvation and the sacramentality of the Church that are regarded as necessary for salvation by Catholics are ruled out.

ascribes to those who are non-Catholic Christians through no fault of their own gracious unity with Christ in faith, hope and love and accords the other ecclesial communities, despite differences in the understanding and scope of the means of grace, the rank of being a medium of salvation (cf. among others *UR 3, NA*). Therefore on the level of visibility, too, especially in the sacrament of Baptism, there still exists a unity of the Church and a visible community of Christians with one another as members of the one Body of Christ even though the *communio* is not complete but is still aiming for full visible unity in the sacramental Church.

The Catholic understanding of ecumenism and Church reform neither sets its sights on a restoration of the status quo ante 1520 nor can it accept the paradigm of a necessary process of pluralization in intellectual history which espouses the status quo of institutionally and confessionally different churchdoms. The latter cannot be accepted because inherent in it is a complete contradiction of the will of Christ, in which the oneness, holiness, catholicity and apostolicity of the Church, whose Head he is, is permanently grounded. The goal of Catholic ecumenism is therefore not one of "reconciled differences"—emphasizing the differences remaining—but rather one of reconciling the contrasts in a deeper communion in Christ: *Unus et totus Christus, caput et membra*. After gratefully recalling the manifold bonds of unity with the non-Catholic churches, the Council continues:

> In all of Christ's disciples the Spirit arouses the desire to be peacefully united, in the manner determined by Christ, as one flock under one shepherd, and he prompts them to pursue this end. Mother Church never ceases to pray, hope and work that this may come about. She exhorts her children to purification and renewal so that the sign of Christ may shine more brightly over the face of the earth. (*LG 15*)

The means of salvation outside the visible communion must likewise not seduce us into no longer regarding the full communion of the visible institutional Church as the goal of ecumenism—for according to Catholic understanding the unity of the Church does not still have to be established by human beings through compromises and negotiations but is already concretely realized in the unity with the Pope and the bishops. This refers to the completeness of the means of salvation, but not to the spiritual and moral lives of Catholics, lives that can be lived in an exemplary manner by non-Catholics and in their communities, too.

While establishing human culpability for the division between Catholics and Protestants, Möhler conjures up the goal of ecumenism: the reconciliation of Christians and the unity of the Church. "This is the point at which Catholics and Protestants will, in great multitudes, one day meet and stretch a friendly hand one to the other. Both, conscious of guilt, must exclaim 'We all have erred—it is the Church only which cannot err; we all have sinned—the Church only is spotless on earth.' This open confession of mutual guilt will be followed by the festival of reconciliation."[55]

Five hundred years of Reformation and schism—not an occasion for either Protestant triumphalism or renewed Catholic feelings of inferiority. After 2017, we ought all to have become more Protestant and more Catholic in the sense of a shared repentance and reconciliation and renewal in Christ.

It is not we who renew the Church of Christ; Christ renews us in His Church. That is reform of the Church: not by us, but *in* us.

---

[55] Johann Adam Möhler, *Symbolik*, 1832, 1884, §37.

6

What Is the Catholic Faith of the Roman Church?

The Rector of the seminary

Your Eminence, I would like to thank you in the name of all those present who are preparing for the priesthood. What does it mean, then, to be Catholic? Does Catholic begin with specific dogmas that we hold in addition to those of other denominations, i.e., beyond what we have in common? In that case, "Catholic" would mean precisely what divides us. But if "Catholic" means "all-embracing" and "universal," then we should speak of what connects us rather than what separates us. Only in that way can we avoid being accused of wanting to force some or other partial tradition on the rest when all Christians are reunited in the one, holy, catholic and apostolic faith. What is integral to the faith? After all, only what has been revealed by God can form the basis for the unity of the Church, not the different traditions based on human law, however valuable they might be.

The Cardinal

Dear confreres, dear young friends,

Let me start with the beginning of Christianity.

When the Church at Jerusalem heard that in Antioch Gentiles (Hellenists), too, had accepted the gospel of Jesus the Lord (cf. Acts 11:1.20f.), they sent Barnabas to this town to consolidate the community there. He and Paul, whom he had fetched over from Tarsus, worked together for an entire year in the community "and taught a great many people" (Acts 11:26). Then follows in the account given in the Acts of the Apostles a sentence that is of immense significance for our question as to the Christian identity:

"And it was in Antioch that the disciples were first called 'Christians'" (Acts 11:26).

So it was not that Jesus' disciples called themselves Christians. They were recognized from outside by a distinguishing feature. The name Christian comes from Christ, not Christ from Christian. So Jesus Christ was not the first Jew to become a Christian; rather, the first Christians were His disciples who professed Him as the Messiah of the Jews "who is called Christ" (Jn 4:25) and as the "the Savior of the world" (Jn 4:42). The Christians receive their name and thus their identity from Jesus the Christ, the Anointed of the Lord.

Jesus Christ — God's last Word to us all

In answer to Jesus' question as to who the disciples think He is — as opposed to the opinions in circulation that He is one of the prophets — Peter replies: "You are the Messiah [or the Christ], the Son of the living God" (Mt 16:16). And this was not just a personal opinion and conviction. Peter said it because Jesus' Father in heaven had revealed it to Him. The Church's profession of Christ reproduces God's self-revelation in the Son. And He reveals Himself as the Father of Jesus Christ. For in His divine nature He proceeds eternally from the Father and is one God with Him and the Holy Spirit. And "no one knows the Father except the Son and anyone to whom the Son chooses to reveal him" (Mt 11:27). The apostles declared their belief in Jesus Christ, Whom they professed in faith as the Messiah of the Jews, the Redeemer and Savior promised by God to His people.

So it was initially the outward impression they made that gave the followers of Jesus the mark of their identity. What was perceived to be the unique character crucially distinguishing them from the Jews and other religions was that they were those who believed in Jesus as the Christ. So Jesus is not one of the many prophets who were preceded by other prophets and followed by yet others. And much less was He a founder of a religion. Its profession of Christ prevents Christianity from being syncretically emptied and falsified.

Not a unified world religion for NGOs

The proponents of constructing a unified religion for the whole world employ every means of propaganda and every psychological trick to combat the finality of revelation in Christ and the uniqueness of His mediation of salvation. Christ, by contrast, the only Son of the Father, did not encourage the natural religious-moral gift in man's free spiritual nature, let alone bring it to its pinnacle in a process of immanent evolution. Instead, He gave it its perfection by raising up nature by grace and giving it a foundation in the transcendence of God. It is not a matter of the human improvement of the world but rather about the final redemption of the world by God and His grace. The beginning of the Letter to the Hebrews expresses the uniqueness, finality and unsurpassability of the coming of Christ: "Long ago God spoke to our ancestors in many and various ways by the prophets, but in these last days he has spoken to us by a Son, whom he appointed heir of all things, through whom he also created the worlds. He is the reflection of God's glory and the exact imprint of God's very being" (Heb 1:1-3). And Luke tells us that an "angel of the Lord" proclaimed to the shepherds in the fields near Bethlehem "good news of great joy for all the people: to you is born this day in the city of David a Savior, who is the Messiah, the Lord" (Lk 2:10f.). Here the three essential soteriological titles are named. Jesus is the Savior and Messiah because he is the Lord, i.e., God in the unity of the Son with the Father in the Holy Spirit.

Roman Encounters

Being a Christian consists not just in an inner conviction but also in an outward profession: "For one believes with the heart and so is justified, and one confesses with the mouth and so is saved" (Rom 10:10). Therefore professing their belief in Jesus unites His followers. As the Head of the Church He is the unity of all Her members, His Body. They are a community in Christ and share the same profession of faith, the same liturgy, and the same universal mission into the whole world. Being a Christian is of inner necessity catholic. The Church is catholic because She bears witness to Jesus' universal mediation of salvation and actualizes it in Her teaching, Her life, and Her sacramental constitution. Against the heretics and schismatics of his time, Pacian of Barcelona put this more concretely in his *Epistola ad Sempronianum de Catholico nomine*: "My name is Christian, my surname is Catholic" (no. 7).

Corresponding to the actions of the Church that are empirically perceptible to the senses is their real spiritual effect with God. For the sacraments signify and bring about the sacred community of life with the Triune God. That means that the Christian identity lies in the community of believers and in carrying out the mission received from Christ. The Christian lives in *communio* with Christ and shares in His universal mission from the Father for the salvation of the world. The Second Vatican Council introduces its definition of the Church as the sacrament of the salvation of the world in Christ as follows: "Christ is the Light of nations. Because this is so, this sacred synod gathered together in the Holy Spirit eagerly desires, by proclaiming the gospel to every creature, to bring the light of Christ to all men, a light brightly visible on the countenance of the Church" (*LG* 1).

In psychology, they speak of identity if a person remains true to himself. In Christian theology, we speak of identity if a person remains true to Christ. For as a Christian I do not have a self-referential identity but rather a relational one. It is not what I was before and outside my encounter with Christ that constitutes the truth of my being and life but rather what I have become *thanks to* my encounter and communion with Him. Before, I was dead as a result of sin, a slave to the old world without God and without hope. But through faith and Baptism I have now become a new creation. In and through Jesus Christ, the Son of the Father, we have been adopted as sons and daughters of God. Therefore we have also become heirs with Him of the Kingdom of God.

The Kingdom of God must not be confused with a secular, politico-ideological rule. It is not a theocracy dreamt up by extreme adherents of Islam or Hinduism in India, i.e., the religious uniformity imposed on a country or the whole world by the use of force and subterfuge. In His Kingdom, God rules through His justice, which manifests itself in peace, freedom and joy. So where peace is threatened and freedom suppressed there is no Kingdom of God. It is not those who use force against their own kind by suppressing their religious freedom and robbing them of their human dignity who can invoke God but those who proclaim to them the gospel of Jesus Christ.

Like no other apostle, Paul experienced a sudden and complete turnaround after his conversion on the road to Damascus, i.e., a re-creation of his personal identity in the encounter with Christ. He says: "For through the law I died to the law, so that I might live to God. I have been crucified with Christ; and it is no longer I who live, but it is Christ who lives in me. And the life I now live in the flesh I live by faith in the Son of God, who loved me and gave himself for me" (Gal 2:19f.).

Our identity is not a question of this or that characteristic of a person or culture, these or those preferences and desires that people obstinately cleave to.

What ultimately matters is not someone's intellectual and artisanal gifts, their membership in ethnic and national groups, or their imperial claims to power. Even less can our identity be defined by negative traits of character such as feelings of superiority, an inability to suppress our urges or irrational prejudices and resentments; on the contrary, these in fact obscure our identity and the unity of our nature with the human person. Identity must be positively determined so that a person can achieve the perfection of his or her calling and destiny.

We should be perfect as our heavenly Father is perfect (cf. Mt 5:48). For this we should bring our gifts, talents and charisms into building up the Body of Christ so that instead of benefitting us, they will benefit others (cf. 1 Cor 12:7). From being lost sinners we shall be turned into saints and friends of God. You do not gain your identity but destroy it if you perfect your negative traits of character, that is, if you change from being a little scoundrel into a big one. God "will repay according to each one's deeds: to those who by patiently doing good seek for glory and honor and immortality, he will give eternal life; while for those who are self-seeking and who obey not the truth but wickedness, there will be wrath and fury" (Rom 2:6ff.).

Instead of losing ourselves in details, we must look at the whole picture. It is a matter of determining the totality of our person, the success or failure of our life, being and nonbeing, eternal life with God or perpetuating the absurdity of finite existence without any hope of seeing God. It is only in relation to God, the origin and goal of all being, that man's question not about this or that in the world but about himself can find an answer. Science and technology can improve the conditions of material existence. And making progress in this sphere is—according to the Christian understanding expressed in Catholic Social Teaching—part of the Church's universal commission. Knowledge of God in faith is the only thing capable of providing an answer to man's existential questions. For man is a living creature like many others, too, but he towers above them all through his intellectual self-knowledge and self-transcendence to the first principle of his being and thinking. And thus man stands before God as a being with intellect and freedom. In the Pastoral Constitution on the Church in the Modern World, Vatican II formulated the fundamental questions that have been asked in every age with ultimate and inescapable acuity: "What is man? What is this sense of sorrow, of evil, of death, that continues to exist despite so much progress? What purpose have these victories purchased at so high a cost? What can man offer to society, what can he expect from it? What follows this earthly life?" (GS 10). And this is the answer that God gives us and which encapsulates the content of our preaching: "The Church firmly believes that Christ, Who died and was raised up for all, can through His Spirit offer man the light and the strength to measure up to his supreme destiny. Nor has any other name under heaven been given to men by which they may be saved" (ibid.).

Being a Christian means, in life as in death, placing all one's hope in God. We believe in God the Creator of heaven and earth, who sent His Son into the world. The Son of the eternal Father is the Word that took on our flesh so that through believing in Him we might have eternal life. In Baptism in the name of the Father, the Son and the Holy Spirit the relations are brought about to the three persons of the God who is one in essence. In giving ourselves to God in freedom we profess our faith in God the Creator, the Redeemer and Perfecter of man. We believe in God Who reveals Himself in His Incarnate Word and in the Holy Spirit poured out over all flesh, Who communicates Himself to us as the truth and life of every human being. Faith is more than a personal choice, an opinion to which I unwaveringly hold fast and for which, if need be, I will even risk my life. When we confess our faith in God, this is a knowing of God in truth and love. He allows us to participate in this knowledge because God in His Word is one indivisible cognitive unit of Father and Son. And in its innermost core, faith is love of God, who introduces us into the mystery of His life as a community of the Father with the Son in the Holy Spirit. The Christian is not faced with a transcendent, distant God towards whom he strives in an endless seeking movement but never finds. Rather, through Christ, God dwells in us and we live in God, Who knows Himself eternally in the divine Logos, the Word, and is eternally united with Himself in love in the Spirit.

To be sure, there are many comprehensive interpretations of the world. We are surrounded by a wealth of different and contradictory philosophies and lifestyles. Their pluralism confuses us. The prevailing opinion seeks in vain to make a virtue out of this necessity. Our finite intellect is incapable of squeezing it together. Only the ideologies of the 19th and 20th centuries imagined themselves able to combine this plurality into one system using a single idea of their finite consciousness and in this way tame it. Hegel regarded everything as *Geist* (spirit/mind) and admitted matter merely as its *Erscheinung* (appearance), whereas his "pupil" Marx tried it the other way around by declaring matter to be absolute and viewing the spirit as a derived phenomenon. But materialism does not do justice to the intrinsic reality and value that belong to matter because it fails to recognize its transcendence towards the spirit. And idealism does not do justice to the spirit because it fails to recognize that it necessarily and positively manifests itself in the created world in matter. The human being as a creature is a substantial unit of spirit and matter, so that the person possesses a spiritual-corporeal nature, which construes itself in space and time and hence essentially has a social and historical dimension. A person extricates himself from the Procrustes bed of the systems thinkers either mutilated or deformed. Repelled by the coercive nature of systems thinking, i.e., the absolutization of individual creaturely constituents, many people today tend towards relativism. But every relativism is at the same time a dictatorship because it denounces any orientation of reason towards truth as intolerance. The compass still points north even when the captain orders a course heading directly for the cliffs. Because truth cannot be squeezed into the grasp of the finite mind, they skeptically or cynically give up seeking the truth. However, truth is not grasped, maintained and claimed by us, but rather reveals itself. The truth of the Christian faith is "the revelation of the mystery that was kept secret for long ages but is now disclosed, and through the prophetic writings is made known to all the Gentiles, according to the command of the eternal God, to bring about the obedience of faith" (Rom 16:25f.). In faith, the finite mind of man obediently subjects itself to the self-revealing God. God gives Himself to us as truth and life. And that is why man does not become lost in the confusion of religious and cultural phenomena. He does not inevitably stop at a non-integrable phenomenalism conflated by theosophical visionaries into a unified religion. A religious Esperanto founders on the question of truth because it reduces religion to its psychological and social usefulness. Anyone who believes in Christ recognizes that in God's Logos, which took on our flesh in Christ, in the *verbum incarnatum*, everything that is "true and holy" (*NA* 2) in religions, philosophies and cultures—despite all the defects of what is human—reflects a ray of God's Logos and is gathered together in Jesus Christ and brought into the light of revelation. In His person He is the unity of mankind with God in love as truth and life. In His human nature He is man's sole way to God and in His divine nature God's sole way to man.

Vatican II declares in the Declaration on Religious Freedom "that God himself has made known to mankind the way in which men are to serve him, and thus be saved in Christ and come to blessedness. We believe that this one true religion subsists in the Catholic and Apostolic Church, to which the Lord Jesus committed the duty of spreading it abroad among all men" (*DH* 1).

And who knows how many religions there have been among the various peoples with their mythologies and cultic rituals. Furthermore there are contradictory theories about the nature and scope of our empirical and transcendent knowledge.

But only a realistic epistemology can open up access to the revealed faith, so that man is neither confronted with the products of his own reasoning and the titanically futile endeavour to justify himself nor gives up on himself up in weary resignation and skepticism, or despairs of himself and perishes.

Only belief in God can take account of the whole of reality because it is a sharing in the infinite mystery of God, which for now only reveals itself "in a mirror, dimly" (1 Cor 13:12). For God's mystery does not stand before us like an impenetrable thicket, a black hole or a nihilating (*nichtend*) nothingness. It is luminous superabundance and pure goodness. We see the world in his light. But we cannot look directly into the sun even though we see everything through its light. In his unfolding of the whole salvation event in the Letter to the Romans, the apostle Paul insists that in their "ungodliness and wickedness" and when they "suppress the truth," people cannot make the excuse of not knowing of the existence of God (1:18). "For ever since the creation of the world his eternal power and divine nature, invisible though they are, have been understood and seen through the things he has made" (1:20). Even the Gentiles, to whom the commandments were not revealed on Mount Sinai as they were to the Jews, know the natural moral law, i.e., that which is accessible to reason, because it "is written on their hearts" (2:15) and their own conscience also bears witness to it (cf. 2:14f.).

This fundamental knowledge of God through the existence of the world and the goodness of created being, which both enable and promote life, gives rise to an attitude of hope that the same God and Creator will reveal Himself as our Redeemer and Perfecter in the midst of the world and of history. In the Declaration on Religious Freedom, the Second Vatican Council states that because every person is equipped with reason and free will, all human beings are linked together — despite all the differences in content between the various religions and interpretations of the world — in their desire to know the truth and thus to know God (cf. *DH* 2).

Man is spirit, and therefore he can truly recognize God analogously as the Creator of the world and then, when God addresses us in His Word, also know Him in the revelation of salvation history. But as finite spirit he cannot make God into an adequate object. God remains the mystery above us. He is the subject of the revelation of His glory in the works of nature and history, through the prophets and finally and unsurpassably in His Son Jesus Christ. But in the Incarnate Word we encounter God from person to person and will one day see Him face-to-face. We can speak *to Him* in prayer and in professing our faith, and the Church can speak *of Him* in dialogical preaching.

Epistemologically, the analogy of being and the analogy of faith as the basis for knowing God's existence, His absolute transcendence towards creation and His absolute immanence in creation rules out two extremes: on the one hand, agnosticism, according to which we can and do know nothing at all about Him and, on the other hand, Gnosticism, according to which we can reduce God to a single concept. There is also relativism, which regards the truth's power of obligation as dangerous because every claim to truth endangers the freedom of anyone thinking differently. The rejection of the biblical belief in the one God and Creator in Judaism and Christianity along with the monotheism of the Qur'an is particularly aggressive because these are purportedly prone to intolerance and, in the extreme case, violence in the name of revealed truth. But people overlook here how violently Jews and Christians have been persecuted both by the polytheistic-political religions of Antiquity and by ideological-political world views in modern times. They also forget that, for example, in Christianity it is not permissible for faith to be coerced in the name of Christ's truth. For it is only through being freely accepted that faith establishes the identity of the Christian with the crucified and risen Christ.

According to his spiritual nature, man is a "hearer of the Word of God" which speaks to him in history in a manner that is accessible and comprehensible to him. It is God's Word in the words of man. This is — so we Christians believe and profess — the person Jesus Christ, the Word, which in the beginning was with God and is God: "And the Word became flesh and lived among us, and we have seen his glory, the glory as of a father's only son, full of grace and truth" (Jn 1:14).

So Christian identity does not consist in our identifying ourselves with the God and Father of Jesus Christ, i.e., grasping Him conceptually from the perspective of our creatureliness, claiming Him for ourselves and possibly even making demands on Him. It is in fact the opposite: it is God who identifies Himself with us. He takes the initiative. He calls us into being. He creates us in His image and likeness and grants us a share in the divine calling. When we identify ourselves with Him, it is not in order to use Him to justify our actions, let alone to commit evil in His name as some terrorists currently do when they invoke the name of Allah. Rather, to identify myself with God means to respond with my whole thinking and life to Him Who spoke to me in His Word and in His deeds for the sake of my salvation and Who met me in a human way in Jesus Christ. My life as a follower of Christ is my reply to God's nearness to me, in Immanuel, God with us.

Christian identity is grounded in the profession of Jesus Christ, our Lord and God, and is executed in discipleship of the suffering, crucified and resurrected Christ. Being a true disciple consists in professing Jesus our Lord and in doing His will. The Sermon on the Mount tells us: "Not everyone who says to me, 'Lord, Lord', will enter the kingdom of heaven, but only one who does the will of my Father in heaven" (Mt 7:21). The use of the term "kingdom of heaven" in Matthew's gospel rather than "kingdom and rule of God" must not mislead us into a diminished understanding. It does not mean heaven as everlasting beatitude after death. It means the realization of God's salvific will in heaven and on earth. Paul says: "For the kingdom of God is not food and drink but righteousness and peace and joy in the Holy Spirit. The one who thus serves Christ is acceptable to God and has human approval" (Rom 14:17f.).

Christian identity is not self-referential but relational. Self-referentiality leads to loneliness, isolation and death. Referentiality to God and other human beings leads to community, joy and life.

I would like to illustrate this with the three essential mysteries of the Christian faith: the Trinity of God, the Incarnation of His Word and the sacramentality of the Church.

The mystery of the Trinity of God

If human reason is left to its own resources and has no powers other than those with which it is naturally endowed, it is incapable of going beyond a philosophical cognition of the existence of God as the author of the world. Our relationship to God rests upon a relationship that God has previously established with us. Which is why He remains sovereign in relation to us in creation and in the first revelation of His glory and wisdom through creation. The Creator is the Lord. But that is precisely what also makes Him free to reveal Himself to *us*, to disclose His identity in what He is in Himself. In Old Testament salvation history, God already reveals Himself to His people in His word and communicates the Spirit of His truth and love to them. His Word and Spirit are not created attributes of God, for that would be in contradiction to His nature.

Nor are they created effects or reflections of God in creation. Expressed in concepts from later theological reflection, God's Word and Spirit are modal relations. The same God acts on the world in the creation and in the leading of His Chosen People in salvation history in the mode of His salvation-creating Word and His life-giving Spirit. But it is only in the Incarnation of God's Word and the eschatological outpouring of the Holy Spirit over all flesh and the infusion of the Spirit's love in our hearts that the One God reveals Himself in the Trinity of the Divine Persons. In the light of God's self-revelation we recognize that God's Word and Spirit are not modes of revelation but rather the revealing God Himself in His life of community of Father and Son and Holy Spirit. In order to get beyond the merely modal relations, which are not person-forming and cannot express the mystery of the Trinity, theology speaks of subsistent relations. This expresses the unity of God in His being and nature just as it does the distinctness (*Eigensein*) of the Divine Persons in their relationship to one another.

Of course, we must note that the purpose of this conceptual clarification is not to presume to take possession of the mystery but precisely to preserve it from rationalization in the heresies of ancient and modern times. After all, the belief of the baptized in God the Father and the Son and the Holy Spirit is not an abstract theory but rather a redeeming knowledge of God in truth and love. Because God is life in Himself in the inner community of being and the mutual interpenetration of Father, Son and Spirit, it is possible for us, too, to relate to the three Divine Persons. Being a Christian does not mean having an external relationship to an other-worldly law-giver but rather having an inner relationship to the Father of our Lord Jesus Christ in the Holy Spirit. The eternal Son of the Father, who took on our flesh, says: "Those who love me will keep my word, and my Father will love them, and we will come to them and make our home with them" (Jn 14:23). God dwells in us and we in Him. What greater intimacy is conceivable between God and man than the mutual indwelling (*Inne-Sein*) of Creator and creature? We do not say just that God loves us, likes us and does a lot of things for us, but that God is love. In the *communio* of Father, Son and Spirit, God's very being, life and activity is love. If God reveals and communicates Himself to us human beings in the Son through the Spirit, then it holds true that: "Whoever does not love does not know God, for God is love" and "God is love, and those who abide in love abide in God, and God abides in them" (1 Jn 4:8.16). In God, truth is Person in the Son and Love is Person in the Holy Spirit. But because the personhood of the Father, the Son and the Holy Spirit is identical with Their relation to one another and their *communio* with each other, the unity of God does not fall apart into three divine beings but is instead enacted precisely through their relations to each other. For, to cite the words of Sacred Scripture, the Son proceeds from the Father through generation and the Spirit from the Father and the Son through spiration.

In and through Christ we are related to God, i.e., are sons and daughters of God and by no means only in name (cf. 1 Jn 3:1). Indeed, the very existence and dynamics of the life of the whole of creation are related to the Father in the Son, both in origin and future. Christ is the beginning and the end, the alpha and the omega. In the Word everything is created and through the Word Incarnate our vocation to eternal salvation is victoriously perfected. Christ is the Mediator of the whole of creation and of redemption. We likewise recognize in the relationship to the Holy Spirit that all life comes from God and is permeated with His truth and goodness. God is love. The meaning of our existence is to be filled with the love that God is in Himself and has for us. By revealing Himself to us, the Triune God takes us up into His trinitarian life when we know and love Him. "For you did not receive a spirit of slavery to fall back into fear, but you have received a spirit of adoption. When we cry, 'Abba! Father!'" (Rom 8:15; cf. Gal 4:6).

Belief in the one and triune God is crucial for the Christian identity. That holds true for our real relationship with God in prayer and in the sacramental life of the Church. We pray in the name of the Father and of the Son and of the Holy Spirit and are baptized, i.e., incorporated into Christ as the Head of all creation and Christ as the Body of His Church, in the name of the Trinity. Our knowledge of God is a participation in the knowledge of God as the Father knows the Son and the Son knows the Father. Our love of God is a participation in that love in the Holy Spirit in which Father and Son are one in the reciprocity of their relation to each other. This is the relational identity of the Christian, who may say to God through the Son in the Holy Spirit: my and our Father.

It is precisely in professing the trinitarian God that the *proprium christianum* is displayed. Belief in the Trinity distinguishes Christianity from the monotheisms of Old Testament Judaism and of the Qur'an as well as the monotheism of the philosophers. The various heresies that have had to be overcome over the course of doctrinal history are proof of the centrality of belief in the Trinity.

Without supernatural revelation, reason can only get as far as knowing of the existence of the omnipotent, omniscient, sovereign and transcendent Creator of the world; hence it is a priori incapable of excluding the possibility of God's being able to make Himself known in His historical revelation in the way the unity of His nature is realized. Unitarian monotheism cannot therefore deny the logic and consistency of trinitarian monotheism. For its consistency lies in the divine logic of love, which enacts God's nature in the relations, not dividing it but realizing it in eternity. This surpasses human understanding, which is nevertheless raised up through God's self-revelation to participate analogously in God's self-understanding in His Word and Spirit, the Logos and the Pneuma. *How* God reveals Himself to us, namely, in the relationship to Word and Spirit, is also *what* He reveals to us, namely, Himself. He is the One God in the three Divine Persons.

The Qur'an's criticism of Christ's Sonship of God, and with it the total misunderstanding of our trinitarian belief, is in fact void. For the begetting of the Son is the eternal — not material and temporal — procession of the Word from the Father. The Sonship of the Word does not split the unity of God and multiply it into two independently subsisting deities. When a human father begets a son, there are subsequently two individual human beings. They do not form a single individual essence but are only connected in their abstractly conceived human nature. God's existence is identical with His essence. Therefore, there is but the one and only God, who, however, enacts his life as love in the internal subsistent relations which, in accordance with revelation, we address and worship with the names Father, Son and Spirit. In the generation of the Word by the Father and the spiration of the Spirit by Father and Son what is realized is the unity of God as the *communio* of love of the three Persons, Who are the one God. If God were not in Himself subsistent knowledge and love, how could He offer Himself to us to know and unite Himself with us in love? What kind of relation would exist between creation and a God conceived of as unitarian? Would creation then be constitutive for God, so that a dialectical relationship would arise between Him and the world?

But because God already realizes His essence in Himself in relationality, He can cause the world to emerge freely from the relation of the Father to the Son without gaining or losing anything through the relationship to the world. It is only on the basis of trinitarian faith that the non-divine finite being of the world can be conceived of consistently as God's creation.

The mystery of the Incarnation
and the sending of the Spirit

Only because the Word proceeds from the Father through genera-tion and is the Eternal Son of the Father, i.e., true God from true God, can the Word assume our flesh. God's Incarnation is possible because the processions within the Godhead expand into the time and space of creation through the sending of the Son in the Incar-nation and the sending of the Spirit in being poured out over all mankind and indwelling in our hearts.

Paul puts it as follows: "But when the fullness of time had come, God sent his Son, born of a woman, born under the law, in order to redeem those who were under the law, so that we might receive adoption as children. And because you are children, God has sent the Spirit of his Son into our hearts, crying, 'Abba! Father!'" (Gal 4:4-6). So as God is eternally immanent in Himself, He also relates in salvation history to us. By freeing us from the slavery of sin, He lifts us up to Him through His grace and makes us into His sons (*per adoptionem*) in the Son, Who is coessential/consubstantial with the Father, and into His friends through the Spirit.

But in the Incarnation Christ did not take on a neutral human nature to serve as an instrument of redemption or of drawing near to us humans. In the kenosis he assumed our nature, and thus all of us together; in this way, he has identified with each one of us. He adopted us who, being subject to the power of sin, are at the mercy of its strength and evil and of death and hopelessness. "For God has done what the law, weakened by the flesh, could not do: by sending his own Son in the likeness of sinful flesh, and to deal with sin, he condemned sin in the flesh" (Rom 8:3).

From the very beginning, the Incarnation has a soteriological orientation. But it does not confine itself just to the forgiveness of sins and the justification of the sinner; rather it goes beyond this and raises up the human being to the relation of a child of God. In the Incarnation of the Son of God the whole meaning of creation is fulfilled, a meaning that despite being obscured by sin could not be obliterated by man. For in Christ we were already chosen before the creation of the world. For "just as he chose us in Christ before the foundation of the world to be holy and blameless before him in love. He destined us for adoption as his children through Jesus Christ, according to the good pleasure of his will, to the praise of his glorious grace that he freely bestowed on us in the Beloved" (Eph 1:4ff.). What is meant here is of course not a temporal priorness to the choosing and to the actual history of salvation but rather the formal aspect of the revelation of His glory, the why and wherefore of creation and the calling to become children of God. The Word became flesh in order that the glory of God might be known and that we might through it be included in the community of love of Father and Son in the Holy Spirit. Before His Passion, Jesus prays in the High Priestly Prayer: "Father, I desire that those also, whom you have given me, may be with me where I am, to see my glory, which you have given me because you loved me before the foundation of the world. Righteous Father, the world does not know you, but I know you; and these know that you have sent me. I made your name known to them, and I will make it known, so that the love with which you have loved me may be in them, and I in them" (Jn 17:24ff.).

What we understand by the Incarnation is not just the act of Jesus' assuming human nature in His conception and His birth from the Virgin Mary through the work of the Spirit of God. The Incarnation reveals itself to us in the whole of Jesus' work of salvation, from the proclamation of the Kingdom of God right up to the full institution of the New and Eternal Covenant in His sacrificial death on the Cross and His salvation-bringing Resurrection. The Incarnation is a fact of revelation and salvation history as well as the life principle of the Church that creates Her identity.

Arising from the Incarnation are both the sacramental form of the mediation of salvation and the Church's global commission. Her commitment to the causes of a life fit for human beings, of social justice as well as freedom of religion and worship is a necessary and logical consequence of the truth that God took up His dwelling among us. Because of the Incarnation, all dualism is overcome between an orientation exclusively towards the next world and a clinging to this, between inward piety of the soul and outward religious-ethical praxis. Whoever has become a child of God in Christ neither negotiates advantages from God his Father nor does he have to blow his own trumpet to the world as a philanthropist.

Particularly in the early years of the Church, the doctrines of the Trinity and the Incarnation triggered violent intellectual battles. They were in fact absolutely essential in order to emphasize the complete novelty and originality of Christianity and to safeguard the mysteries of revelation from being rationalistically narrowed or made more superficial. We cannot go into the details here. The important thing is that those who upheld the full and complete reality of the Incarnation triumphed. If Jesus Christ is not really and truly God and consubstantial with the Father, then He would not have been able to redeem us. For only God can redeem. But if Christ is not true man, with a human soul and a human body like us, really born of a woman, who lived on this earth at a specific time and in a specific place, then nor are we human beings adopted by God and called to be His sons and daughters in the Son.

In that case there would be no Christian identity either. For all the Manicheans, Gnostics, Platonists and Idealists it was and is to this day a ghastly concept that the eternal, exalted God, the purest of all Ideas, the Absolute Spirit, should have taken on our corruptible flesh, allowed Himself to be worshipped by stinking shepherds in the stable at Bethlehem and ended up as a criminal on the Cross, disfigured and dishonored, besmirched with loathsome sweat and blood. The idea of the Son of God as a baby in a manger and as a young man on the pillory of the Cross is for sensitive, spiritual persons "a stumbling-block" and for the finely educated and for cynical realists" it is "foolishness" (1 Cor 1:23).

It also belongs to the Christian's identity to know that Jesus identifies Himself with the poor, the despised, the beggars and the victims of physical and psychological violence. For what you did to the least of my brethren, you did it to me (cf. Mt 25:40). Billionaires are fond of establishing charitable foundations and are praised as philanthropists for doing so. But Christ, who in His divinity was infinitely rich, became poor in the sacred exchange so that by His poverty we might become rich (cf. 2 Cor 8:9). It is He who suffers hunger and cold in the poor and looks at us out of their eyes.

With regard to the Incarnation, one principle emerges that sums up the Christian identity: "*Caro cardo salutis* — the flesh is the pivot of salvation" (Tertullian, *De carnis resurrectione* 8,2).

We believe in God the Creator of spirit and matter, who created man as a being made of flesh; we believe in the Word that became flesh and we believe in the resurrection of the flesh. That is our Christian identity. We are no Gnostics, Manicheans, idealists and materialists. We use our religion neither to flee the world nor to idolize it. We do not venerate the perishable world like God but know rather that the perishability of the world will one day be embraced by the imperishability of God and delivered from all suffering, pain and death. And because the Incarnation exists, so does the bodily resurrection from the dead.

The mystery of the sacramental Church

The Dogmatic Constitution on the Church *Lumen Gentium* does not start — as is frequently erroneously assumed — with the chapter on the People of God but with "The Mystery of the Church." Its ecclesiology does not begin sociologically, so to speak from below, but from God's revelation. In Her ground and essence, the Church is a mystery, a reality of salvation and of the sacramental mediation of salvation. From the Incarnation it necessarily follows that Christ's grace is communicated through visible signs, words and actions that correspond to the corporeal and social nature of man. They come towards us just as God comes towards us: humanly in the humanity of His Son. This takes place in the seven sacraments of the Church: Baptism, Confirmation, Eucharist, Penance and Reconciliation, Anointing of the Sick, Holy Orders, and Matrimony.

The sacraments are not just outward signs that indicate to us what is actually going on between God and man inwardly, i.e., in faith, hope and love. Rather, they are efficacious signs and true means of grace. In Christ, God has identified Himself with our corporeality and our nature as communal beings. The Incarnation is incompatible with both an idealization of the mediation of salvation and its reduction to the interiority of the relationship to God and with an exteriorization (reification) of grace, which would amount to treating God like a business partner. You don't do deals with God. We are not His business partners but rather "children of God, and if children, then heirs" (Rom 8:16f.). In the sacraments, Christ makes present the salvation that He Himself is. But it is up to us whether we give ourselves to Him in faith, hope and love and thus also become aware of the spiritual effect of the sacraments.

The sacraments are celebrated in the Church and administered by Her. Therefore the Church is, in Christ, Herself a sign and instrument of man's "very closely knit union with God and of the unity of the whole human race with one another" (LG 1). In Christ, the Church is "the universal sacrament of salvation" (LG 48).

Because of the Incarnation, "in him [Christ] the whole fullness of deity dwells bodily" (Col 2:9). Therefore: "He is the head of the body, the church" (Col 1:18) because He saved Her. Through

His love and self-giving, Christ, the Head of the Church, unites Himself with the Church as His Body just as the bridegroom enters into an indissoluble relationship with His bride at marriage, a relationship of body, life and love (cf. Eph 5:21-27). From this arise the unity and holiness of the Church, coming as they do from Christ, which remain irrevocable in spite of the sins and flaws of individual members because the Incarnation is final and unsurpassable. This Church also participates in the universality of Christ's mediatorship of salvation, which She makes present in word and sacrament through the hierarchically ordered community. The Church is also apostolic because She is built on the foundation of the apostles and their teaching and dynamically continues their universal mission. The Pope and bishops are the successors of Peter and the apostles. So there is a continuity of the Church in time and an identity in content and form of the Church of all ages with the Church of the apostles.

It is for this reason that being a member of the pilgrim Church is necessary for salvation. "Whosoever, therefore, knowing that the Catholic Church was made necessary by Christ, would refuse to enter or to remain in it, could not be saved.

"They are fully incorporated in the society of the Church who, possessing the Spirit of Christ accept her entire system and all the means of salvation given to her, and are united with her as part of her visible bodily structure and through her with Christ, who rules her through the Supreme Pontiff and the bishops. The bonds which bind men to the Church in a visible way are profession of faith, the sacraments, and ecclesiastical government and communion" (*LG* 14).

So let me now conclude. The identity of the Christian is not self-referential. The Christian does not want to be autonomous and self-sufficient, a complacent member of the educated classes and a proud free thinker who imagines he has himself to thank for everything and that he can be his own god, lord, creator and redeemer.

The Christian owes everything to God. His is a Eucharistic existence, thanking God for the life and body, the intellect and freedom he has been given. He gives thanks for the world, for his parents and friends, and does not sit down smugly at a well-laid table without saying grace. He does not enjoy Sunday just as a day of pure leisure but renders thanks to his Creator and Redeemer on the Lord's Day, which is after all God's gift to him. The Christian addresses God as his Father, who in Christ has called him to be His son and heir. He rejoices in the Holy Spirit at being delivered from death and corruption and called to eternal life. The Christian gives thanks for the communion of the Church and for being incorporated into Her Body, whose members are the faithful.

Being a Christian is relational identity in God, the Father, Son and Holy Spirit in the communion of His Church.

The unity of ecclesial and sacramental communio

The connection between Church and Eucharist is constitutive of the life and creed of the Catholic faith. Hence sacramental communio in the Eucharist can as a matter of principle only be received by those of the baptized who are in full ecclesial communion with the "the one Church of Christ which …, constituted and organized in the world as a society, subsists in the Catholic Church, which is governed by the successor of Peter and by the bishops in communion with him" (*LG* 8).

Anyone who disputes this revelation-based truth in theory or abrogates it in practice thereby enters into open contradiction to the Catholic faith.

I would like to show the connection between sacramental and ecclesial communion by using only the precepts contained in revelation as it is faithfully and fully preserved in the Catholic Church and without going into the recommendations that are to be expected from the German Episcopal Conference. For we are living in times when ideology is valued more than theology, or rather theology is subordinated to ideological or ecclesio-political goals. Instead of arguments being exchanged in open debate, individuals are discredited. Every problem is personalized and thereby neutralized. No matter if someone knows the whole of Sacred Scripture by heart, has studied all the Church Fathers and is well qualified in modern philosophy and science, all it takes is for one journalist from the provinces or a mediocre hobby theologian to denigrate him as conservative or even arch-conservative and all his knowledge is cancelled out in the same way as the finest wine is rendered unfit for consumption if some idiot mixes poison with it. Every newly appointed bishop is tested and then labelled as conservative or liberal, whatever that might be, depending on whether he is personally "for or against" women's ordination, "for or against" the blessing of homosexual couples, "for or against" priestly celibacy and "for or against" Holy Communion for "remarried divorcees." Other topics are of no interest, and differentiated arguments don't count with the "evergreens." Thus there is a shift from factual discussion to the imputation of personal ideological bias. Those who loosen the connection between ecclesial and sacramental communio in order to purportedly make the faith easier for people today then accuse their critics of having closed minds and rigidly clinging to dogmas that the secularized Christian can no longer understand.

There is an anti-dogmatic climate that also has a negative effect on the understanding of the sacraments. They are no longer the signs instituted by Christ and celebrated in the Church that bring about invisible grace in the rightly disposed recipient. They morph into psychological and social props for inner mystical experiences with a "Christ" made in our own image and likeness in our consciousness. To be sure, the grace of the sacrament is not a reward for good moral behavior, but it is even less a justification for immoral behavior and a life that is contrary to God's command-ments. Between grace and morality there is no either-or but rather an *et-et*, and so Vatican II states: "It is through the sacraments and the exercise of the virtues that the sacred nature and organic structure of the priestly community [of the Church] is brought into operation" (*LG* 11).

The reason why many people today are, as Romano Guardini already noted at the *Katholikentag* in Mainz in 1948, "incapable of liturgy" (*liturgieunfähig*) lies in their viewing Christianity as a his-torical variant of the religious sense of some vague transcendence instead of tracing the Church back to the fact of the Incarnation in Her dogma and life. The nature, the manner of working and the effect of the sacraments are only disclosed in the light of the Incarnation and the historical and real mediation of salvation in the Cross and Resurrection of Christ, God's Incarnate Word. Any-one proceeding from this principle immediately senses how totally un-Catholic the way of thinking is of those who say: "That may be right in dogmatics, but it's no good for pastoral work."

For in the Church's awareness of faith, dogma expresses the truth received in revelation which we have to accept with our intellect and free will in the divine and Catholic faith for the sake of our salvation. This is something quite different from the theory of the philosophers who, according to the dictum of Karl Marx, have hitherto only interpreted the world in various ways whereas the point now is to change it. Christ, the teacher of the truth that is God Himself, Who reveals Himself to us to know and love, is the same as He Who, as the Good Shepherd (*bonus pastor*) and "guardian [*episkopos*] of our souls" (1 Pet 2:25), gave up His life for us on the Cross. Therefore, there can be no double truth in Catholic dogma. For what is dogmatically false will have a damaging effect for the salvation of souls if employed pastorally in accordance with erroneous principles.

Rarely has St. Paul's warning to Timothy, the prototype of the Catholic bishop, been more pertinent than today: "proclaim the message; be persistent whether the time is favorable or unfavorable.... For the time is coming when people will not put up with sound doctrine, but having itching ears, they will accumulate for themselves teachers to suit their own desires" (2 Tim 4:2f.).

Precisely in an age of social media, digital communication and totalitarian mainstreaming, it is not a matter of whether the Pope and bishops come across well to the people but rather of whether, through their message, Christ comes across to the people as the truth and life of God. For this reason, the Church's unique and indivisible Magisterium bears the ultimate responsibility for ensuring that no ambiguous signs and unclear teachings emanate from the Pope and the bishops which might confuse the faithful or give them a false sense of security. It is an occupational hazard for the Pope and the bishops to be pilloried by the opinion leaders and powerful of this world as unworldly, hostile to life or medieval. If the prophets were already persecuted, why then do the bishops as the successors to the apostles imagine that it is due to getting their media policy wrong if people utter "all kinds of evil against you falsely" (Mt 5:11) on Christ's account?

In an age of dogmatic relativism, which quickly turns into a verbal and physical persecution of the witnesses to the revealed truth, it takes a clarity of theological thinking and the courage of the martyrs in order to bear witness to the truth as Jesus did before Pilate. The Church's concern in discipleship is God's truth, not the power of the world.

But we want to testify to the Catholic faith and live it in such a way that we can journey together with Christians from other churches and denominations on the way to the full unity of the Church that Christ Her founder wishes to exist.

When He instituted the Eucharist, Jesus did not answer in detail all the individual questions that would come up on later reflection. But all the Church's dogmatic elucidations are founded on the nature of this sacrament as it was instituted by Jesus. Whoever wishes to receive the sacramental Body and Blood of Christ must already have been incorporated through the profession of faith and sacramental Baptism into the Body of Christ, the Church. There is therefore no mystical and individualistic community of feeling with Christ, who is always the Head of His Body, the Church, that bypasses Baptism and membership of the Church. "The cup of blessing ..., is it not a sharing in the blood of Christ? The bread that we break, is it not a sharing in the body of Christ? Because there is one bread, we who are many are one body, for we all partake of the one bread" (1 Cor 10:16f.). Whoever visibly belongs through faith and Baptism to the Church and thereby also participates in the supernatural community of life with God because the Church is in Christ a sign and instrument of the most intimate union between man and God (*LG* 1) must also be conformed to Christ in his religious and moral life so as to receive Christ in sacramental communion to his salvation and not to his judgement (cf. 1 Cor 11:27). "You cannot partake of the table of the Lord and the table of demons" (1 Cor 10:21).

In his First Apology (ca. A.D. 150), the philosopher and martyr Justin already formulated the three conditions for the rightful and worthy reception of the spiritual nourishment of the Eucharist, saying no one is allowed to partake of it "but the man who believes that the things which we teach are true, and who has been washed with the washing that is for the remission of sins, and unto regeneration, and who is so living as Christ has enjoined" (1 *Apol.* 66). For this is not common bread that binds us together as in an agape or some random religious meal; it is the flesh and blood of Christ that the Logos assumed at the Incarnation. And we too are nourished by this sacred food and transformed into the Body of Christ by being conformed to Him and strengthened in our membership of the Church. We really receive Christ, the Head of the Church, in the sacrament, and we are symbolically joined more and more to His ecclesial body to the extent that the Church is a visible community through which we share in the invisible community of grace with God. A few decades earlier, Ignatius of Antioch speaks of docetic Christians who stay away from the celebration of the Eucharist or are excluded from it because they reject the corporal, real presence of Christ in the sacrament and in general wish to understand the salvific events of the Incarnation, Cross and Resurrection of Christ purely metaphorically and not in a realistic and corporal way, thus robbing themselves of salvation. The only thing that helps against heretical beliefs and schisms from the unity of the Church is unity with the bishop and the visible Church. "You should regard that Eucharist as valid which is celebrated either by the bishop or by someone he authorizes [presbyter]. Where the bishop is present, there let the congregation gather, just as where Jesus Christ is, there is the Catholic Church. Without the bishop's supervision, no baptisms or love feasts are permitted" (*Letter to the Smyrnaeans* 8, 1f.).

These pointers to the indissoluble connection between the sacraments and membership of the visible, sacramental and episcopally ordered Church express the essential elements of the Catholic understanding of Church and Eucharist. Since Justin's time it has been clear to every Catholic that only full communion with the ecclesial Body of Christ in the profession of faith, the sacraments and the hierarchical constitution of the visible Church can be the prerequisite for the permissible and fruitful reception of the Body and Blood of Christ in Holy Communion. In addition to this, the Catholic must be in a state of sanctifying grace, i.e., the person must sincerely repent of any mortal sin committed since Baptism and confess it — combined with the resolve not to sin again — and in this way normally be freed through sacramental absolution from the guilt that radically separates him or her from God and the Church. Membership of the pilgrim Church is a prerequisite for salvation for every one of the baptized, albeit with the further proviso that "Whosoever, therefore, knowing that the Catholic Church was made necessary by Christ, would refuse to enter or to remain in it, could not be saved" (*LG* 14).

When the Popes and Councils excommunicated heretics and schismatics, they excluded them from Eucharistic fellowship until the day that they repented and were reconciled with God and the Church. Conversely, those who held false beliefs but regarded themselves as being orthodox believers, for their part denied Catholics ecclesial fellowship by not granting them Eucharistic Communion.

Up until the Leuenberg Concord signed between Protestant churches in Europe (1973), even Lutherans and Reformed did not share any fellowship of pulpit and table because they held fast to the early Church principle of community of sacrament and Church. But not all ecclesial communities derived from the Reformation joined this church fellowship because the controversy over the Real Presence of Christ at the Lord's Supper had been settled by it in favor of a more Calvinistic view and so a true unity of faith on the question of the Lord's Supper had yet to be achieved.

In spite of significant progress in the dialogue with various Protestant communities, the Catholic Church cannot depart from the essential doctrines about Her own mission and the sacraments mediated through it without being disloyal to Christ. And it is not enough for non-Catholic Christians to selectively accept a number of the Church's teachings for themselves and reject others or regard them as unimportant. In the doctrine of the Eucharist there is almost complete agreement with the Orthodox churches (the

Real Presence, the sacrificial character of the Mass, the ordained priest without whom there is no Eucharist) and partial agreement with several Protestant communities, especially the Lutherans. However, for both Orthodox and Catholic thinking, the mutual requirement of ecclesial community and reception of the Eucharist is indispensable. The sacraments are not merely signs for us of a justification of the sinner that has already come about in faith alone, but rather signs that effect what they signify. If in some circumstances it is not possible to celebrate the sacraments of grace as visible symbolic actions as well, God nevertheless gives those who open themselves completely to Him in faith, hope and love the grace of these sacraments. He does this for the person's salvation, not in order to relativize the visible sacramental mediation of salvation that is grounded in the Incarnation and in conformity with human nature.

People who now interpret their spiritual hunger for God and His grace using psychological instead of theological categories run the risk of confusing pagan magic and Christian sacrament. The Eucharist is "the medicine of immortality" (Ignatius of Antioch, *Eph* 20, 2) because of supernatural faith and grace, not a pharmaceutical remedy for psychodramatic experiences and traumas. The latter call for the natural treatments of medicine and therapy. Nor can it, as it were, physically restore lost ecclesial communion unless a supernatural unity has already been achieved by virtue of a shared profession of faith, sacraments and visible unity with the Pope and bishops. The call not to be so scrupulous about this and to leave it at the pious feelings and good will of those who simply come forward for Holy Communion and should not be excluded actually only appears to be displaying generosity whereas in reality it reveals a disdain for the revealed faith entrusted to the Catholic Church. To simply replace a striving after an understanding of the Catholic faith with a pronouncement made by individual episcopal conferences with the tacit approval of the Pope constitutes an undermining of itself by the Magisterium. For the latter's authority does not lie in administrative power; rather, it has "the task of authentically interpreting the word of God, whether written or handed on.... This teaching office is not above the word of God, but serves it, teaching only what has been handed on, listening to it devoutly, guarding it scrupulously and explaining it faithfully in accord with a divine commission and with the help of the Holy Spirit, it draws from this one deposit of faith everything which it presents for belief as divinely revealed" (*DV* 10).

God instituted only one teaching office in the Catholic Church. The idea that there could be a conflicting variety in matters of faith and in the praxis of the sacraments and that even episcopal conferences or individual bishops could possess a teaching office capable of interpreting revelation in a dogmatically binding manner without being linked to the Pope and the entire body of bishops not only displays a frightening lack of theological literacy but also represents nothing other than a monstrous attack on the revealed unity of the Church in Christ that has been given to us. The fact is that for the universal Church and the whole body of bishops the Pope — and by analogy the bishop for the local church — is the principle and foundation of unity in faith and communion in the grace of the sacraments (*LG* 18; 22) and not the reason for them to split into autocephalous national churches. The secular principle of the decentralization of political power can only be applied analogously to purely organizational aspects of governing the Church but absolutely not to the truth that unites all the faithful in God when they devote themselves "to the apostles' teaching and fellowship, to the breaking of bread and the prayers" (Acts 2:42).

Nevertheless, in an extreme situation where it is a matter of immediate preparation for individual judgement and eternal life, i.e., in a case of mortal danger, the Church cannot refuse a non-Catholic baptized Christian pastoral assistance if the person seriously requests it. This can only occur when respect is shown for the person's religious convictions. For most non-Catholic Christians have not made themselves guilty of heresy or have become apostate of their own accord. Christians belonging to ecclesial communities derived from the Reformation do in any case have a real connection to the Catholic Church as a result of their Baptism and many other Church-building elements (*UR* 3f.). It is not communion as such that is lacking but just full communion with the visible Church and all her means of grace. When a Christian asks a Catholic priest for sacramental forgiveness of sins and also for Holy Communion as a viaticum in a case of grave necessity that affects his eternal salvation and must not be confused with socio-psychological con-straints, then that person may be given the sacraments of grace if he at least implicitly affirms the Church's belief regarding these two sacraments because God bestows the grace of the sacraments (*res sacramenti*) on him on the grounds of his faith, hope and love. Any appearance of denominational relativism must be avoided. It is not permissible to, for example, arbitrarily stretch the concept of "grave necessity" (CIC 844) so that de facto a sacramental communion of the Catholic Church comes about with communities that are not joined to Her in full unity. Church law is to be interpreted on the basis of revealed faith and, where the *ius mere ecclesiasticum* is concerned, also corrected. And by the same token the faith cannot be de facto overruled by positive canons of ecclesiastical law. A disparity between the teaching and practice of the faith is impossible if we wish to remain Catholic. For the goal is not intercommunion between visible churches that remain separate but rather the visible unity of the Church which is represented and realized in the unity of faith, sacraments and the recognition of the office of teaching and governance exercised by the Pope and the bishops (*UR* 4).

Roman Encounters

Although a denominationally mixed marriage and family pose a great challenge to the spouses and children, this can even offer an ecumenical opportunity for Christians to grow together on the way to Church unity; however, it is in itself on no account a case of "grave necessity" that would make the sacraments of the Catholic Church necessary for the non-Catholic members for the sake of their souls. If a Protestant becomes inwardly convinced of being able to affirm the whole of the Catholic faith and its ecclesial form in his or her conscience, then the right course of action is to seek full visible communion with the Catholic Church. From experience in my own country of Germany, which has been denominationally divided for 500 years, so that every Christian there has relatives of a different denomination, I know that there are loyalties and attachments to one's own original denomination that cannot be undone simply by being received into the Catholic Church. For some it would mean being robbed of their economic existence, too. Anyone wanting to pass judgement on their fellow Christians should ask themselves just how courageous they would be about their faith in a non-Catholic environment. But there is no call here for regulation by episcopal conferences and self-congratulation by ecclesial bureaucracies that allow themselves to be praised by the media for their ecumenical openness. A good pastor knows what advice given to a person's conscience he can take responsibility for in the *forum internum*.

With respect to the Orthodox Churches the questions are dogmatically and theologically quite different since they share with us an understanding of the Church as a sacramental reality. Like us, they have the valid sacraments and sacramental priesthood as well as the valid ordination of bishops, who are then true and legitimate successors of the apostles. Therefore in a grave emergency, i.e., when the salvation of his soul is at stake and he cannot reach a Catholic priest, it is permissible for a Catholic to ask an Orthodox priest for the sacraments of Penance, Anointing of the Sick and the Eucharist as a viaticum. A Catholic priest is also permitted to administer these sacraments to an Orthodox Christian under the same conditions. The other way around, the Orthodox are more cautious; this is because in sacramental teaching they have not invariably and consistently implemented the conclusions drawn by the Catholic Church in the 4th and 5th centuries from the fundamental decision taken against the Donatists. According to this decision, even a heretical or schismatic priest, or one not living a morally impeccable life, can, if he is validly ordained, validly administer the sacraments if he celebrates them according to the mind of the Church.

In the case of the competence of the episcopal conferences, one must not look just at legal competences as they have been positively laid down canonically between Rome and the local authorities. Of far greater importance is the insight that neither the bishops nor the Pope have any competence to interfere with the substance of the sacraments (Trent, *Doctrine and Canons on Communion*: DH 1728) or to tacitly initiate processes that establish errors and confusion in practice, thus endangering the salvation of souls.

It is also not possible to leave the wording of a doctrine unchanged but, by employing an changed fundamental hermeneutic, attribute a completely different or even contradictory meaning to it. For example, a differentiated theological explanation of the sacrificial nature of the Mass does not relativize it but rather shows it in a light that brings out more clearly the real unity of the Sacrifice of the Cross and the Sacrifice of the Altar as well as their liturgical difference. Or when categories other than those of Aristotelian philosophy are also employed in order to explain the somatic Real Presence, then the awareness of the problem of the doctrine of Transubstantiation that has been achieved (Lateran IV, Trent) cannot be subverted by a less consistent theory of a professor of theology and his epigones. Ecumenism must aim to overcome the doctrinal differences in the matter itself and not content itself with a scarcely sustainable compromise on formulation.

If you make things easy for yourself by holding that academic theology is to blame for the divisions in western Christendom, all this does is promote indifference in matters of faith. And that would be an ecclesiological nihilism into whose abyss "the church of the living God, the pillar and bulwark of the truth" (1 Tim 3:15) would be bound to fall.

7

The Unity of the Church's Teaching Office

Dear Confreres in the Sacred College of Cardinals,

You have asked me for a contribution on the nature and purpose of the Church's teaching office. For the opinion exists that a reform of the curia comes down to destroying the power of this unloved Roman apparatus of government. The Pope must, they argue, take over the governance himself and could do everything alone with a few trusted advisers. The College of Cardinals, which represents the Roman church in its shared responsibility for the universal Church, could be replaced by a regular Synod of Bishops. In between, the Secretariat of the Synod of Bishops would take on the task of lending the Pope collegial and synodal support. Above all, the overemphasis on doctrine must be relinquished in favor of giving priority to pastoral concerns. In the individual countries, the episcopal conferences, or their chairmen and secretariats, could assume the role of the Roman Magisterium. That, they say, is decentralization. I fear, however, that fundamental theological concepts are being wrongly used here and that the result could be a political distortion of the Church. Some people in the Vatican's Communications Center imagine that it is possible to push aside the doctrine of the Roman primacy so as to replace it with a modern personality cult around the person of the Pope. But that is not how you modernize the papacy; rather, it is how you destroy it. After all, the papacy does not exist for its own sake, but rather in order to unite the Church daily in Her profession of Christ, the Son of the living God and the sole Mediator of salvation. Whether or not Catholics know much about the biography of the reigning Pope is of no interest whatsoever for their faith. For the Church is Christocentrically constructed. So let me now offer a few thoughts on the unity of Pope and bishops in the teaching office of the Church. I shall not argue politically but theologically.

The new impulse of *Evangelii Gaudium*

One can only talk of the Church on the basis of the question about God and the knowledge of His human presence in Jesus Christ for the world.

In view of the global and daily tragedies facing us today in civil wars and terrorism, in poverty and exploitation, in the distress of refugees, in drug deaths, in the increasing suicide rates and the addiction to pornography afflicting 20% of today's youth, and in the crisis of meaning and intellectual and moral disorientation experienced by millions, the Church of God finds Herself confronted with the momentous task of restoring people's hope. But the Church Herself is not the light; She can only bear witness to the light that is the light of all people, to Jesus the Son of God and Redeemer of all mankind. Knowing God is what decides whether or not man becomes aware of his divine calling and still has a future in this world and beyond.

A Church that only revolved around Her own structural problems would be dreadfully anachronistic and out of touch with the world. For in Her being and mission She is nothing other than the Church of the Triune God, the origin and goal of every human being and of the cosmos. Any readjustment of the autonomy and collaboration between the local churches or of the collegiality of the bishops and the primacy of the Pope must never lose sight of the momentous challenge of the question of God. In his Apostolic Exhortation *Evangelii Gaudium*, Pope Francis speaks of a sound "decentralization." The life of the Church cannot be concentrated in such a way on the Pope and his Curia as if what goes on in the parishes, communities and dioceses ranks only as of secondary importance. The Pope and bishops point rather to Christ, Who alone gives hope to mankind. It is neither possible nor necessary for the Pope to record centrally from Rome the great variety of living conditions that manifest themselves for the Church in the individual nations and cultures and to himself solve every problem in situ. "Excessive centralization, rather than proving helpful, complicates the Church's life and her missionary outreach" (*EG* 32). Hence a new evangelization of the kind that was the subject of the last Synod of Bishops (7-28 October 2012) also calls for a reformed exercise of primacy. This applies to the institutions of the universal governance of the Church, especially the dicasteries of the Roman Curia which the Pope draws on when exercising supreme, full and immediate power in the universal Church. These "therefore, perform their duties in his name and with his authority for the good of the churches and in the service of the sacred pastors" (*Christus Dominus* 9). For the purpose of new evangelization, the bishops, synods and episcopal conferences must also exercise greater responsibility, including "a certain magisterial competence," which accrues to them through ordination and canonical sending and not through special papal authorization. "Bishops, teaching in communion with the Roman Pontiff, are to be respected by all as witnesses to divine and Catholic truth" (*LG* 25). The papal magisterium does not replace the teaching office of the bishops and their working together on a national or continental level (e.g. the documents of CELAM: Puebla, Medellín, Santa Domingo, Aparecida) but rather presupposes it and promotes it in its responsibility for the whole Church (*EG* 16). The Pope refers specifically to the Motu Proprio *Apostolos Suos* (1998), in which John Paul II had offered a detailed description of the tasks of the episcopal conferences based on the Second Vatican Council.

In marked contrast to superficial interpretations, this does not give the signal for a change of direction or a "revolution in the Vatican." The Church could only afford power struggles and arguments about competence by paying for them with a loss of Her missionary task. The ecclesiological synthesis of Vatican II rules out an antagonistic or dialectic interpretation of the relationship between the universal and the particular church. The historical extremes of papalism/curialism on the one hand and episcopalism (conciliarism/ Gallicanism/ Febronianism/ Old Catholicism) on the other only go to show us what does not work and that the absolutization of one element of the constitution at the expense of another contradicts our profession of the *una sancta ecclesia catholica*.

The collegial and fraternal unity of the bishops of the universal Church *cum et sub Petro* is grounded in the sacramentality of the Church and is thus of divine law. It would only be at the cost of desacralizing the Church that it would be possible to conduct a power struggle between centralistic and particularistic forces. All that would remain in the end would be a secularized and politicized Church that differed only in degree from an NGO. That would be an exact contradiction of the Apostolic Exhortation *Evangelii Gaudium*. According to its literary genre, this papal document is not a dogmatic text but rather a paraenetic one. It presupposes as its dogmatic basis the teaching on the Church set out with ultimate magisterial authority in *Lumen Gentium* (*EG* 17). The Pope's concerns are to overcome the lethargy and resignation encountered in the face of extreme secularization and to put an end to the paralyzing disputes within the Church between traditionalist and modernist ideologies. In spite of all the storms and adverse winds, the Barque of Peter is once again to hoist sails of joy at

Jesus' presence with us. And the disciples will pull strongly at the oars of a missionary Church.

If we offer an outward image of disunity and enmity, no one can be expected to perceive the Church as a credible witness to God's love and to venerate the Church as the Bride of Christ and learn to love Her as their mother.

The origin of unity in Jesus Christ

In the Dogmatic Constitution on the Church *Lumen Gentium*, the Second Vatican Council does not start with a sociological-immanentist purpose of the Church as if the Church were constituted as a result of the will to form a community of members sharing the same religious and moral convictions.

Instead, the inmost origin of the Church is to be found in the procession of the Son from the Father. In the Son all people are from all eternity already predestined to share in the divine life. Man's communion with God, which becomes a reality with his creation, was already prefigured in Christ from the beginning of human history. In the history of salvation, it was prepared in the People of the Covenant, finally constituted in the Christ event and the outpouring of the Spirit, and made manifest in the Church of the new and ultimate covenant (*LG* 2).[56]

Since the Church is not a purely human institution, asking about the status of Her foundation by the "historical" Jesus according to the law governing associations is factually misguided and for the purposes of a theological hermeneutic of historical revelation also anachronistic. Rather, as a community of life with Jesus, the Church is grounded in His divine nature and His Son-relation to

---

[56] On the definition of the relationship between the NT and OT, cf. the new document published by the Pontifical Biblical Commission, *The Jewish People and their Sacred Scriptures in the Christian Bible* (May 24, 2001) (= VAS 152).

the Father and is historically revealed in what He did as a man. For in His person the Kingdom of heaven has come. To this belongs the gathering of disciples to whom He gives a share in His authority and mission. As the eschatological Mediator of God's rule, Jesus (1) through both His preaching and His salvific acts as well as His fate in the Cross and Resurrection founded the eschatological covenant people as the communio of mankind with God, and (2) gave the community of those who believe in Him a share in His mission.

So it is the two elements of *communio* and *missio* that consti-tute the community of Jesus' disciples as a sign and instrument of mankind's oneness with God and with each other. The Church is therefore, as the servant and mediator of this union, essentially one, a single reality, unique, an original with no copies. The Church is not the retrospective sum of individuals in their autonomous and direct relationship to God. The Church is already organically one with Christ, like the body with the head. Christ as the Head constitutes the principle of the unity of all the members. Only in this way can all rejoice or feel compassion when another rejoices or suffers. The plurality of members of the Body of Christ is with respect to the Head *unus* with Christ (Gal 3:28): *totus Christus, caput et corpus*, the one and only Mediator of the whole of creation and eschatological man, the New Adam. All are taken into His Son relation to the Father in the Holy Spirit (cf. Gal 4:4-6). The word *ekklesia*, which already appears in the Septuagint (LXX) as the Greek designation for the assembly of the people of God and is usually rendered in English with "church," is always encountered in the singular when referring to God the Father, Christ the Son and the Holy Spirit: the one and only People of God, the one and only Body of Christ, which is the Church, and the one and only Temple of the Holy Spirit.

This Church stands in the service of Christ's unique, unifying and universal mediation of salvation, which is in its nature and mission necessarily universal, in Greek *katholikos*. For the Church proclaims salvation to all humanity. The gospel of Christ liberates human beings from their Babylonian captivity and diaspora and calls them into the pentecostal unity of the one People of God from out of the many peoples and cultures, and forms them into a new humanity in Christ, the Head of the Church and the whole of creation.

The one Church in her universal mission and local concretization

The sacramentality of the Church is grounded in the Incarnation. Analogously to the divine-human unity of Christ, the one, holy, catholic and apostolic Church exists as a spiritual and invisible community of life with God and as a visible, hierarchically constituted society. The unity is displayed in the shared apostolic teaching, the sacramental life and the hierarchical constitution. Therefore She cannot be merely the illustration of a supratemporal idea that binds peoples together, a *civitas platonica*. As a Church for human beings in their spiritual-corporeal constitution and historical-social form of existence, She takes on Her concrete form in accordance with the cultural conditions under which people live and with the coordinates of space and time. The Church of the Word of God who entered space and time is realized both universally and locally. The one and universal Church that is governed by the Pope and the bishops in communion with him consists in and of the particular churches. This is the meaning of the formula: "*in quibus et ex quibus una et unica Ecclesia catholica existet*" (LG 23).

Christ's mission applies to all people in every place and time. And yet He Himself lived in one of many places on earth and at a tiny space of time in the history of humanity. But this mission was realized historically uniquely in the human being Jesus of Nazareth, who lived and worked at a particular time and place in the world. Even pre-paschally, we encounter the tension between universal mission and local presence. Jesus chose the apostles in order to send them to all the places He could not go to Himself. After Easter He sends the apostles out to every location in the world and promises His presence to all of them together and to each individually, so that in the mediation of the many apostles the one Christ is present in every place in the world mediating salvation and unifying humanity. In this sense, the term "church" can also be used for the multitude of local churches. The one and only Church of God is present as the universal Church in the churches of God in Corinth, Rome, Thessalonica, etc. And what the faithful interact with locally is none other than the one Church of Christ in which the Holy Spirit unites all the baptized with one another and incorporates them into the unity of the Body of Christ so that all are one in Christ and, as sons and daughters of God in Christ, represent the one *familia Dei.*

So there is not first an interim spiritual mandate which, once the political and strategic expediencies have been weighed up, is then divided between the Pope and the bishops, the universal Church and the particular churches. Rather, Christ called the apostles as a body. He Himself placed the apostle Peter at their head as the principle and foundation of the unity of the one apostolic mandate and mission for the whole Church. Episcopal ordination also displays the collegial nature of the episcopal office in the assigning the individual bishop to the whole college and at its head the Pope, without whom the college cannot exercise any universal authority in its teaching and pastoral office. "This collegial union is apparent also in the mutual relations of the individual bishops with particular churches and with the universal Church. The Roman Pontiff, as the successor of Peter, is the perpetual and visible principle and foundation of unity of both the bishops and of the faithful. The individual bishops, however, are the visible principle and foundation of unity in their particular churches, fashioned after the model of the universal Church, in and from which churches comes into being the one and only Catholic Church. For this reason the individual bishops represent each his own church, but all of them together and with the Pope represent the entire Church in the bond of peace, love and unity" (*LG* 23).

Any attempt to define the relationship between universality and particularity will only be successful if undertaken from a consistently Christological and ecclesiological perspective. There is nothing analogous to be found in state and non-state forms of organizing human societies and business corporations with which it could be compared. The universality of the Church is indeed concretely realized in the local church, which is why a widely scattered personal parish can never be, in the strict sense, a local church, just as every local church is by its very nature nothing other than the universal Church in that locality. This mutual indwelling is the Catholic communio of the Church, which is constituted as the *communio ecclesiarum*.

The unity of primacy and episcopacy

Chapter 3 of *Lumen Gentium* describes the unity of universality and particularity. This is premised on the apostolic structure of the local church. It means that the local church is no more constituted through individual Christians wishing to form an association than is the Church of Christ in general. It would be completely uncatholic to imagine the Church as a loose aggregate of national churches. The outcome of such a constellation would be that instead of election by the Roman Church (through the College of Cardinals), the chairmen of the national churches would choose themselves a president; the latter could then even be allowed to retain the traditional title of 'pope' in order to conceal the complete destruction of the Catholic doctrine of the Church.

In fact, however, it is Christ Himself Who, through His apostles and their successors (in the *munus predicandi, sanctificandi et gubernandi*), grounds the universal Church in and from the particular churches as a *communio ecclesiarum*, thus making them into the *corpus Christi visibile*. One can only speak of a local or particular church if it visibly realizes in its bishop, the successor to the apostles, both its unity with the other local churches and its unity with the origin of the Church in Christ and the apostles. This is displayed in the unity of the apostolic profession of faith and the sacramental-liturgical making present of salvation in Christ. Hence the doctrine of the bishops as successors to the apostles, of their collegial unity with one another and their unity with the successor of Peter as the visible head of the entire Church and of the College of Bishops is constitutive for the Catholic concept of Church. Pope and bishops do not relate to one another in the same way as, for example, the Superior General to the Father Provincials in the Society of Jesus.

Only in this way is it possible to properly appreciate the following description of universality and particularity as the realization of the unity and uniqueness of the Church of Christ: "Just as in the Gospel, the Lord so disposing, St. Peter and the other apostles constitute one apostolic college, so in a similar way the Roman Pontiff, the successor of Peter, and the bishops, the successors of the apostles, are joined together....

"But the college or body of bishops has no authority unless it is understood together with the Roman Pontiff, the successor of Peter as its head. The pope's power of primacy over all, both pastors and faithful, remains whole and intact.... This college, insofar as it is composed of many, expresses the variety and universality of the People of God, but insofar as it is assembled under one head, it expresses the unity of the flock of Christ. In it, the bishops, faithfully recognizing the primacy and pre-eminence of their head, exercise their own authority for the good of their own faithful, and indeed of the whole Church, the Holy Spirit supporting its organic structure and harmony with moderation. The supreme power in the universal Church, which this college enjoys, is exercised in a solemn way in an ecumenical council.... This same collegiate power can be exercised together with the pope by the bishops living in all parts of the world, provided that the head of the college calls them to collegiate action, or at least approves of or freely accepts the united action of the scattered bishops, so that it is thereby made a collegiate act" (*LG* 22).

The individual local churches form the one Catholic Church of God in the *communio* of churches governed by their bishops. Every particular church has a share in the universal Church through its unity with Her and Her apostolic origin, through unity in the profession of faith, the Church's Sacred Scripture, Her liturgical-sacramental forms of mediating grace, and through the apostolic authority embodied and guaranteed by the bishop and stretching back from the bishop to the apostles in the apostolic succession. This unity does not impede but rather promotes the richness that is manifested through inculturation to different peoples and different historical epochs. The local church of Rome is one among many local churches, but with the distinctive feature that its apostolic foundation through the *martys* (= witness) *verbi et sanguinis* of the apostles Peter and Paul has given it a primacy in the overall witness and the unity of life of the *catholica communio*. Because of this *potentior principalitas*, every other local church must agree with this church.[57] As far as the substance of the faith is concerned, the two Vatican Councils did not have anything further to say about catholicity and particularity, about the collegiality of the bishops and about being guided by the *Cathedra Petri* in matters of doctrine and discipline.

[57] Cf. Irenaeus, *haer* II,3,2.

Roman Encounters

The Pope and the whole body of bishops
in the service of unity and truth

It is, however, important to understand episcopal service itself as a sacramental reality in the sacramental Church and not to confuse it with a moderator of purely human associations.

For the episcopate is an office instituted in the Church in perpetuity by God (*LG* 18). The bishops, whom the Holy Spirit has made overseers (*episcopos*) (cf. Acts 20:28), have charge of Christ's flock in God's stead (*LG* 19). In sacramental ordination, the Spirit effects "that bishops in an eminent and visible way sustain the roles of Christ himself as Teacher, Shepherd and High Priest, and that they act in his person" (*LG* 21). They are "vicars and ambassadors of Christ" in the exercise of their duties (*LG* 27).

The very fact that at the sacramental ordering of a successor reference is made to "neighboring bishops of other churches" demonstrates the collegial dimension of the episcopal office and that it belongs to the universal Church. It is not that an individual community constitutes itself and its office. Rather, the episcopal consecration integrates the bishop symbolically into the College of Bishops and confers on him a responsibility for the one worldwide Catholic Church, which consists in the *communio ecclesiarum*.

In his local church the bishop is "the visible principle and foundation of unity" (*LG* 23). This applies to the communio of all the faithful and the college of presbyters, deacons and other ecclesiastical office holders. The one episcopal office does not swallow up the diverse forms of mission and ministry. Instead, it not only prevents the individual ministries from falling apart but also promotes the diversity of ministries in the individual members and guarantees the unity of the mission of the one Church in *martyria*, *diakonia*, and *leiturgia*.

Since the episcopal office serves the unity of the Church, it must itself bear the principle of its unity within it. This can only be embodied in the bishop of a local church, not the president of a federation *made up of* regional or continental churches. Nor can the principle be a purely objective one (majority decision, delegation of rights to an elected governing body, etc.). Since the inner essence of the episcopal office is one of personal witness, the principle of the unity of the episcopate itself is embodied in a person. According to Catholic thinking, the personal principle of unity is given in the Bishop of Rome, in its origin as well as in its present realization. As bishop he is the successor of Peter, who as the first apostle and the first witness to the Resurrection himself embodied in his person the unity of the apostolic college. What is crucial for a theology of primacy is a characterization of the Petrine ministry as an episcopal mission along with the understanding that this office is not of human but rather divine law inasmuch as it can only be exercised in the Holy Spirit and on Christ's authorization by virtue of a personally given charism. "And in order that the episcopate itself might be one and undivided, [the eternal Shepherd Jesus Christ] placed blessed Peter over the other apostles, and instituted in him a permanent and visible source and foundation of unity of faith and communion" (*LG* 18; cf. DH 3051).

What the Pope has in mind in *Evangelii Gaudium* is an improved praxis better suited to today's global, digitalized civilization. Although primacy and episcopacy are essential features of the Church, the forms in which they are realized in history are necessarily different. The Pope's call for a renewed perception of episcopal collegiality is the opposite of a relativization of the task given him directly by Christ of serving the unity of all the bishops and faithful in the revealed faith, the shared life lived from sacramental grace and the mission to communicate the unity of the whole human race in God (*LG* 1). Since the episcopal office is of a collegial nature, a share in the care and responsibility for the wellbeing of the universal Church is also conferred on him by virtue of his consecration and canonical sending: "The task of proclaiming the gospel everywhere on earth pertains to the body of pastors. . . . From this it follows that the individual bishops, insofar as their own discharge of their duty permits, are obliged to enter into a community of work among themselves and with the successor of Peter, upon whom was imposed in a special way the great duty of spreading the Christian name" (*LG* 23).

In recognition of the fruitful apostolate carried out by the hitherto existing episcopal conferences and wishing to see these bodies established everywhere, the Second Vatican Council offers a kind of brief definition of their role: "An episcopal conference is, as it were, a council in which the bishops of a given nation or territory jointly exercise their pastoral office to promote the greater good that the Church offers mankind, especially through the forms and methods of the apostolate fittingly adapted to the circumstances of the age" (*CD* 38,1). The theological and practical implementation of the ministry of the episcopal conferences in the service of the universal Church and of the particular churches belonging to them is further developed and concretized in the motu proprio *Apostolos suos*. This also includes a teaching competence on the part of the totality of bishops belonging to such a conference (cf. *AS* 21; *CIC* can 753). This serves the unity of the faith and its concrete implementation within a particular cultural sphere. Reference to the Successor of Peter, the visible principle of the unity of the Church and of the entire episcopate of the Catholic Church, is constitutive for every ecumenical council, every particular synod and every episcopal conference; it is also a matter of divine law, the principle that must underlie all codified law. An episcopal conference can never make separate dogmatic pronouncements, let alone relativize defined dogmas and constitutive sacramental structures (e.g. make its own teaching and pastoral office dependent on bodies that are established purely by ecclesiastical law).

Separatist tendencies and prepotent behavior damage the Church. Revelation has been entrusted for faithful preservation to the one universal Church which is governed by the Pope and the bishops in unity with him (*LG* 8; *DV* 10). The Catholic Church is the *communio ecclesiarum* and not a federation of national churches or an alliance of denominationally related ecclesial communities which from purely human tradition respect the Bishop of Rome as their honorary president. For nation, language and culture are not constitutive principles of the Church which in Christ testifies to and realizes the unity of the nations; nevertheless they are in a regulative sense indispensable media through which all the riches and fullness of Christ are unfolded in the redeemed.

Evangelii Gaudium was intended to draw the Church inwardly together so that the people of God do not stand in their own way in their missionary service of a humanity that is so greatly in need of salvation and help.

8

Statement on the Limits of Papal Authority

Following the above talk, the Cardinal receives a visitor. A confrere asks him to clarify one question.

A confrere from the Sacred College

In the discussion about the post-synodal apostolic exhortation *Amoris Laetitia* the question remains unanswered as to whether the Pope can change valid Catholic teaching if it is defined as *de fide divina et catholica*. In other words, it is about what belongs to the revealed divine and Catholic faith. That formula is used to express both the origin of the belief in God and the fact that it has been clearly proclaimed by the highest teaching office of the Catholic Church. Considerable doubts also exist regarding the formal procedure as to whether an acknowledgement published in the *Acta Apostolicae Sedis* confirming that the Pontiff has received a pastoral handout produced by a local episcopal conference is magisterially binding, especially if nothing has been dogmatically clarified in it. For example, a simple statement that a Catholic in a state of mortal sin can worthily receive Holy Communion would be plainly heretical. Surely all you have to do is ask whether or not someone is in a state of mortal sin and point out that, if there is any doubt, that person must not reject the help of the sacrament of Penance.

Roman Encounters

It really is the case that — put ironically — with the new Pope "a marvellous exchange" has taken place. Those who, being ardently anti-Roman, would previously reject whatever came from Rome now never tire of the joys of a super-papalism that would have been the envy of Vatican I maximalists. I fear that both extreme parties do not know what the Catholic faith says about the papacy, above all about what it says it is not.

The Cardinal

I shall respond to you in the form of a statement that I gave to a Catholic journal.

On 4 March 1875, Pope Pius IX sent an important Apostolic Letter to the German episcopate. In it he confirmed with supreme authority that the German bishops had explained the dogmas of papal infallibility and primacy of jurisdiction completely in accordance with the definitions of Vatican I.

This had been preceded by a "Circular Letter" from the German Chancellor Otto von Bismarck employing a monstrous misinterpretation of papal primacy in order to justify the brutal persecution of German Catholics in the *Kulturkampf* (culture struggle).

In the Pope's words, the German bishops show quite clearly in their written response "that there is absolutely nothing in the attacked definitions that is new or that changes anything at all with regard to our relations with civil governments or that can offer any excuse to persist in the persecution of the Church" (DH 3117). One must, of course, also be aware of the intellectual background of Bismarck and his liberal and nationalistic supporters in the *Kulturkampf*. Even though they had often already given up the contents of the Protestant Reformation, the prejudice nevertheless remained that the Magisterium of the Pope and the councils put itself above God, threatened the immediacy to God of the Christian's faith and conscience, and placed itself as a heterogeneous authority between the citizen and the State, which, of course, ascribed to itself a total authority that was even divorced from natural moral law. Comparable to Bismarck's *Kulturkampf* in Germany is the struggle conducted against the Church by liberals in Italy under the pretext of not being against the faith but only against clericalism. With the introduction of *Laïcité* as the State ideology in France with the Law on the Separation of the Churches and the State[58] under Prime Minister Émile Combes, an ex-seminarian, we find the same motifs of "liberalism" as a struggle against seeing Christianity as originating in a supernatural revelation. In the name of freedom of religion, the purportedly "liberal" state laid claim to the highest authority even over the truth conscience of its citizens. God as a higher authority than the laws of the State stands in the way of seizing power over the knowledge and conscience of the governed. On this I can warmly recommend the book by Manuel Borutta, *Antikatholizismus: Deutschland und Italien im Zeitalter der europäischen Kulturkämpfe*.[59] He describes the self-contradiction of liberalism torn between the demand for freedom and the claim to exclusive validity.

The liberals were agreed that the Pope with his authority could arbitrarily present the Church, and thus the subjects of foreign sovereigns, with something that was to be believed on pain of excommunication and even the loss of eternal life. Against the completely inappropriate interpretation of the *plenitudo potestatis* as absolute papal sovereignty over the Church and the possibility of demanding absolute obedience, the German bishops argue: "The pope cannot change the constitution given to the Church

---

[58] Jean-Paul Cahn, Hartmann Kaelbe (Ed.), *Religion und Laizität in Frankreich und Deutschland im 19.und 20. Jahrhundert. Religions et laïcité en France et en Allemagne aux 19e et 20e siècles*, Stuttgart 2008.

[59] Göttingen 2008.

by Her divine Founder.... In all essential points the constitution of the Church is based on divine directives, and therefore it is not subject to human arbitrariness" (DH 3114). It follows from this that the Church's teaching authority "is restricted to the contents of Holy Scripture and tradition and also to the dogmas previously defined by the teaching authority of the Church" (DH 3116). The spiritual authority of the Magisterium is displayed in its ability to freely and unimpeded by any earthly power (freedom of religion) guarantee the allegiance of the faithful to revelation (infallibility).

From this is derived the subordinate, serving role of the teaching office of the Pope and bishops compared to the Word of God in the historical presence and fullness it has in Jesus Christ, the *Verbum incarnatum*.

Christ is the "one instructor" (Mt 23:10), who proclaims to us "the words of eternal life" (Jn 6:68). In relation to Him, Peter, the apostles and all the baptized are his disciples and pupils; and in relation to each other they are brothers and sisters with the one heavenly Father.

Nevertheless this on no account precludes Jesus' choosing some from among His disciples to be His apostles and conferring on them the authority to teach and to govern. These are entrusted with the message of reconciliation, acting "as ambassadors for Christ, since God is making his appeal through [them]" (2 Cor 5:19f.) for the salvation of the world. The risen Lord, to whom is given all power in heaven and on earth, sends the apostles—and with them their successors in the office of bishop with the successor of Peter, the Pope, at their head—out into the whole world to make disciples of all who believe and baptize them in the name of the Father and of the Son and of the Holy Spirit. And Christ makes clear that it is His teaching that is to form the content and the criterion of truth in their teaching (cf. Acts 2:42). He instructs the apostles to teach "them to obey everything that I have commanded you"

(Mt 28:20). In this lies the certainty of the Christian faith that the human word of the apostles and bishops is the divine word of salvation, which is testified to by human mediators but does not originate from them (cf. 1 Thess 2:13).

As the terminology that has been firmly established since Irenaeus of Lyon in the 2nd century puts it, the content of revelation is communicated to us through Sacred Scripture and the Apostolic Tradition, and the formal authority of the witnesses and proclaimers of revelation is part of this. This is the ecclesial teaching office of Pope and bishops. Against the Reformation principle of *sola scriptura*, i.e., the bible as both the principle of the content and the formal principle of certainty, the Council of Trent stresses "that it belongs to her [the Church] to judge the true meaning and interpretation of Holy Scripture—and that no one may dare to interpret the Scripture in a way contrary to the unanimous consensus of the Fathers" (DH 1507).

Vatican II takes up this fundamental hermeneutic of the Catholic faith and concludes from it: "This teaching office is *not above* the word of God, but serves it, teaching only what has been handed on, listening to it devoutly, guarding it scrupulously and explaining it faithfully in accord with a divine commission and with the help of the Holy Spirit, it draws from this one deposit of faith everything which it presents for belief as divinely revealed" (*DV* 10).

A consensus exists that Sacred Scripture is and contains the word of God. Since it is transmitted in human language, it does not possess the evidence (*quoad se*) that Protestants wish to ascribe to it. Rather, it requires interpretation on the part of the teachers of the faith authorized by the Holy Spirit who also represent its authority in human words and decisions for the hearers of the word of God (*quoad nos*). For this reason the Magisterium is an essential part of the Church's mission. Only with the aid of the living Magisterium of Pope and bishops is it possible for the word of God which creates unity and transmits truth to be passed on unabridged and unaltered to believers and possible hearers of the gospel until the end of time. The act of believing refers to God, in whose existence we believe (*Deum esse*), in whom we in faith place all our trust (*credere Deo*) and in whom we believe in his Trinity and Incarnation (*credere in Deum*).

The human words we use in the Creed to recognize God (in act and content) as the true object of our faith and to profess our faith in Him and the way in which we defend the faith against errors are subject to a certain amount of change in how we express it. St. Thomas clearly states the reason for this: "*Actus credentis non terminatur ad enuntiabile sed ad rem*"[60] (*S.th.* II-II 1, 2, ad 2). Because the teaching of the apostles and of the Church is God's word expressed in human words, there is also a development and refining of God's word in the faith awareness of the Church resembling the development of the human mind in the history of ideas under the guidance of the Holy Spirit (cf. Jn 16:13). Therefore, there exists both for the individual Christian in his or her personal faith history and for the Church as a whole a certain progress in the conceptual cognition and spiritual grasp of the truths of salvation. "This tradition that comes from the apostles develops in the Church with the help of the Holy Spirit. For there is a growth in the understanding of the realities and the words which have been handed down. This happens through the contemplation and study made by believers, who treasure these things in their hearts (cf. Lk 2:19, 51), through a penetrating understanding of the spiritual realities which they experience, and through the preaching of those who have received through episcopal succession the sure gift of truth. For as the centuries succeed one another, the Church

---

[60] The act of the believer does not terminate in the proposition but in the reality.

constantly moves forward toward the fullness of divine truth until the words of God reach their complete fulfillment in her" (*DV* 8). This "dogmatic history" does not, however, bring us substantially new contents of faith because revelation reached its unsurpassable climax and complete fullness in Christ. The statement of the Council of Nicaea and subsequent councils on the divinity of Christ, declaring Him to be of one substance with the Father (*homoousios*) and one being with the Father and the Holy Spirit is merely the linguistically correct formulation of a fact that was clearly testified to in the early Church and in Sacred Scripture, namely, that Jesus is in his divine pre-existence the Son of the eternal Father. This is an example of the homogenous development of dogma in which the dogma presents and interprets the word of God with certainty in the Church's profession of faith. But when—under the influence of Enlightenment rationalism, which a priori regards the Incarnation as metaphysically and ethically impossible—Jesus is updated as the epitome of our consciousness of God and when he is made comprehensible to "modern" man as simply a moral and social role model (exactly within the framework of Rationalism), then what we are dealing with is not a development of dogma but rather a corruption of the revealed truth and thus also a deconstruction of the Christological dogma altogether.

It belongs to the Pope as head of the teaching office of the bishops and as principle of the unity of the Church in the truth both to preserve the whole truth of revelation and to draw up new conceptual formulations of the *symbolum* in order to bring it up to date. He can neither add anything to the revelation that is presented to us in Scripture and Tradition nor change the content of earlier dogmatic definitions. However, he has the right and the duty, under certain circumstances and in order to preserve the unity of the faith and the Church, to frame the profession of faith in a new way (*nova editio symboli*). As Thomas Aquinas explains:

"The truth of faith is sufficiently explicit in the teaching of Christ and the apostles. But since, according to 2 Peter 3:16, some men are so evil-minded as to pervert the apostolic teaching and other doctrines and Scriptures to their own destruction, it was necessary as time went on (*temporibus procedentibus*) to express the faith more explicitly against the errors which arose" (*S.th.* II-II 1, 10 ad 1).

The Magisterium relies here both on the Spirit-filled sense of the faith of the people of God with all believers and under the guidance of their pastors (*LG* 12) and also on the theologians. Without the theological groundwork of St. Athanasius and the Cappadocians there would have been neither the declaration of faith of Nicaea nor its defense and clarification at the subsequent councils; no more would the decrees of Trent have been possible without the prior groundwork of the most learned theologians of the time. When elucidating the faithful historical transmission of revelation in its entirety by the Magisterium in the charism of the infallibility of Pope and council, Vatican II does not neglect to add: "The Roman Pontiff and the bishops, in view of their office and the importance of the matter, by fitting means diligently strive to inquire properly into that revelation and to give apt expression to its contents; but a new public revelation they do not accept as pertaining to the divine deposit of faith" (*LG* 25). But this must not limit living faith, as act and content, to the defined dogmas. For just as the car driver does not confuse the goal of his journey with the signposts yet also does not separate the way from the goal, it is not the dogmas themselves that the Christian believes in but rather God in the word of his self-communication in grace and truth. The dogmas are always to be read in the greater light of the fullness of God's word, which is the source of our knowledge of God. Hence the study of the history of the Church's dogmas and of the dogmas themselves does not obviate the need to study Holy Scripture, the Church Fathers and the Doctors of the Church. But no one can make the strings of a violin sing without the instrument's resonance chamber. So as a Catholic you cannot go back behind the developed doctrine of the Church to the purportedly pure teaching of Scripture. To do so would mean either decomposing or recomposing the Church's teaching. The Parable of the Prodigal Son, for example, is not a catechetical representation of the Sacrament of Penance and Reconciliation in its matter (repentance, confession, satisfaction) and form (absolution by the priest), so it is not possible to conclude from the fact that the son did not confess his sins that we do not have to submit ours to the Church's sacramental penitential court. To set Scripture against the Church in this way would be a serious abuse of the word of God, who after all entrusted the entire *depositum fidei* to the faithful safekeeping of the apostles with Peter at their head. We must continually draw from the source again and again, but we cannot dam up the flow of the history of revelation and faith or make the waters flow back uphill.

The Pope was placed by Christ over the other apostles as the visible head of his Church; and Christ "instituted in him a permanent and visible source and foundation of unity of faith and communion" (*LG* 18).

This refers particularly to the Church's teaching but also to the administration of the means of grace in the sacraments. In the decree regarding the reception of Communion under only one species the Council of Trent declares that "the Church has the authority to shape the external rite of the sacraments but denies her the right and the power to touch the substance of the sacraments—*salva illorum substantia*" (DH 1728).

When the Council of Trent defines (DH 1673-1683; 1704) that three acts on the part of the penitent belong to Sacrament of Penance (contrition with the resolve not to sin any more, confession and satisfaction), then the Popes and bishops of future times are bound by this. They are not at liberty to grant the sacramental forgiveness of sins or to give priests the authority to grant absolution for sins that have not been repented or when the penitent directly refuses to resolve not to sin again. For no one can resolve the inner contradiction between the effect of the sacrament, namely, the new community of life with Christ in faith, hope and love, and the missing disposition of the penitent — not even the Pope or the Council because they have no authority to do so. Nor could they ever receive any such authority because God never charges man to do something that is self-contradictory and antithetical to God.

It must also be borne in mind that dogmatic definitions are to be accepted "with divine and Catholic faith." The doctrinal statements carry different amounts of weight. Accordingly, the degrees to which assent to them is binding (theological grades of certainty) also differ. It is also *e contrario* clear that the Pope or bishop must never demand of anyone an action or teaching that goes against natural moral law. No one can be forced to act against his or her conscience, not even if it should be an erring conscience.

Hence the obedience of the faithful towards the ecclesial superiors is not an absolute obedience and the superior cannot demand absolute obedience because both are brothers under the same Father and both are pupils under the same teacher. That is why it is harder to teach than to unteach because it involves greater responsibility before God. For the Church, too, and especially for Her, the words apply: "We must obey God rather than human beings!" (Acts 5:29). With respect to the principle of absolute obedience in the Prussian army and state, the German bishops in their response to Bismarck insisted: "it is certainly not the Catholic Church that has embraced the immoral and despotic principle that the command of a superior frees one unconditionally from all personal responsibility" (DH 3115).

When private opinions or intellectual and moral limitations are allowed to influence the exercise of ecclesial authority, this calls for objective criticism and personal fraternal correction especially from fellow bishops. It lies at the very heart of the tasks of the Roman church in the form of the Sacred College of Cardinals or the Congregation for the Doctrine of the Faith to support the Pope in his teaching office and adjust any imbalances.

Like St. Augustine before him, St. Thomas Aquinas, whom no one will accuse of relativizing papal primacy and the virtue of obedience, interpreted the incident in Antioch (Gal 2:11) thus: "This shows that the fraternal rebuke of one apostle by another or criticism of a superior is in certain circumstances not just a right but also even a duty" (*Comm in Gal* 2:11, cap. II lect. 3). It does not mean that a person is permitted, on the basis of his own private opinion, to downgrade the Magisterium to a private opinion so as to dispense him- or herself from the binding force of authentic and defined doctrines of the Church (cf. *LG* 37). Nor is this contradicted by the example given by St. Ignatius in No. 365 of his *Spiritual Exercises* when he says of the complete conformity of our thinking and perceiving with the Catholic Church (*sentire cum ecclesia*): "What seems to me white, I will believe black if the hierarchical Church so defines." This is no reason for the anti-Jesuit polemic on account of their blind obedience such as was heard in, of all places, the *Kulturkampf* in absolutist Prussia. For the mysteries of the revealed faith cannot be understood with the principles and power of natural reason, but only through the supernatural light of the Holy Spirit. Our physical eyes cannot see that "In the Cross is salvation"; however, despite appearances, with the eyes of our faith we do see it. It is not a matter of the certitude of a sensory perception in itself but rather of its relationship to a supernatural truth.

Nonetheless, the monastic vow of obedience, and the Jesuits' special vow of obedience to the Pope, must be strictly distinguished from the ecclesial and religious obedience all the faithful owe to their bishop and to the Pope. If the Pope is personally formed by the spirituality of his order, when discharging his office he must make a clear distinction between this and the generally binding obedience that he may expect of the bishops and priests and also the cardinals of the Holy Roman Church. Finally, a further point needs mentioning, namely, that the civil authority of the Pope in the Vatican State with its institutions and those of the Holy See must be completely separated as a subject under international law from his religious authority over the universal Church, meaning that in the former capacity he may only expect loyalty from the employees of the State but not from the faithful.

What the fullness of apostolic authority specifically does not mean is an unrestricted plenitude of power in the secular sense; rather, it means the opposite, namely, the strict limitation of this power to the preservation of the Church's unity in the identity of her belief in God's Son, whom he sent in "the fullness of time" (cf. Gal 4:4-6). This authority lies in being bound in the closest possible way to revelation. But it is only through the power of God that Peter can keep the whole Church firmly held in Her fidelity to Christ when Satan shakes and sifts Her in order to separate the wheat from the chaff: "But I have prayed for you that your own faith may not fail — *ut non deficiat fides tua*" (Lk 22:32). And there can be no power on earth that will prevent the Pope from fulfilling the command to strengthen his brothers: "*tu conversas confirma fratres tuos*" (ibid.).

Summa Summarum

A reform of the Church can only happen as a renewal in Christ. As Her Head He is the ground and innermost heart of Her unity. The Pope and bishops must take their bearings from Him and not from the opinions of the mass media. More faith and witness, less politics and power games — that is what is called for now. Accordingly, all roads should lead to Rome, to the graves of the apostles and martyrs Peter and Paul, *ad limina apostolorum*, who from the Lord Jesus Christ "have received grace and apostleship to bring about the obedience of faith among all the Gentiles for the sake of his name" (Rom 1:5). And the Apostle to the Gentiles addresses this letter "To all God's beloved in Rome, who are called to be saints," adding: "I thank my God through Jesus Christ for all of you, because your faith is proclaimed throughout the world." (Rom 1:7f.). That is the service that the Roman church with the Pope and cardinals must not fail to render to the faith and the unity of the Church to this very day.

In his supreme teaching office, the Pope unites the whole Church and Her bishops in the same profession: "You are the Messiah, the Son of the living God" (Mt 16:16). And it is precisely this that makes him the rock upon which the Lord Jesus continues to build His Church until the end of the world. Jesus handed the keys to Peter so that he could open for mankind the doors to the Kingdom of Heaven, to the Kingdom of God, which Jesus is in person. In truth, it is the Son of God Himself in the human nature He assumed Who is the gate leading to the sheep that belong to God's flock (cf. Jn 10:2). He appointed Peter and the bishops in communion with him to feed them (cf. Jn 21:16). He alone remains the Savior of all humanity, and the Pope, bishops and priests are merely servants of the sole Mediator between God and mankind. They themselves do not mediate grace but simply administer the sacraments of grace.[61]

The Church in Her visible form serves the invisible community of salvation in the Triune God:

> As the assumed nature inseparably united to him serves the divine Word as a living organ of salvation, so, in a similar way, does the visible social structure of the Church serve the Spirit of Christ, who vivifies it, in the building up of the body.
>
> This is the one Church of Christ which in the Creed is professed as one, holy, catholic and apostolic, which our Savior, after his Resurrection, commissioned Peter to shepherd, and him and the other apostles to extend and direct with authority, which he erected for all ages as "the pillar and mainstay of the truth" (1 Tim 3:15).
>
> This Church, constituted and organized in the world as a society, subsists in the Catholic Church, which is governed by the successor of Peter and by the bishops in communion with him, although many elements of sanctification and of truth are found outside of its visible structure. These elements, as gifts belonging to the Church of Christ, are forces impelling toward catholic unity.

---

[61] Thomas Aquinas, *S.th.* suppl. q.36 a.3.

… The Church, embracing in her bosom sinners, at the same time holy and always in need of being purified, always follows the way of penance and renewal. The Church, 'like a stranger in a foreign land, presses forward amid the persecutions of the world and the consolations of God, announcing the Cross and death of the Lord until he comes." (*LG* 8)

About the Author

Cardinal Gerhard Ludwig Müller served as Prefect of the Congregation for the Doctrine of the Faith from 2012 to 2017. He was appointed Bishop of Regensburg in 2002 by Pope John Paul II. Müller was elevated to Archbishop in 2012 by Pope Benedict XVI and to Cardinal in 2014 by Pope Francis.

Prior to being named Prefect, Müller served on the Pontifical Council for Culture, the Congregation for Catholic Education, and the Pontifical Council for Promoting Christian Unity. After his appointment as Archbishop and Prefect, he also became *ex officio* President of the Pontifical Biblical Commission, the International Theological Commission, and the Pontifical Commission *Ecclesia Dei*.

Müller retired in 2017. He has written more than six hundred works on various topics, including dogmatic theology, revelation, ecumenism, and the diaconate. Pope Benedict XVI personally entrusted him with the publication of his complete works (sixteen volumes).